FAILED EVIDENCE

Failed Evidence

Why Law Enforcement Resists Science

David A. Harris

NEW YORK UNIVERSITY PRESS
New York and London

To Larry Solan —
My fellow DR show guest —
With best wishes and thanks
for your important work —

NEW YORK UNIVERSITY PRESS
New York and London
www.nyupress.org

References to Internet websites (URLs) were accurate at the time of writing.
Neither the author nor New York University Press is responsible for URLs that
may have expired or changed since the manuscript was prepared.

Library of Congress Cataloging-in-Publication Data
Harris, David A., 1957-
 Failed evidence : why law enforcement resists science / David A. Harris.
    p. cm.
Includes bibliographical references and index.
ISBN 978-0-8147-9055-7 (cl : alk. paper)
ISBN 978-0-8147-9056-4 (ebook)
ISBN 978-0-8147-4466-6 (ebook)
1. Criminal justice, Administration of—United States. 2. Law enforcement—United States.
3. Science—United States. I. Title.
HV9950.H396 2012
363.250973—dc23
                            2012010674

New York University Press books are printed on acid-free paper,
and their binding materials are chosen for strength and durability.
We strive to use environmentally responsible suppliers and materials
to the greatest extent possible in publishing our books.

Manufactured in the United States of America

CONTENTS

ACKNOWLEDGMENTS

Understanding the issues discussed in this book presented a great challenge, and I could not have managed to find my way into the many layers that surround this subject without the help of those individuals who were willing to talk with me and share their experiences, knowledge, and wisdom. They included present and former prosecutors, police officers, defense lawyers, scientists, forensics experts, and judges. I am especially grateful to those people from the law enforcement community who spoke to me; their contributions were fundamental to my understanding. Some of the people I spoke with appear in this book; others do not. But all of them should know that their willingness to speak candidly with me was incredibly valuable. Thank you, one and all.

There is a widespread misconception about writing a book. The common image of the writer is the lone man or woman working for hours on end in solitude, putting the words down, editing them, and producing a finished product that might get published some day. There is some truth to this quaint image, but it captures only one part of the endeavor. There is so much more to a book than the author writing it; anyone who has done it knows that it takes a whole team. Pitt Law's helpful and sharp library staff was always game for the challenge of finding the obscure sources I needed. Pitt Law's Document Technology Center staff went above and beyond the call of duty many times to get my manuscript in shape. Research Assistant Emily Boardman (Pitt Law Class of 2012) and Library Fellow Derek Candela (Pitt Law Class of 2011) both did a great job helping me assemble basic research materials. My colleagues at Pitt were always willing to listen to me and make suggestions as I formed the ideas that found their way into this book. As always, my ace in the hole has been my secretary, Patty Blake, who has saved me from more errors than I can count. Most of all, I thank Professor Andrew Taslitz of American University Washington School of Law and Deborah Gershenowitz, my editor at NYU Press. Both of them believed in this project from the very beginning, and helped me understand the book I needed to write, as opposed to the one I started with. Both Andy and Debbie helped me through the inevitable rough spots, and guided me along. I can't thank either of them enough.

I am grateful for the support of the University of Pittsburgh School of Law, which gave me the time and resources necessary to write this book.

I am most thankful for the support of my wife, Rebecca, and my children, Alicia and Sam, all the way through this process. And I am lucky beyond measure to have Zappa, an extraordinary dog and the best writing companion I could imagine.

1

Introduction: Science-Driven Policing, or Police Indifference to Science?

In 2010, and for the previous nine years running, *CSI: Crime Scene Investigation* ranked among the most popular shows on television in the United States.[1] The program became a hit so quickly after its premiere in 2000 that the original series, set in Las Vegas, spawned two clones: *CSI: Miami* and *CSI: New York*. These shows put a new twist on the old police procedural drama. The *CSI* officers solved crimes with high-tech forensics: gathering DNA, lifting fingerprints with revolutionary new techniques, and using science to reconstruct the paths of bullets. Watching these programs, the viewer knows that policing has changed. For every member of the *CSI* team using a gun, more wield test tubes, DNA sampling equipment, and all manner of futuristic gizmos designed to track down witnesses and catch the bad guys.[2] The show signals a break with the past, because it revolves around the way police use modern science to find the guilty and bring them to justice.

CSI reflects the emergence of DNA evidence as a powerful tool since it first appeared in American criminal courts in the late 1980s. With DNA and other formidable forensic techniques on our side, little could escape our

scientific police work. In this new world, in which science could tell us definitively that the police had the right guy, with a probability of millions or even
billions to one, the game had changed for good. The "just the facts, ma'am"
approach of Sergeant Joe Friday, and the slow and inexact old-school ways
that might or might not turn up evidence, began to seem like quaint relics of
a bygone era. Sure, some real-world police protested that *CSI* raised unrealistic public expectations of both forensic science and the police,[3] but *CSI* simply put a drama-worthy sheen on the way that police departments liked to
portray themselves in the age of DNA: using the best of what science had to
offer to construct air-tight criminal cases. Police frequently announced that
they had used DNA to catch guilty people, sometimes for crimes far in the
past, attracting wide public notice and bolstering law enforcement's science-
based image. With headlines like "State, City Police Laud Increase in Arrests
Using DNA"[4] in Baltimore, "Georgia DNA Solves 1,500 Cases"[5] in Atlanta,
"DNA Databanks Allow Police to Solve at Least Four Murders"[6] in Memphis, and "With Added Lab Staff, DNA Tests Resolve String of Old Killings"[7]
in Milwaukee, the direction and approach of police work now seem woven
together with the latest scientific advancements. Science has given police and
prosecutors an enormous, unbeatable advantage.

But this all-too-common view of modern police work using science to
move into a gleaming, high-tech future turns out to be a myth. When we
strip away the veneer of television drama and the news stories about how
DNA has helped police catch another killer or rapist, the real picture concerning law enforcement and science actually looks much different. With the
exception of DNA (and then, only sometimes), most of our police and prosecutorial agencies *do not* welcome the findings of science; they *do not* rush
to incorporate the latest scientific advances into their work. On the contrary,
most police departments and prosecutor's offices *resist* what science has to
say about how police investigate crimes. The best, most rigorous scientific
findings *do not* form the foundation for the way most police departments
collect evidence, the way they test it, or the way they draw conclusions from
it. Similarly, most prosecutors *have not* insisted upon evidence collected by
methods that comply with the latest scientific findings in order to assure
that they have the most accurate evidence to use in court. Like police, most
prosecutors have resisted. And this resistance comes despite a nearly twenty-
year drumbeat of exonerations: people wrongly convicted based on standard
police practices, but proven irrefutably innocent based on DNA evidence.
These DNA exonerations, now numbering more than 250 nationwide, prove
that traditional techniques of eyewitness identification, suspect interrogation,

and forensic testing contain fundamental flaws that have resulted in miscarriages of justice.

Yet the resistance continues. At best, police and prosecutors have used advances in science selectively, when it helps their cases. At worst, they have actively opposed replacing questionable investigative methods with better, empirically proven techniques, sometimes even insisting on retaining flawed methods. As a matter of principle and logic, this indifference to improved practices that will avoid miscarriages of justice seems puzzling and irresponsible, since we know for certain that we can do better than we used to. As a matter of concrete cases, when we see that the failure to use our best methods sometimes leads to both the punishment of the innocent and the escape of the guilty, indifference can become a catastrophe for our system of justice. It is this resistance to sound, science-based police investigative methods that forms the heart of this book.

Brandon Mayfield and the Infallible Science of Fingerprinting

Brandon Mayfield's case makes a striking example. In March of 2004, terrorists bombed four commuter trains in Madrid, killing 191 people and wounding approximately eighteen hundred. Spanish police soon found a partial fingerprint on a plastic bag in a car containing materials from the attack. Using a digital copy of the fingerprint sent by the Spanish police, a senior FBI fingerprint examiner made "a 100% identification" of Brandon Mayfield, an Oregon attorney, whose prints appeared in government databases because of his military service and an arrest years earlier.[8] Three other fingerprint experts confirmed the match of Mayfield to the print found on the bag: FBI supervisory fingerprint specialist Michael Wieners, who headed the FBI's Latent Print Unit; examiner John Massey, a retired FBI fingerprint specialist with thirty years of experience; and Kenneth Moses, a leading independent fingerprint examiner.[9] The FBI arrested Mayfield, and at the Bureau's request, a court incarcerated him for two weeks, despite the fact that he did not have a valid passport on which he could have traveled to Spain; he claimed he had not left the United States in ten years.[10] When the FBI showed the Spanish police the match between the latent print from the bag and Mayfield's prints, the Spanish police expressed grave doubts. The FBI refused to back down, even declining the request of the Spanish police to come to Madrid and examine the original print.[11] Only when the Spanish authorities matched the print with an Algerian man living in Spain did the FBI admit its mistake. The Bureau issued an apology to Mayfield[12]—an action almost unprecedented in the history of the FBI—and later paid him millions of dollars in damages in an out-of-court settlement.[13]

The extraordinary apology and the payment of damages may help to rectify the injustice done to Mayfield and his family. But for our purposes, what happened *after* the FBI admitted its mistakes and asked the court to release Mayfield shows us something perhaps more important. The Mayfield disaster occurred because, among other things, the verification of the original FBI match of Mayfield's print—a procedure performed by three well-regarded fingerprint experts—ignored one of the most basic principles of scientific testing: the verification was not a "blind" test. The three verifying examiners knew that an identification had already been made in the case, and they were simply being asked to confirm it.[14] No scientific investigation or basic research in any other field—a test of the effectiveness of a new over-the-counter medicine, for example—would ever use a nonblind testing procedure; yet nonblind verification is still routine in fingerprint identification. Further, the FBI conducted proficiency testing of all of the examiners involved in the Mayfield case—but only *after revelation of the errors,* not before. At the time of Brandon Mayfield's arrest, the FBI did no regular proficiency testing of its examiners to determine their competence, even though such testing routinely occurs in almost any commercial laboratory using quality-control procedures. Further, and perhaps most shocking of all, the fingerprint comparison in the Mayfield case relied not on rigorously researched data and a comparison made under a well-accepted set of protocols and standards, but on the unregulated interpretations of the examiners.

Yet, confronted by an undeniable, publicly embarrassing error that highlighted the crying need for fingerprint analysts to adopt standard practices used in every scientific discipline, the experts refused to yield. Their answer was resistance and denial: resistance to change, and denial of the existence of a problem. Months after the humiliating exposure of the Mayfield debacle, some of those involved continued to insist that the matching of prints to identify unknown perpetrators could not produce mistakes—*ever.* In an article on the Mayfield case and other instances of mistaken forensic identification, Agent Massey, who had verified the print as belonging to Mayfield, told the *Chicago Tribune* that he and his fellow analysts had just done their jobs—nothing more. He acknowledged that when he verified Mayfield's print, he knew that another examiner had already declared the print a match; in other words, he had not performed a blind verification test. Nevertheless, he said, "I'll preach fingerprints till I die. They're infallible."[15] Another examiner interviewed about the Mayfield case made an almost identical, unequivocal statement: "Fingerprints *are* absolute and infallible."[16] When another false fingerprint match led to the two-year incarceration of a man named Rick Jackson, *CBS News* correspondent Lesley Stahl confronted another FBI agent on the news program *60 Minutes*. The agent's words eerily echoed Agent Massey's declarations of fingerprint infallibility. After a demonstration of fingerprint identification by the agent, Stahl asked, "What are the chances that it's still not the right person?" Without hesitation, the agent replied, "zero," because "[i]t's a positive identification."[17]

As an institution, the FBI did no better at accepting its error and changing its practices. The Bureau announced that it would conduct an investigation of the practices of its Latent Fingerprint Unit, with an eye to "adopting new guidelines." (The Latent Fingerprint Unit conducted this investigation itself.) As these words are written, more than six years after a mistaken fingerprint match almost sent Brandon Mayfield to prison for the rest of his life, the FBI laboratory's fingerprint identification division does not use standard blind testing in every case. The laboratory widely considered to have the best fingerprint identification operation in the country continues to resist change and remains in denial, and has refused to move toward practices and safeguards that the scientific world has long considered standard.

How We Got Here

To understand how we got to this point, we must start with DNA. DNA analysis did not develop in the context of police-driven forensic investigation, but rather as a wholly scientific endeavor. This helps explain why DNA testing has always included fully developed standard protocols for its use and the ability to calculate the probability of its accuracy based on rigorously analyzed data.[18] This made courts willing to allow its use as proof. Despite its obvious complexity, DNA analysis had been thoroughly tested and was well grounded in scientific principles. As long as forensic scientists followed proper protocols for handling and testing the evidence, DNA could "individualize"—indicate whether a particular person had or had not supplied a tiny piece of tissue or fluid—with a degree of precision unimaginable before. The potential for solving crimes, particularly murders and rapes by strangers in which police might find some fragment of the assailant's DNA left behind, seemed limitless. Defendants who might have escaped detection and conviction got the punishment they deserved. Even decades-old "cold cases" would yield to this marvelous new tool providing that enough testable biological material still existed, and advances in testing rapidly made accurate analysis of ever smaller samples possible.[19]

Soon enough, though, police and prosecutors found that the great sword of DNA had two edges: it could confirm guilt like nothing else, but it could also exclude a suspect that the authorities believed had perpetrated the crime. Sometimes the prosecution had already tried the suspect and obtained a guilty verdict. DNA could convict, but it could also throw police investigations, charges, and even convictions into the gravest doubt. A pattern emerged: many of the cases upended by DNA rested on well-accepted types of evidence, like identifications by eyewitnesses, confessions from suspects, or forensic science producing a "match" with a perpetrator. Thus DNA began to demonstrate that these traditional methods actually did not have anything like the rock-solid basis everyone in law enforcement had always imagined. The very basis for trusting these standard types of evidence began to erode.

By early 2010, DNA had resulted in the exoneration of more than 250 previously convicted people, some of whom had spent years on death row.[20] By far, the single most common factor, found in 75 percent of these cases, was incorrect eyewitness identifications;[21] the second most common type of error was inaccurate (or sometimes downright fraudulent) forensic testing.[22] Perhaps most surprisingly, DNA also proved that some suspects did something most people considered unimaginable: they confessed to serious crimes that they had not committed.[23] All in all, the DNA exoneration cases showed, beyond any doubt, that we simply had to rethink some of our fundamental assumptions about the most basic and common types of evidence used in criminal cases. An eyewitness who expressed absolute certainty when identifying the perpetrator could actually be wrong. A person who confessed to a crime might not actually have done it. And forensic analysis, including fingerprint matching, was not invariably correct.

With DNA exonerations continuing every year in the 1990s and 2000s, more and more research on traditional police investigative methods began to come to prominence. The research had earned acceptance in the scientific community, sometimes decades before, through peer review, publication, and replication by other scientists, but most of it had remained obscure except to a small circle of researchers. With the advent of DNA exonerations, the science became important to anyone interested in the integrity of the criminal justice system. Decades of these studies, it turned out, pointed out flaws in the ways that police conducted eyewitness identifications. Other research showed that the most widely used method of interrogating suspects rested upon assumptions shown to be deeply flawed, and that common interrogation methods created real risks of false confessions.

DNA's precision and scientifically sound foundation effectively raised the bar for every other forensic technique and investigative method. Experts and researchers began to call traditional (i.e., non-DNA) investigative methods into question.[24] The full scope of damage to the credibility of police investigative tactics became visible in 2009, with the National Research Council's report on forensic sciences, *Strengthening Forensic Science in the United States: A Path Forward.*[25] In this landmark report, discussed in detail in chapter 2, a large group of the most knowledgeable people in forensic science and related fields declared that, aside from DNA and a few other solidly scientific disciplines such as toxicology, almost none of the forensic science disciplines could claim any real scientific basis for their results. Most of the forensic work done in the United States did not follow the standard scientific precautions against human cognitive biases. Striking at the core of forensic science, particularly fingerprint analysis, the report stated that (again with the exception of DNA and some other disciplines based firmly in the hard sciences) none of the common forensic disciplines could proclaim themselves rigorously reliable, let alone infallible.[26]

But this sudden exposure of the shortcomings of traditional police investigation tactics also had another, more positive side. The same bodies of research that demonstrated the failings of traditional eyewitness identification testimony, interrogation methods, and forensics also revealed better, more accurate methods to solve crimes—or, at the very least, improved ways to investigate that would greatly reduce the risks of incorrect charges and convictions. These new methods could help guard against mistakes, both by producing more reliable evidence and by eliminating common human cognitive biases from police and forensic investigation. Many of these improved methods would cost very little—sometimes nothing. Thus, the research on traditional investigative methods did not just point out flaws; it pointed the way to better, more reliable tactics. A few examples make this plain.

- Research by cognitive psychologist Gary Wells and others demonstrated that eyewitness identification procedures using simultaneous lineups—showing the witness six persons together, as police have traditionally done—produces a significant number of incorrect identifications. This is the case because showing the six persons to the witness simultaneously encourages witnesses to engage in relative judgment: they make a selection by asking themselves, "Which of the people in the lineup looks *most like* the perpetrator, even if I can't say for sure that the perpetrator is there?" Wells discovered that if he showed the persons in the lineup to the witnesses sequentially—one at a time, instead of all six together—a direct comparison of each individual person in the lineup to the witness's memory of the perpetrator replaces the flawed relative judgment process, reducing the number of false identifications significantly.

- Research has demonstrated that interrogations that include threats of harsh penalties ("Talk, or we'll ask for the death penalty.") and untruths about the existence of evidence proving the suspect's guilt (a false statement by police asserting that they found the suspect's DNA at the scene) significantly increase the prospect of an innocent person confessing falsely. By eliminating these tactics, police can reduce false confessions.[27]
- Fingerprint matching does not use probability calculations based on collected and standardized data to generate conclusions, but rather human interpretation and judgment. Examiners generally claim a zero rate of error—an untenable claim in the face of publicly known errors by the best examiners in the United States. To preserve the credibility of fingerprint examination, forensic labs could use exactly the kinds of proficiency testing and quality assurance standards scientists have crafted for other fields. These methods have become widely available; scientists, engineers, and researchers all use them for work that requires high levels of reliability.[28]

The Reaction: From Indifference to Hostility

In light of all of the challenges that science now poses to established methods of police investigation, highlighted by what DNA tells us about the (in)accuracy of the procedures police have long used, we ought to have seen wholesale changes by now in the basics of the procedures used by police to investigate crimes. We might also have expected to see at least the beginnings of changes in forensic science practices—a willingness to embrace proficiency testing, for example, or a wholesale reexamination of some of the disciplines, such as bite mark analysis, that seem to have little scientific basis and a notable track record of producing convictions of innocent people.

But as the discussion of the Mayfield case shows, we have seen very little change at all. To be sure, in a growing but still relatively small group of police departments and prosecutors' offices, one now sees an openness to new, scientifically proven methods of investigation that minimize the risk of sacrificing the truth. But, as described in chapter 3, the reaction in law enforcement overall has been disappointing. Most police departments and prosecutors' offices have ignored the new science on forensics, eyewitnesses, and interrogation, preferring the status quo. Others have actively resisted change, even fought against it. Some agencies have proclaimed the soundness of discredited methods even in the face of undeniable failures, just as those who mistakenly matched Brandon Mayfield to the Madrid bombings continued to proclaim fingerprints infallible. This represents not just a missed opportunity to do better, but a likely source of future cases in which the train of justice derails and the wrong people pay the price for crimes they did not commit while the real predators and perpetrators remain free to strike again.

The resistance to these new approaches takes different forms. First, those in policing or prosecution sometimes see the new science behind eyewitness identification, interrogation, and forensics as just a way in which slick defense lawyers can help guilty defendants avoid punishment. These new methods might interfere in some way with the constant battle to arrest criminals, law enforcement says, and this means society cannot afford to accept these new approaches. They may lead to more guilty people escaping justice—something no society should tolerate, let alone encourage. Second, police and prosecutors sometimes distrust or deny outright the correctness of the scientific findings and their implications for investigative work as police currently do it. Scientists may find these new methods proven and sound, police say, but that means nothing; a clever academic can make statistics say anything. Science remains too unsettled to allow law enforcement to rely on it, too fluid to build a conviction on, and too laboratory-centric and divorced from the realities of the street, where real police work takes place. Science that criticizes police work seems fundamentally elitist to many in law enforcement, overvaluing experiments and undervaluing the lived experience of police officers. The need to prove everything in terms of hard data, they often say, fails to appreciate the special intuitive skills of experienced police officers, which allow them to spot lies, identify suspicious activity, and see potentially criminal behavior that the rest of us do not recognize. Third, some law enforcement officials take the new information science has provided as a personal attack on them—"you're saying that police are corrupt"—or as an attack on the law enforcement profession and its abilities as a whole. "We know how to do police investigation," the argument goes; "we've been doing this for years, and no bunch of pointy-headed ivory tower types will convince us of anything different." Fourth, some police and prosecutors simply do not understand science and the scientific method. Therefore, they do not recognize the power of the scientific method to help us appreciate how well the investigative procedures police use *actually* work—as opposed to how well police and prosecutors *think* these procedures work. They also object to the costs of these new ways of investigating cases, both the direct costs of implementing these changes and the indirect costs of greater manpower and new training.

But none of this explains—let alone justifies—the refusal to accept solid evidence that has shown that serious flaws exist in the ways we have always investigated crimes, and the battle on the part of many—not all, to be sure, but many—in law enforcement to resist improved and tested methods. Given the solid evidence that exists, we can no longer pretend that our methods of interrogation, our ways of using eyewitness testimony, and our forensic testing all work as well as we have always thought they did. We can no longer credibly contend that innocent people never confess, that eyewitnesses always provide reliable evidence, and that forensic matching of things like hair, shoe prints, bite marks, and or even fingerprints have a scientific basis. The facts simply do not support these and so many other assumptions, no matter how strongly, or for how long, police, prosecutors, and others have believed them. Yet much of the law enforcement establishment still holds fast to those views. And none of the reasons why they continue to believe could outweigh the obligation to make determinations of guilt and innocence in the most reliable fashion that we can.

Thus, if neither the feared acquittals of the guilty, nor costs, nor distrust of science, nor limiting police officers' ability to utilize their intuition can justify this resistance, we must ask why the resistance occurs and continues. Surely, no one enters the police academy or takes a job as a prosecutor with the aim of arresting or convicting the wrong people. Why, then, would law enforcement leaders and prosecutors resist changes in investigation procedures in the face of a steadily growing body of evidence that the ways they do and have long done these basic law enforcement tasks produce a noticeable number of miscarriages of justice, with the wrong people punished and the guilty free to victimize others? Why resist change when the data we have proves not just that the old ways work poorly at times but also that new ways can work better, without costing the innocent their liberty? Why has law enforcement not only failed to embrace advances that could help improve police work but actively fought against acceptance of these improvements?

At least two sets of explanations account for this resistance. The first set, described in chapter 4, focuses on *cognitive obstacles to change*: the ways that human beings think. First, consider police culture. Police officers tend to regard each other as members of a closed fraternity; those who do not wear the badge cannot fully understand what it means to do so, and therefore can never claim membership in the clan. Police culture remains notoriously insular, and those who belong regard outsiders with suspicion. This culture does not welcome change or new ideas that challenge established ways of thinking or operating. Cognitive science tells us that this kind of situation will induce *group polarization*: those who associate only with like-minded others will tend toward an extreme version of their beliefs. They hear only one side of the argument; even more importantly, agreeing with other group members becomes a mark of group loyalty and identity. And group identity is especially strong in both police departments and prosecutors' offices. Strong group identity also breeds an intense *us-versus-them mentality*; therefore, anything that helps "them" (suspects, defendants) must hurt "us" (the law enforcement fraternity). When new knowledge coming from outsiders appears to undermine the tried and true approaches police have used for decades, this constitutes a direct *threat to the social status of police*. Police view themselves as having special talents that laypersons do not have: the ability to spot a lie, to see suspicious activity the rest of us would not recognize, and to identify potentially criminal conduct in what looks like innocuous behavior. This special type of expertise gives police officers claims to higher social status, and with it entitlement to greater authority and autonomy. Thus the new science that challenges these supposed special abilities stiffens any natural hesitation to accept change. The new science on police investigation may also cause *cognitive dissonance*. Police officers and prosecutors see themselves as the good guys, making the world safe by arresting, charging, and trying criminals. The research on police investigation that has emerged, including the documented cases of wrongful convictions, could appear to point in a very different direction: the possibility that individuals in law enforcement may have had some role in convicting innocent persons in the past. This would create a strong cognitive conflict: people who believe themselves fundamentally good and associated with the right side of the struggle would have to confront the possibility that, perhaps inadvertently, they have participated in grave injustices. Thus, to avoid this cognitive dissonance, police and prosecutors will filter out information that indicates this could be true, and will resist change. Change from the status quo also brings *wealth effects* into play: the natural sense that movement away from the tried and true will bring loss of what one has in the present. Since individuals feel losses more painfully than they feel denied gains, they resist change.

The second set of reasons for resistance to change, discussed in chapter 5, involves professional and institutional barriers. First and foremost, we must consider the institutional and professional incentives built into the jobs of both police officers and prosecutors. In the United States, police officers live by the imperative of arrest. Their careers thrive or fail to prosper according to how many cases they can close by arresting perpetrators. Arrests are measurable—one can easily count their numbers (if not their quality). Arresting criminals, and thereby closing cases, has therefore become the single important measurement within police departments of whether an officer does his or her job well. For prosecutors, convictions constitute the parallel metric. Those with the best conviction rates advance; their peers regard them as stars of the office staff. Obviously, police want to arrest the right people—the real perpetrators. Similarly, prosecutors want high conviction rates, though presumably only of the truly guilty. The problem is that any reform that looks as though it might disturb the police officer's or prosecutor's chances of achieving arrests or convictions runs counter to the strong incentives built into the very core of the way they perform their work. Thus, if the traditional ways in which police interrogate suspects, work with eyewitnesses, and utilize forensic testing bring them results by which they benefit, they may be, at best, indifferent to the new scientific knowledge that suggests better ways to perform these tasks. If they perceive these new methods as a threat to what has always worked for them, they may be not just indifferent but actually hostile to the idea of moving in those new directions and away from the tried and true. *Police unions* and other groups concerned with police working conditions may resist change because they fear that changing the status quo in any way may endanger gains they have already secured for their members. They will resist giving away such gains in any context; trading them away for possible gains that accrue to someone else—a criminal suspect, no less—seems unthinkable. *The law-and-order orientation of the media* also plays a role. While the media have covered numerous stories of wrongful convictions in ways that help the public understand the reality of these miscarriages of justice, most news reports on criminal justice issues still err on the side of a vastly oversimplified presentation of local crime and criminals. This creates the impression of an increasingly dangerous environment for everyday citizens. Media organizations, especially television outlets, have presented this impression for years, even in the face of irrefutable evidence that crime has actually *decreased* overall for nearly two decades. This media misrepresentation can make bringing about reform in existing police procedures devilishly difficult. *Political ambition* may also play a role in generating resistance to reform, along with *lack of representation of voices for reform* in legislative settings.

Why Single Out Police and Prosecutors for Blame?

Why focus on police and prosecutors? Police seek out the evidence, collect it, and, at least initially, interpret it. They decide in the most direct way whether a suspect has committed a crime, and if so of what nature. Prosecutors take the evidence police bring them and make independent determinations concerning whether cases will or will not proceed, and with what charges. Thus most of what happens in the criminal courts originates with the actions of police and prosecutors, and those actions shape every individual case as well as the long-term trends across the system. Because of the primacy and importance of their input, police and prosecutors have the ability to shift their own efforts and the entire criminal justice system toward better practices that science has shown will produce fewer erroneous convictions and miscarriages of justice. To be sure, other actors share some of the blame when things have gone wrong. Defense lawyers have failed to challenge the basic science behind police procedures. Judges have failed to act as "gatekeepers" against the use of junk science in criminal courts. Nevertheless, police and prosecutors have the dominant position and the most leverage in shaping the way criminal justice works in our country, whether focusing on individual cases or on systemic issues. For that reason, this book focuses primarily on them.

This does not mean police or prosecutors have intentionally caused wrongful convictions by using discredited forensic testing or investigative methods. Some cases of outright fraud or knowing creation of false evidence have occurred, but the vast majority of police do not want to bring cases against the wrong suspects. Prosecutors have no reason to want to convict those who have done nothing, instead of the actual guilty parties. But even if most use of poor investigative or forensic methods does not constitute intentional wrongdoing, the actions of police and prosecutors still deserve special scrutiny. They serve as the collectors (police) and presenters (prosecutors) of evidence in our adversary system of criminal justice. The object is not a perfect criminal justice system that never makes an error; no system created and run by human beings could function perfectly. Rather, we should strive to do the best that imperfect human beings can do, using all of the knowledge, energy, and creativity at our disposal, to minimize the risk of the conviction of the innocent. If our police and prosecutors do their jobs according to the best practices we have, according to the strongest evidence and the most current scientific research, the criminal justice system as a whole can do the best possible job of excluding the innocent from accusation, trial, and punishment—the ultimate nightmare, because an undeserving person would suffer and because the guilty party would remain free to harm other victims. The public has every right to expect that those who carry the awesome responsibility of arresting, charging, and trying suspects will do their jobs using the best possible tactics and methods we have, in order to steer clear of the mistakes that imperfect human beings can avoid. If, instead, they use methods that researchers have found to have no scientific basis, that do not work as advertised, or that actually create significant risks of producing faulty evidence, when better practices can become part of law enforcement's arsenal without significant cost, police and prosecutors do not serve the public properly. Doing justice may be hard, but no task has greater importance to our nation's values, and for that reason alone our public officials must at least attempt to carry out their difficult responsibilities in the most accurate ways available. And that responsibility leaves no room for ignoring new methods scientifically proven to produce more accurate evidence. The integrity of the criminal justice system must, at all times, remain paramount, and we should not tolerate anything that subverts it.

Accurate proof of facts has always been the lifeblood of this process. And we depend on our police and prosecutors to do the best that they can to assure that only accurate evidence comes before judges and juries. In the end, we cannot be absolutely certain that any of us—members of juries, police officers, judges, or prosecutors—know the ground truth; we cannot know for certain whether the conclusions we draw from the evidence we bring to court are in fact accurate. But we can know whether we have obtained the evidence we use by methods and processes that *minimize the risk* of bringing into the record false confessions, or incorrect identifications by witnesses, or misleading or mischaracterized or incorrect forensic test results. And we can also know whether we have used methods that our best scientific minds have proven will *minimize the chances* that the wrong person will go to jail, with the real criminal remaining free. That is what is at stake in this debate. If we choose to let the resistance to new methods stand, we will not have not done what we as human beings can to ensure that we are right when we judge the guilt or innocence of our fellow men and women. And when we can see the result of that—miscarriages of justice, lost years in prison for someone undeserving of punishment, and the destruction of the trust and confidence citizens need to have in police, prosecutors, and the rule of law itself—we see there is simply no excuse. We must persuade our law enforcement officers and our prosecutors of the necessity of doing what is right, and if we cannot persuade them, we must bring them along anyway in the march toward better practices.

What Must Happen? How Do We Make It Happen?

What must we do to make this happen? Chapter 6 explains that at this point, scientists and researchers have given us a reasonably good map of how the system must change. In the forensic sciences, the most questionable fields, such as hair analysis, bite mark comparisons, and shoe and tire impressions, must become unusable in courts, until they can establish their reliability through empirical research. For more established disciplines, such as fingerprint comparisons or tool marks comparisons involving firearms, we must begin constructing databases and a set of protocols to standardize comparisons, and we must use these tools to render a true picture of the accuracy of these disciplines. Basic processes to eliminate human cognitive bias and proficiency testing (for individual evidence examiners) and quality assurance procedures (for laboratories) must become standard. For interrogation, we must make electronic recording a requirement. We must prohibit certain tactics—threats, promises of leniency, and lies about test results—that dramatically raise the risk of false confessions. For the handling of eyewitnesses, the list of scientifically proven approaches includes blind administration of lineups, sequential presentation of live suspects and photos, prohibition on any statements by the lineup administrator before or after the lineup, the taking of a "level of confidence" statement from a witness who makes an identification immediately afterward, and electronic recording of the process.

If that is what we must do, the tougher question remains how to accomplish it. After all, the research recommending these changes is not new, and yet the improved practices the research supports have not spread across the entire field. Making it happen will take a multipronged approach. Above all, we will need the right leadership, which must usually come from the law enforcement establishment and from the political Right. A movement for the reform of police and prosecutorial methods led by criminal defense lawyers and civil liberties advocates may sometimes succeed, but will often find itself undermined by criticism that it is self-interested; a group advocating reform led by prosecutors will, by contrast, seem to have the kind of disinterested credibility that will persuade many others in law enforcement to join. As a persuasive strategy, we will also have to focus more on the future than on the past, while at the same time institutionalizing mechanisms for review of old miscarriages of justice that cry out for correction. The key concept is the integrity of the criminal justice system. Wrongful convictions eat away at the public confidence that the legal system must have in order to survive.

We must also concentrate on the three other things: creating best practice standards that all law enforcement agencies would need to follow; using public money as leverage; and sharpening the contours of judicial control over evidence while creating the judicial spine to use it. As for best practices, the federal government and professional law enforcement organizations should set best practices in all three of these areas—forensic testing, identification by witnesses, and suspect interrogation. In some cases, this work has already advanced; the framework for these practices already exists. The Department of Justice issued guidelines followed by an academic white paper two years later, setting out best practices in witness identification in 1999; a distinguished group of researchers did the same for interrogation practices in 2010. For the forensic sciences, the National Research Council's report, issued in 2009, will provide more than a starting point. Professional groups, such as the International Association of Chiefs of Police and the National District Attorneys Association, should become part of this process, and studies by the National Institute of Justice, such as one focusing on improving the reliability of fingerprint examination and comparison, can make vital contributions to this process. Money will help motivate almost any set of actors and institutions, and law enforcement agencies in the United States receive considerable funding from both state and federal governments. Receipt of all of this funding should become contingent on adopting all of the best practices in this area; in other words, federal standards should require that if an agency wants any federal funding for its operations, it must comply with best practices regarding the interrogation of suspects, the making of witness identifications, and the conduct and use of forensic testing. In addition, federal funding should be made available for any department that wishes to retrain its officers in the new best practices to be adopted. In the courts, the beginning point is the U.S. Supreme Court's decision in *Daubert v. Merrell Dow Pharmaceuticals, Inc.* from 1993, which designated judges as the gatekeepers in their courts to guard against junk science. They have carried out this responsibility vigorously in civil cases, but for whatever reason, they have failed miserably in this role in criminal cases. To put it simply, this must change.

There is hope that these new, science-driven methods will overcome the resistance of most police and prosecutors. As we will see in chapter 7, in a small but growing number of states, police departments, prosecutors' offices, and forensic laboratories, new ways of doing things have taken root. For example, in decades past, no jurisdictions required audio or video recordings of the interrogation of suspects. Now, a small number of states require it, and an increasing (though still relatively small) number of police departments and prosecutors swear by it—even some of those who resisted it mightily in the past. Similarly, a number of jurisdictions have imposed changes in the way their personnel conduct eyewitness identification procedures— requiring blind administration of the process, and even using sequential as opposed to simultaneous lineups. All of this tells us that, with the right push forward, we can indeed hope for better tactics and methods, and overall better evidence.

The purpose of this book is not to condemn police officers or policing, or to paint prosecutors as intransigent. Police officers do a very difficult and often thankless job, frequently under the most trying circumstances. Prosecutors work in the public sector, sacrificing the high incomes they might make in private law practice in order to serve the public by putting criminals in jail. Neither job is easy. But the institutions involved—police departments and prosecutors' offices or, more generally speaking, the law enforcement establishment—must become more open to the advances that scientists and professionals in a variety of fields have brought to bear on the work of criminal investigation. There is much to lose by resistance; there is much to gain by embracing the future.

2

Science and Traditional Police Investigative Methods

A Lot We Thought We Knew Was Wrong

When we think about the usual methods police use to investigate crimes, three things usually come to mind. First, when evidence leads police to a suspect, officers may interrogate the person. Second, officers may conduct identification procedures such as lineups, during which police display a group of six or eight similar-looking people for the witness to view, with instructions to pick out the person who committed the crime. Third, investigators may use forensic science to gather evidence that will help to put the perpetrator in jail. This may include everything from collecting DNA specimens to lifting and comparing fingerprints to matching a bullet recovered from a crime scene to a particular firearm. Any given case may include one or more of these procedures as part of the investigation; they are so common that television, movies, and books have made them staples of the cops-and-crime genre.

Other methods of evidence gathering also appear regularly in run-of-the-mill cases: police may use informants to obtain evidence, or officers may utilize electronic surveillance, such as wiretaps, hidden cameras, and infrared imaging to gain intelligence or find the defendant. But interrogations of suspects, identification by eyewitnesses, and forensic testing make up the most common aspects of evidence gathering. The science of the past several decades has taught us that much of the common wisdom concerning these types of evidence turns out to be wrong. What's more, misconceptions about these methods have caused miscarriages of justice—cases in which juries have convicted innocent people.

Forensic Science: Is It Really Science, or Something Less?

For years, forensic scientists have used science and the tools of the laboratory to help police officers and prosecutors find evidence that could help build the case against an accused. The identification of materials, such as suspected contraband substances or trace evidence like gunpowder residue, makes use of classic techniques of chemical analysis. The matching of bullets to particular guns utilizes microscopic examination; so does the forensic comparison of hairs and fibers. Arson investigators apply knowledge of the way fire starts and burns, and the way various substances can serve as fuel or accelerants. Serologists give us information that allows us to know whether the blood found at the scene might have belonged to the suspect under scrutiny. Other specialists use their expertise to match shoeprints to particular shoes, tire tracks to particular tires, and bite marks to the teeth of specific individuals. Fingerprint analysis tells us that the impressions of the unique ridge patterns that make up each person's fingerprint may be "matched" for identification purposes. This has long represented the gold standard in forensic science: fingerprint analysts with sufficient training, knowledge, and expertise could match a print left by an unknown person at a crime scene to a known sample. Perhaps only the perpetrator and the victim of the crime had been present when the crime occurred, but with fingerprint analysis—and other forensic disciplines—the forensic scientist would know who did the crime. But DNA testing changed almost all of this: it upended the certainty and the safe assumptions that forensic science had rested on for almost a century.

Most of forensic science had not, actually, come from true scientific work or the experimental laboratory. Rather, the forensic disciplines other than DNA and chemical analysis originated with criminal investigation, not the scientific method. Many of the common forensic science disciplines "have never been exposed to stringent scientific inquiry" to gauge their accuracy, limitations, and foundations.[1] This means that these methods do not really qualify as science, and thus do not deserve the kind of respect that the law and the courts generally give to information derived from real scientific exploration. So we should ask, just what, exactly, qualifies as real science?

What Does "Real Science" Mean?

Adherence to the principles of the scientific method enables a researcher to reliably and rigorously infer knowledge from uncertain, otherwise unexplainable information, and it greatly enhances the trustworthiness of any answers derived through those principles. A good description of the way this process works comes from the National Academy of Sciences.

> The scientific method presumes that events occur in consistent patterns that can be understood through careful comparison and systematic study. Knowledge is produced through a series of steps during which data are accumulated methodically, strengths and weaknesses of information are assessed, and knowledge about causal information is inferred. In the process, scientists also develop an understanding of the limits of that knowledge (such as the precision of the observations), the inferred nature of relationships, and key assumptions behind the inferences. Hypotheses are developed, are measured against the data, and are either supported or refuted. Scientists continually observe, test, and modify the body of knowledge. . . . Methods to reduce errors are part of the study design. . . . Throughout scientific investigations, the investigator must be as free from bias as possible, and practices are put in place to detect biases (such as those from measurements, human interpretation) and to minimize their effects on conclusions.[2]

When people think of science, they picture hard science—disciplines like chemistry, biological sciences, and physics. And when we think of these disciplines, we automatically think of the tools of hard science: beakers and test tubes, laboratory instruments and precision measuring gear. Hard-science disciplines do use the scientific method to test hypotheses in laboratory environments. But the National Academy of Sciences' description of the way science works shows that real, rigorous science results from following the principles and processes of the scientific method, not from using particular physical tools. Rather, the question about any method is not whether it involves a single test tube or microscope, but whether it uses the scientific method. The failure to understand this, and to think that "science" can only mean hard science, illuminates a critical problem: some people do not accept social science as real science.

Andrew Taslitz, a law professor at American University and an expert in the law of evidence and criminal procedure, recalls that he once presented the latest social science findings on eyewitness identification at a state's annual seminar for all of its judges.[3] Taslitz presented the judges with all of the most important scientific work on eyewitnesses from leaders in the field, and discussed new procedures that the research suggested would make for more accurate identifications. During the question and answer period, one judge in the audience raised his hand. "All of this, everything you've said, that's just social science, isn't it?" The judge continued, "You can make social science say anything you want. I'm not going to give any credence to that." Taslitz remembers that not all the judges agreed with the man, but "there were a significant number of judges who were totally with this guy." Taslitz argued with the judges, explaining what makes good science and how such work is done, but he encountered "real skepticism."

Experiments in the social sciences, dismissed by these judges as soft or not real science, can be just as rigorous, as reliable, and as important as any experiment done with a flask full of chemicals. When performed according to the principles and procedures of the scientific method, social science is unambiguously real science. This becomes critically important because much of what science can tell us about how basic aspects of police investigation actually work—for example, how utilizing eyewitnesses in certain ways raises the risk of false identifications—comes from social science, particularly cognitive and behavioral psychology. Though the judges described in Professor Taslitz's story might consider this work soft and unworthy of acceptance, it exhibits all of the principles of scientific investigation described here: reliance on data, not intuition; the development and testing, and then the confirmation or refutation, of hypotheses; and the peer-reviewed publication of results, which others can then duplicate. Thus the properly constructed work of experimental psychology and other social sciences qualifies as rigorously scientific in every way.

Forensic Science: How Scientific?

In the 1980s, the potential of DNA as a tool for identification began to emerge, but some raised concerns about the validity and reliability of the methods used to capture and analyze DNA samples.[4] A 1990 study by the Congressional Office of Technology Assessment declared that DNA testing was both valid and reliable but that exacting standards and quality control procedures needed to be put in place before it came into wide use.[5] The National Research Council followed with a report in 1992, which stated that while DNA stood on valid scientific ground, "[n]o laboratory should let its results with a new DNA typing method be used in court, unless it has undergone . . . proficiency testing via blind trials"[6]—exactly what the scientific method would call for to guard against error and bias in testing. A third report, also by the National Research Council, addressed the question of the likelihood that two matching samples might come from different people—an issue critical to fully understanding DNA's power to make identifications—by recommending key statistical calculations that factored in population structure.[7] The report also called for independent retesting, observance of high standards of quality, proficiency testing, and accreditation. Thus when DNA finally emerged as evidence in criminal courts, with its laboratory testing, refinement, and precision, it was in every sense real science. It had been rigorously vetted in blind trials. Scientists had formed falsifiable hypotheses; tested them through proper experiments; published their results in order to receive criticism from their peers; and had their results borne out through replication by others. This process had generated agreed-upon protocols for the proper use of DNA[8] and sufficient justification for DNA's extraordinary power to make an identification of the source of almost any bodily substance. With this kind of scientific muscle, DNA had the ability to identify any person who had left fluid or tissue at a crime scene.

This strengthened law enforcement investigation immensely—even as it also began to raise doubts about most other forensic disciplines. DNA not only inculpated suspected perpetrators, making their guilt certain for all practical purposes; it also exculpated others. And sometimes those exculpated had already become suspects or been charged or even convicted and incarcerated, based on evidence from other types of forensic science. Suddenly, DNA proclaimed that in some of these cases, the great emperor of criminal justice called forensic science actually had no clothes—or at any rate, seemed far too lightly dressed.

Thus began the long march toward a thorough examination of the bases for all of the forensic disciplines. Exonerations through DNA began with two cases in 1989. An Illinois jury convicted Gary Dotson of a 1977 aggravated kidnapping and rape, based on a composite sketch from the rape victim and two types of forensic evidence: an examination of fluids by a serologist, and a pubic hair found on the victim that an expert called "similar" to Dotson's.[9] Both experts badly missed the mark: the presence of type A blood should have excluded Dotson, and the hair-similarity testimony had no empirical basis. The victim later recanted her testimony, admitting that no rape had occurred. But only DNA testing that excluded Dotson persuaded the courts to order a new trial, and the state then decided not to retry him in 1989, effectively setting him free.[10] That same year, David Vasquez, convicted of second-degree murder in Virginia, was freed when DNA testing showed that another man, who had committed two other rape/murders, had also committed the homicide for which Vasquez had gone to prison.[11] Vasquez, a borderline mentally impaired man, had supposedly given a confession to the crime, but forensic science had played an important role in his conviction: as in Dotson's case, an expert in hair analysis called a pubic hair found on the victim consistent with those of Vasquez, a claim that—just as in Dotson's case—the science simply did not support.[12]

In the next four years, 1990 through 1993, twelve more exonerations took place in the United States, and in each year after that, the numbers surged, never dropping below five per year.[13] In 2002 alone, twenty-four people were exonerated; an average of eighteen exonerations took place each year in the first decade of the twenty-first century.[14] Enough of these cases have come and gone—as of the first half of 2010, more than 250 people have left prisons and even death row—that we can now see the commonalities in the great sweep of these cases. The sources of these errors have varied, but the most common causes appear over and over: faulty eyewitness identification[15] and erroneous forensic testing.[16] So when DNA began not just to suggest but to prove that some forensic disciplines did not, in fact, deserve the kind of respect and deference that scientifically derived facts usually received, an inquiry into the very foundations of forensic science became inevitable. By 2005, enough members of Congress had become convinced of the existence of a problem that they directed the National Academy of Sciences to investigate which forensic disciplines needed work and how to improve them for the good of the country.[17] The National Academy established a committee of distinguished scientists, forensic practitioners, judges, academics, and lawyers to undertake the task, and the committee held eight hearings around the country. It received testimony from federal agency executives, from federal, state, and local law enforcement officials, from academics, researchers, scientists, medical examiners, heads of public and private crime laboratories, forensic science practitioners, and many other interested parties. The committee members reviewed numerous published studies, reports, and materials of all kinds on the relevant topics, and also conducted their own independent research.

The resulting 2009 report, *Strengthening Forensic Science in the United States: A Path Forward*,[18] shook the ground on which forensic science had rested for decades. "Research is needed to address issues of accuracy, reliability, and validity in forensic science disciplines," it said; the forensic disciplines needed peer-reviewed research "establishing the scientific bases demonstrating the validity of forensic methods."[19] The authorities should also fund research to develop "quantifiable measures of reliability and accuracy," as well as the limits of the methods under review to deliver accurate and reliable results.[20] Additionally, the government should fund "the development of quantifiable measures of uncertainty in the conclusions of forensic analyses."[21] The report also recommended research into "human observer bias and sources or human error"[22] and the establishment of protocols for forensic work that "reflect best practices and serve as accreditation tools for laboratories."[23] The sterile language of the report masks a high-impact message: DNA and some of the other science-based disciplines (such as testing the chemical composition of suspected drugs) aside, forensic science lacks the basics of what real science is and does, and this has resulted in errors—some of them catastrophic, with the wrong people in jail for years while the actual predators have remained free.

Fingerprint Identification

Among all of the forensic sciences devoted to determining the source of evidence, fingerprint identification has always stood alone for its reliability and dependability. Fingerprint evidence can claim a high degree of public trust,[24] but it also shares many of the conceptual, theoretical, and practical problems of other forensic disciplines. That makes it an excellent place to begin exploring doubts raised by science about non-DNA forensics generally, because if real issues exist in fingerprint identification, we can hardly expect other newer and less well-grounded forensic disciplines to perform better. In fact, most do not perform as well.

For its adherents, a "match" between an unknown fingerprint left at a crime scene and the known print of the accused establishes guilt beyond any dispute. No less a source on the investigation of criminal matters than the FBI itself has said that "[o]f all the methods of identification, fingerprinting alone has proved to be both infallible and feasible."[25] Courts have accepted fingerprints as evidence of identification for a hundred years.[26] As we saw in the Brandon Mayfield case, most fingerprint experts do not admit any possibility of error; they routinely state that, unlike other experts, their error rate is not small, not low—it is zero.[27] Disturbingly, the Mayfield case was not the first but the second exposure of a fingerprint mistake in a notorious case in that same year, 2004. In January 2004, a court released a man named Stephan Cowans after he had served almost seven years of a 30- to 45-year sentence for shooting a police officer.[28] Cowans's conviction rested on fingerprint and eyewitness evidence, but a DNA test showed that he did not commit the crime; Boston police admitted that they had made a mistaken fingerprint identification.[29] Unfortunately, the Mayfield and Cowans cases do not stand alone.[30]

The task of fingerprint identification is source attribution:[31] the process of determining the origin of a piece of evidence. It is a quest for "individualization":[32] determining that a piece of evidence —here, a fingerprint left at the crime scene—came from exactly one single human being, among all other possible sources. The basics of fingerprint identification begin with the acronym ACE-V. The letters stand for the steps that fingerprint examiners take—Analyze, Compare, Evaluate, Verify—when they compare an unknown print from a crime scene (often called a "latent" or a "latent print") to some number of known samples.[33] First, examiners analyze the unknown print, closely examining the quality and quantity of discernible ridges, loops, and other features. This stage performs a critical screening function, because not all latent prints come to print examiners large enough, clear enough, or with sufficient detail to allow a comparison. Police and evidence technicians obtain unknown latent prints not in the laboratory or in the relative calm of the police station booking room but out in the world, where randomness and chance rule. The examiner then performs the same kind of analysis on the known print: typically, a print taken from the person police suspect. Known prints for suspects may be on file from previous cases, or taken just for the purpose of the comparison. The process goes forward from this point only if, in the examiner's judgment, both the unknown and known prints have enough detail of sufficient quality to allow comparison. If not, the examiner classifies the prints as "no value" and the process ends.[34] Assuming prints suitable for evaluation, the examiner proceeds to a visual comparison between the unknown and known prints. Comparison seeks to determine which details of the unknown and known fingerprints correspond with each other.[35] Noting these corresponding details, the examiner then proceeds to the evaluation of the points of agreement between the unknown and known prints. The evaluation determines whether sufficient agreement exists between details to allow the examiners to make an identification—a match between the unknown and known prints, definitively determining whether the unknown print came from a known source.[36] As a result of the evaluation, the examiner will make one of three pronouncements: a source determination, i.e., a match; exclusion, meaning that the process indicates sufficient disagreement between the unknown and known print; or inconclusive, because the examiner could not make either a match or an exclusion.[37] Verification constitutes the final stage. During verification, another fingerprint examiner repeats the analysis, comparison, and evaluation stages of the unknown and known print. Verification supplies validation if the second examiner comes to the same conclusion as the first one.[38]

ACE-V constitutes the standard methodology that fingerprint examiners follow[39] to make their absolute and infallible identifications. Therefore, we should note several characteristics of the ACE-V method. First, since making an individualization—a match—between a known and an unknown fingerprint requires sufficient matching between the details of the prints, we need to know what "sufficient" means. We can find a definition in the description of acceptable fingerprint examination methodology codified by the FBI's Scientific Working Group for Friction Ridge Analysis, Study, and Technology, or SWGFAST, a standard-setting body in the field. According to SWGFAST, "Sufficiency is the examiner's determination that unique details of the friction skin source area are revealed in the [print]."[40] In other words, whether a comparison shows a sufficient or insufficient number of correspondences depends on the examiner's own determination—not really a standard at all. Second, there exists no consensus among fingerprint examination experts on the number of characteristics that the known and unknown prints must have in common in order for an examiner to declare a match. Rather, "considerable disagreement" remains, and different countries have adopted varying standards on this crucial point.[41] For example, France and Italy both require sixteen matching characteristics; Australia requires twelve; Brazil and Argentina require thirty.[42] But in the United States, fingerprint experts operate under a different standard: there is no minimum number of corresponding points of identification necessary for an identification. Both the FBI[43] and the International Association for Identification,[44] the professional certifying organization of fingerprint examiners, have adopted this nonstandard, and it forms the basis for what every examiner in the United States does when making a determination of a match. According to the National Academy of Sciences, "In the United States, the threshold for making a source identification is deliberately kept subjective, so that the examiner can take into account both the quantity and quality of comparable details. As a result, the outcome . . . is not necessarily repeatable from examiner to examiner."[45] This gives fingerprint examination an inherent subjectivity.[46]

Thus, when declaring a match between the latent print collected from the crime scene and the known print, the fingerprint examiner says, with absolute certainty, that the latent print could have come from only one source in the world: the same source that supplied the known print. This constitutes a fundamentally probabilistic judgment. The examiner making a match says, in effect, that the probability that the unknown print came from a particular known person is 100 percent; the probability that the unknown print came from someone else is zero.[47] But this judgment comes not from comparisons of data that would ground the probabilistic judgment in statistics, as it should, but from the judgment of the human being making the comparison. In fact, the fingerprint examiners' professional organization forbids members from stating this fundamentally probabilistic judgment in any form that uses explicit statements of probability; professional examiners may only testify that the accused is the only possible source for the fingerprint, or is not the source, or that the source of the print is inconclusive.[48] They cannot testify that they have made an identification with X percent certainty.

The verification stage of ACE-V also presents an issue. At the verification point in the process, a second fingerprint examiner looks at the unknown and known prints that the first examiner has identified as having come from the same person, and repeats the process. The verification occurs if and when the second examiner comes to the same conclusion as the first. But one critical aspect of verification deserves special notice: the second examiner generally knows of the conclusions reached by the first examiner. Thus the usual fingerprint verification—described by some in the profession as "peer review" built into the method—is not blind; the verifying examiner knows the "right" answer from the beginning. Because blind testing produces solid, highly defensible results on which we can safely rely, it constitutes the norm in the sciences. Nonblind testing does not. Suppose researchers want to know if a new over-the-counter medicine will reduce pain. The researchers conduct blind experiments in which the subjects do not know whether they are receiving the medicine or a placebo. A person working for the researchers, who also does not know whether the subject has the real medicine or a placebo, asks the subject about the effects experienced after having taken the medicine (or what appeared to be medicine). We blind the subject and the researchers' assistant to whether or not the subject has actually received the medicine not because we think the subject or the assistant is dishonest but because we know that both subjects and researchers try to make the study come out "right." Subjects vary their responses according to subtle, usually unconscious signals from the researchers' assistant. As discussed later in this chapter, blinding helps us eliminate the human bias toward finding the "right" answer. This built-in bias works the same way in fingerprint examination. If the examiner serving as a verifier knows that the first examiner—perhaps a colleague in the same laboratory—has already decided that the unknown and known prints came from the same source, this will influence the verifying examiner; it will bias her toward confirming what the first examiner has already found.

The thinking behind the ubiquitous use of blind experiments in the sciences demonstrates an important principle: to conduct any inquiry in a way rigorous enough to learn the truth, we must guard against cognitive biases: errors in reasoning that all human beings fall into in the regular course of thinking. This happens not because of flaws in our characters—for example, that we harbor attitudes of bigotry or unfairness—but simply because human beings "unconsciously pick up cues from our environment and factor them in an unstated way into our mental analyses."[49] We also make unsupported and unnecessary assumptions, and approach our thinking with an unjustified degree of confidence in its correctness.[50] All people suffer from cognitive biases to one degree or another, so scientists make great efforts to avoid biases by utilizing strict procedures specifically designed to minimize them. These procedures make experimental results valid, stronger, and more useful. Failing to do this weakens results, because one loses the ability to tell whether the experimental variables or the cognitive biases account for the results. For these reasons, one always sees rigorous efforts to eliminate cognitive biases at the highest levels of the scientific enterprise.

Fingerprint examiners do not believe that they exhibit these biases, because, as highly trained and experienced professionals, they are unaffected by the biases that affect an average person. Veteran examiners, this thinking goes, would not be influenced by the simple fact that another examiner has already declared a match; they would make their own judgments, on the basis of the prints. But empirical testing does not support this belief. In a small but ingenious experiment, Itiel Dror and his colleagues from the University of Southampton set out to see whether context might influence expert fingerprint examiners in their conclusions.[51] Five experts, from a variety of agencies and countries and with a collective eighty-five years of experience, served as subjects. For each expert, unbeknownst to them, Dror and colleagues obtained a pair of fingerprints that the expert had identified as a conclusive and definite match in the regular course of his work five years earlier.[52] Two other independent experts, not involved in the experiment as subjects, verified that the pairs did indeed match. The subjects then received the same pairs of prints at a random time over the succeeding months in the regular course of their work. When the subjects received the prints, they were asked to examine them and were "told that the pair of prints was the one that was erroneously matched by the FBI as the Madrid bomber"—the prints from Brandon Mayfield's case—"creating an extraneous context that the prints were a non-match."[53] Of the five experts, only one said the prints matched—the same judgment the expert had come to before. The others all changed their opinions. One decided that insufficient evidence existed to allow a match or an exclusion; three decided that the prints did not match.[54] According to Dror and colleagues, this "shows that fingerprint identification decisions of experts are vulnerable to irrelevant and misleading contextual influences" and that "the extraneous context in which fingerprint identifications occur can determine the identification decision."[55] This experiment does not demonstrate errors by the experts due to negligence or carelessness. Rather, the results "reflect cognitive flaws and limitations in conducting objective and independent processing and evaluation of the information"— in other words, basic faults in the way the human mind works,[56] against which we must maintain some level of vigilance by using proper procedures. While Dror's experiment used only a small number of subjects, a larger follow-up study produced even stronger results.[57]

Given Dror's results, it seems difficult to imagine that allowing the verifier in the ACE-V process to know that the first examiner made an identification would not influence the verifier's own results. Just like the veteran examiners in Dror's studies, the verifier would receive a strong message telegraphing the "right" answer: the one arrived at by the first examiner. And without a process blinding the verifier to the earlier results, the verifier would not have to be corrupt or incompetent or negligent for the earlier results to influence the verification. Rather, she would just have to be human. The lesson here is not that fingerprint experts harbor biases; it is that fingerprint experts are humans, and all humans come with the full complement of biases and thinking distortions found in the brains of all of us. Yet not until 2011 did SWGFAST (the standard-setting body) create protocols for blind verification. And those it did create did not apply to every case and did not bind any law enforcement agency.

This does not mean that fingerprint identification does not work or always errs. In fact, it does allow law enforcement to make identifications of unknown prints in a high percentage of cases, and provides immeasurable assistance to prosecutors attempting to prove cases. But what the science and scholarship of the last fifteen years tells us is that, contrary to the usual claims its proponents make, it does not always work. It is, as practiced, fallible; mistakes get made, and we cannot even tell for certain how often this happens. It is not a science in any true sense of that word—certainly not compared to something like DNA identification. Most importantly, we now know how law enforcement could improve the use of fingerprint identification: by screening out human biases and moving toward a scientific, data-based approach. Holding fast to the old conceptions of a flawless method based on wisdom that needs no change or improvement seems, at best, untenable.

As we examine other disciplines in forensic science, the same themes that surface in fingerprint identification emerge repeatedly. Aside from DNA and identification of contraband and other substances through the techniques of analytic chemistry, most of forensic science comes down to a matter of human judgment, infused with considerable subjectivity. These other forensic disciplines do not rest on data, rigorously analyzed through valid statistical techniques, but rather on the experience-based decisions of individual human beings. Not enough—and sometimes, nothing—is done to guard against common cognitive biases. Experts in these disciplines cannot state their standard rates of error and often overstate their conclusions.

Firearms Identification

When most people think about matching a bullet or shell casing to a particular weapon, they use the term "ballistics," but the art of identifying firearms is really the study of tool marks. Tools make marks on objects whenever they come into contact with softer objects. Tools, in this sense, include things we think of as tools (screwdrivers, crowbars, hammers, or pliers) but also include the internal metal parts of a firearm, which make contact with the (softer) brass or lead components of ammunition. The marks that the firing pin, the barrel, and other parts of a gun leave on bullets and shell casings come within the broad classification of tool marks. These marks will depend on the manufacturing of the gun's inner workings and the materials of which they consist, as well as the tiny individual imperfections in these parts that develop over the course of the weapon's use. Marks will show up on the bullet from the spiral grooves cut into the inside of the gun barrel, and the brass of the cartridge case receives marks from the firing pin, the breech face, and the extractors and ejectors that push out expended ammunition and bring in new rounds ready for firing. Examining these marks, in order to try to match a fired projectile or spent cartridge to a particular weapon, constitutes one of the more common functions of forensic laboratories.

The markings on bullets and cartridges may disclose either class characteristics or individual characteristics. Class characteristics consist of distinguishing features shared by many, but not all, objects of the same type. For example, all knives by a certain manufacturer may have a distinctively serrated blade different from the edge used by all other manufacturers on their knives. For firearms, the number of grooves cut into the inside of the gun's barrel might distinguish one gun maker's products from all others. Class characteristics allow the examiner to narrow down the possible categories from which the object comes. For example, class characteristics may allow a firearms examiner to determine that the recovered bullet came from a gun of the type that the defendant possessed upon arrest. The examination then focuses on individual characteristics: microscopic markings that come from the very small individual imperfections in a firearm resulting from use and wear over its life. This examination consists of a visual comparison using two microscopes connected together to allow a side-by-side comparison of tool marks on the surfaces on known and unknown bullets or cartridge casings.

This sketch of the process describes what happens in most firearms identification scenarios, but it should not disguise an important fact: no mandatory protocol for firearms identification exists that would guard against errors, ensure that proper procedures are followed, and require that examiners conduct tests the same way every time. The federal Bureau of Alcohol, Tobacco, Firearms, and Explosives (ATFE) has created no such protocol for examining firearms, bullets, and casings.

The Association of Firearm and Tool Mark Examiners (AFTE) has established a governing standard for examiners to use in making an individualization, i.e., offering an opinion concerning whether a particular firearm or other tool made the particular markings the examiner observed. Under the standard, an examiner can declare that a particular gun left a particular set of tool marks on a bullet or cartridge when "sufficient agreement" exists in the pattern of the compared sets of marks.[58] According to the standard, "sufficient agreement" exists "when it exceeds the best agreement demonstrated between tool marks known to have been produced by different tools and is consistent with the agreement demonstrated by tool marks known to have been produced by the same tool."[59] The standard does not define "exceeds the best agreement" or "consistent with" and does not take into account, much less resolve, questions of "variability, reliability, repeatability, or the number of correlations needed to achieve a given degree of confidence."[60] The AFTE acknowledges that examinations based on this standard will rest on subjective judgments that largely depend upon the individual examiner's skill and experience. This standard recalls the definition used by fingerprint examiners to describe the judgments they make; it comes down to the same type of self-referential rule.

In its review of firearms identification and tool marks, the National Academy of Sciences report described the discipline's strengths and shortcomings. New technologies, such as ballistic imaging and expanded databases, might help examiners find a pool of possible matches. But in the end, "the final determination of a match is always done through direct physical comparison of the evidence by a firearms examiner."[61] The decision made by that examiner "remains a subjective decision based on unarticulated standards and no statistical estimation of error rates."[62] As with fingerprint examination, it is not the case that firearms identification is always wrong or can never help; on the contrary, it often supplies useful evidence that can form a key part of a prosecution. But when looked at with clarity and without the cloak of science it often wears, this discipline lacks a real standard by which to make judgments and relies on subjective human interpretation, not well-analyzed data and statistics. This leaves us without a way to estimate the accuracy of the technique, and without any prescribed protocol.

Impression and Pattern Evidence: Shoeprints and Tire Marks

With impression evidence from shoes and tires, analysts attempt to identify a specific source for the impression. In general terms, this process closely resembles the method used by tool-marks examiners, and the goal is the same: narrowing the source of the impression to one particular object. First, analysts attempt to identify the class characteristics of the object that left the impressions. If the class characteristics bring the object within the possible universe of objects in question, the examiner then looks for random individual identifying characteristics that result from the specific wear and tear that the object has undergone during use. For example, for a shoe, "individual identifying characteristics . . . result when something is randomly added to or taken away from a shoe outsole that either causes or contributes to making that shoe outsole unique."[63] These characteristics could "include cuts, scratches, gouges, holes, or random inclusions" like rocks or wads of gum.[64]

With this analysis of individual characteristics, the analyst may make or rule out identification according to the number of characteristics the evidence shares with the suspected source. But just as with the identification of fingerprints and tool marks, the National Academy of Sciences tells us that "there is no defined threshold that must be surpassed, nor are there any studies that associate the number of matching characteristics with the probability that the impressions were made by a common source."[65] One authoritative source says that many matching characteristics must be found before the comparison merits a positive identification, but the most important factors are other things: the examiner's experience, the clarity of the impression, and the uniqueness of the characteristics seen.[66] Training, qualifications, and the terminology used to describe the conclusions of the examiners vary widely.[67] As the National Academy of Sciences says,

> there is no consensus regarding the number of individual characteristics needed to make a positive identification . . . [nor is there] any data about

the variability of class or individual characteristics or about the validity or reliability of the method. Without [these] studies, it is impossible to assess the number of characteristics that must match in order to have any particular degree of confidence about the source of the impression.[68]

The experts in the field may get a sense of the probabilities of different individual characteristics through experience, but "it is difficult to avoid biases in experience-based judgment, especially in the absence of a feedback mechanism to correct an erroneous judgment."[69]

Analysis of Hair and Fiber

Forensic science can provide some useful evidence from hair and fiber found in connection with a crime scene. But analysis of hair and fiber shares many of the same problems plaguing other forensic disciplines. Both humans and animals shed hair continuously. Characteristics of hair vary between individuals, so that forensic scientists can include or exclude certain individuals from the pool of possible suspects, but forensic examiners analyzing hair cannot match hair to a particular person the way DNA analysis can. No statistical foundation, built upon real and rigorously analyzed data, exists to make these kinds of definitive statements. Yet hair examiners have often made strong identification claims based on their experience, only to have these assertions proven grievously wrong later by DNA analysis.

Hair analysis has exhibited major problems with accuracy. In an FBI study, hair examiners found eighty pairs of hair samples "associated" through microscopic examination of their characteristics. When scientists performed mitochondrial DNA analysis on the samples, test results showed that 12.5 percent of the pairs actually came from different sources.[70] This illustrates two fundamental problems with hair analysis. First, forensic examination of hair characteristics remains imprecise, and cannot dependably move beyond a class identification—that is, whether a particular hair does or does not belong to the same class of persons to which the accused belongs. Second, imprecise terminology can muddy the waters in this and other forensic fields. By "associated," did the hair examiners mean something like "match"? Did they mean that the hairs shared a certain number of class characteristics? Or did they mean something between these two possibilities?

According the National Academy of Sciences, hair analysis carries with it many of the same problems we have already seen in other forensic disciplines. "No scientifically accepted statistics exist about the frequency with which particular characteristics of hair are distributed in the population. There appear to be no uniform standards on the number of features on which hairs must agree. . . . The categorization of hair features depends heavily on examiner proficiency and practical experience. . . . [T]estimony linking microscopic hair analysis with particular defendants is highly unreliable . . . [there is] no scientific support for the use of hair comparisons for individualizations in the absence of nuclear DNA."[71]

Analysts can examine natural fiber (from botanical sources) and synthetic fiber (such as polyester or nylon) microscopically, just as they do with hair. These examinations will suffer from the same kinds of limitations that hair does: their physical characteristics can give examiners ways of comparing them to known samples of carpets, fabrics, or ropes, but these microscopic analyses will yield only class-level comparisons.[72] (The only exceptions might consist of examinations of samples in which one looks to have been torn from the other; this might allow comparison of the mating edges and any patterns in cloth, which would make it possible to associate a torn sample with the garment from which it was ripped.)[73] The analysis of fibers can become more precise than that of hair because scientists can use analytic chemistry to examine them and probe their makeup, giving the results a stronger scientific footing than a microscopic examination alone. Still, fiber examiners generally agree that they can only make class, not individual, identifications of these materials.[74] While professional guidelines exist for fiber examinations, they contain no set standards for the number and quality of characteristics that samples must share in order to justify a conclusion that fibers came from the same manufacturing batch. Thus a "match" in a fiber examination "means only that the fibers could have come from the same type of garment, carpet, or furniture"[75]—in other words, only class evidence of limited use.

Forensic Odontology

Forensic odontology, often called forensic dentistry, has two main uses in criminal cases. First, it can make a positive identification of unknown human remains, assuming the availability of teeth with the body and dental records of a known person to which to compare the teeth. This is a well-established and relatively uncontroversial use of science. The second use to which this discipline is put is the comparison of bite marks, and this has become as

controversial as any forensic technique could ever be, because of its sometimes outlandish claims and incorrect results.[76]

Bite marks occur most often in cases of homicide, sexual assault, and child
abuse. The American Board of Forensic Odontology (ABFO) has approved
guidelines for the collection of bite mark evidence, both from victims and
biters.[77] The bite marks collected come from human skin, but these marks on
the skin change with time and undergo distortions because of swelling, healing, unevenness of the bite, and skin elasticity. Therefore, even though certain methods of collecting bite marks from the skin have become accepted
(photography, dental casts, electron microscopy, etc.), the condition and
variability of the skin in which the marks rest "may severely limit the validity
of forensic odontology."[78]

The ABFO guidelines list a number of methods of analysis that forensic
odontologists might use to study bite marks, but they say nothing about the
criteria for using each method to match a bite mark to a particular person's
teeth, or the required degree of probability of any such match. No studies
exist to quantify the reproducibility of results between different examiners,
or between the same examiners over time.[79] Even when using the ABFO
guidelines, examiners have reported "widely differing results and a high
percentage of false positive matches of bite marks using controlled comparison studies."[80] No large-scale studies have demonstrated the uniqueness
of bite marks: a critical assumption necessary for the identification of any
individual through a bite mark. Most comparisons are made between the
bite mark found at the crime scene and a cast of the teeth of an individual
already suspected. Blind comparisons and verification by another expert do
not usually occur. Add the fact that police find bite mark evidence in highly
sensationalized or grisly cases, with police under pressure to announce or
confirm a suspect, and one can see how easily substantial biases may enter
the investigation.

A 2001 review of bite mark analysis stated that an examination of the field
"revealed a lack of valid evidence to support many of the assumptions made
by forensic dentists during bite mark comparisons."[81] The National Academy
of Sciences reported that in the course of gathering facts and testimony for
its 2009 report on forensic science, it "received no evidence of an existing
scientific basis for identifying [a bite mark from] an individual to the exclusion of others." All of this, the academy report said, "has led to questioning of
the value and scientific objectivity of such evidence."[82]

Bloodstain Pattern Analysis

The analysis of the patterns made by blood exiting the body has gained enormous currency in recent years. Dr. Henry Lee, a pathologist often retained in high-profile cases, has gained lasting fame as an expert in blood pattern analysis; he testified for the defense in the O. J. Simpson murder trial in the 1990s. And television programs such as the *CSI* shows make frequent use of "blood spatter" analysis as a way to solve cases.

Bloodstains occur in a wide variety of crimes. Many variables influence the form and pattern of a stain, making interpretation of bloodstains much more complicated than it might at first seem. Reading these patterns takes not only experience but significant education in the physics of fluid dynamics and the pathology of wounds. The National Academy of Sciences cautions that "the opinions of bloodstain pattern analysts are more subjective than scientific," and since requests for bloodstain pattern analysis often originate with either prosecutors or defense attorneys as a way to bolster their cases and not to simply investigate the facts, problems with bias constantly recur.[83] Science does support some aspects of bloodstain pattern analysis, but some experts in the field seem comfortable extrapolating far beyond what the science will support.[84]

Bottom Line: Most of Forensic Science Lacks a Basis in Science

With the exception of DNA testing and other forensic disciplines grounded in chemical analysis, most forensic science does not qualify as science in any true sense of that term. Disciplines like fingerprint analysis, firearm tool-mark analysis, and bite mark analysis have no basis in data or statistics, and do not originate in inquiry conducted according to scientific principles. Rather, they rely on human judgment grounded in experience, but practitioners in the field exercise that judgment without reference to rigorous and agreed-upon standards. Without any scientific foundation, analysts of these types of evidence lack any basis upon which to estimate the probability that their "matches" are correct; they cannot explain to a judge or jury what rate of error to expect, and therefore they cannot justify whatever degree of confidence they might express in their results. Instead, they substitute claims of zero error rates or vague terms like "associated with," neither of which has any real meaning and both of which can badly mislead the jury. Though scientists have long understood the influences of cognitive biases in scientific experimentation, and have created standard practices to avoid and guard against these biases, the forensic sciences have done little or nothing to address biases. Therefore, it is fair to say that much of forensic science could be much more useful if standardized, performed, and checked according to scientific principles.

Police Interrogation of Suspects: The Practice and Science of Asking Questions

A crime occurs. Police respond, find a suspect, and begin to question him. The suspect usually talks to police,[85] attempting an explanation or trying to deflect blame. Some of the information the suspect conveys may help police; some of it may not. For police, the best thing that may come out of questioning a suspect is a confession—a statement that admits guilt.

Detectives want a confession from every suspect; prosecutors want to see a confession in every case that goes to court. Confessions constitute powerful evidence—perhaps the most powerful evidence one can imagine. When the defendant admits to committing a crime, the confession removes all doubt about his guilt. While the prosecution in the American system of justice always has the burden of proving each element of the crime beyond a reasonable doubt, a confession—especially a confession studded with details of the crime and insights into the perpetrator's mental processes that only the person actually responsible for the crime would know—will go a long way toward carrying that burden, almost by itself. Unquestionably, it helps the prosecution to have evidence other than a confession, and without a confession, police obviously must have other evidence. But if there is a confession, this other evidence will often prove unnecessary because everyone understands something basic and important about confessions: absent mental infirmity, intoxication, or blatant physical abuse, no sane, sober adult would confess to a crime she did not commit. And the more serious the crime in question, the less likely that a suspect would falsely confess to it. Taking the rap for possession of a small amount of marijuana for a friend on probation? Maybe. Admitting to guilt for a horrible rape or murder that one had no part in? No way.

Yet DNA analysis has proven that this rock-solid certainty no longer holds true in every case. DNA test results have pushed us far from our baseline assumptions concerning confessions. As a result, we now know two things. First, we know that innocent people sometimes do confess, even in the absence of physical mistreatment, intoxication, or mental illness.[86] Second, we know that confessions retain a unique, almost overwhelming power to persuade—even in the face of DNA that directly contradicts the confession.

These two points seem contradictory, but then we look at the case of the Norfolk Four, and we understand how these ideas can coexist.

The Norfolk Four: The Confession Is King, Never to Be Dethroned

In July of 1997, someone raped and murdered a young woman named Michelle Bosko in the apartment she and her husband shared near the naval base in Norfolk, Virginia.[87] Police immediately focused on Danial Williams, a navy man like Michelle's husband, who lived in an apartment across the hall. Though he had no previous criminal record, police had Williams come to the police station. Over the course of an all-night interrogation session, police questioned Williams, summarily dismissing his denials and repeatedly stating they already knew of his certain guilt. Police falsely told him that he had failed a polygraph test he willingly took and that a witness had seen him leaving the victim's apartment at a critical time.[88] When he insisted he could not have done the crime, officers suggested that he had repressed the memory of it, causing Williams to doubt his own recollection.[89] For ten hours, Williams maintained his innocence, until a senior detective began to question him much more aggressively—yelling at him, poking him in the chest, insisting loudly on his guilt of rape and murder, even threatening him with the death penalty, all the while telling Williams that a confession could mean that the detective could get the capital murder charge reduced.[90] His resistance worn away after eleven hours of continuous questioning without sleep or food, Williams broke. He made up a story about how he committed the rape and murder that he thought the police wanted to hear, in order to stop the interrogation. Just hours later, however, the police discovered that much of Williams's tale did not square with important details they learned when they received the autopsy report. So they brought him back into the interrogation room and got him to make a second confession, this one consistent with the autopsy report. But later, when the report on the DNA recovered from the rape investigation came back, the investigators got a surprise: the test showed that Williams had not left the semen found in Michelle Bosko's body. The DNA test excluded him.[91] Rather than take this powerful scientific evidence seriously and ask whether they had the right man, the police fell into one of the most well-known cognitive biases: they discounted the evidence that did not support what they already believed, and instead went hunting for evidence that bolstered their case. To do this in a case in which irrefutable DNA evidence contradicted Williams's confessions, police now began to say that he had acted with an accomplice—even though neither the first nor the second confession Williams made had mentioned this crucial fact.[92] The police zeroed in on Williams's roommate, Joseph Dick, as the likely source of the DNA found on the victim, and quickly pried a third confession out of Williams, this time implicating Dick. They then subjected Dick to the same interrogation tactics that had ensnared Williams: a marathon questioning session, positing his guilt with absolute certainty despite his denials, lying to him about evidence against him, and threatening him with the death penalty if he did not confess. When Dick finally confessed, police believed they now had the two perpetrators—until further DNA tests showed that Dick was not the source of the semen, either. Concluding, again, that others must have been involved, police repeated this process—they obtained revised (false) confessions by both Williams and Dick, implicating yet more men, two more of whom then also confessed falsely. All told, the police used confessions they got from the four who confessed to charge seven men—despite the fact that the DNA did not match a single one of them. Of the four who confessed, three served eleven years in prison, and one served eight. The other three who did not confess spent between seven and ten months in jail before prosecutors dropped the charges.[93] The real perpetrator, a man who knew the victim and had been in her apartment, confessed in a letter from prison (he was incarcerated on another charge) that he had committed the crimes and had acted alone. When police interviewed him, he repeated his confession in the first twenty minutes that the officers spoke with him.[94] This man's DNA matched the semen recovered from the victim. Yet the police insisted that he must have acted in conjunction with the seven other men, and they refused to accept a confession from him until he agreed to say that he acted as part of an eight-person gang rape—even though no physical evidence existed that a gang rape occurred.[95]

To this day, the prosecutors and police involved in the case insist that all eight men committed the crime together, despite the DNA evidence found in the victim's body that implicates only the man who confessed from prison, and the lack of any physical evidence to tie the other seven to the crime.[96] With powerful DNA evidence so directly contradicting all of the confessions, many prosecutors would at least consider dropping the charges.[97] But the prosecutors in the Norfolk cases, D. J. Hansen and Valerie Bowen, did not. Asked if he thought suspects might ever confess falsely, Hansen replied, "certainly not [in this case],"[98] despite the presence of multiple contradictory confessions in the evidence, all unsupported by the DNA. He remains convinced of the guilt of the seven defendants; asked whether the DNA results affected his thinking on whether they had had been at the crime scene, Hansen said "not at all."[99] Bowen claims that "a lot of corroborating evidence" existed to support the guilt of the defendants despite the DNA results, but "I can't even go into all of [it] now, it would just take too long."[100] Hansen has no second thoughts. "Everything fits together. . . . It just makes so much sense when you look back on it."[101]

We cannot be sure that we know the "ground truth" in the case—the actual truth of what happened to Michelle Bosko. But with DNA telling a story very different from the confessions, and with an actual perpetrator who has made a confession of acting alone supported by DNA results, the state's version of how the crime occurred and who did it seems preposterous. Yet the power of the confessions overwhelmed even multiple DNA results. This makes the interrogation process vitally important.

The Structure of Police Interrogation: The Reid Technique

To understand police interrogation, we need to start with the dominant interrogation technique used in American police departments, which comes from John E. Reid & Associates. The firm describes its method as "the leading interview and interrogation approach used today in both law enforcement and business communities."[102] Known as the Reid Technique, this method comprises nine specific steps that, its proponents say, identify the guilty without the danger of inducing false confessions from the innocent.[103]

Created in the 1940s and 1950s by lawyers John E. Reid and Fred E. Inbau,[104] the Reid Technique aimed to replace the use of physical force in police interrogation—the so-called third degree—with a scientific process.[105] Their book, *Criminal Interrogation and Confessions*,[106] now the most well-known book on police interrogation in the United States, contains the complete explanation of the Reid Technique,[107] and it still dominates the field.[108]

The book begins with a crucial distinction: the difference between an interview and an interrogation.[109] According to the book, "[a]n interview is nonaccusatory" in approach and tone, and its "purpose is to gather information" through a free-flowing, loose style.[110] The interview typically occurs early in an investigation, and can take place in a variety of settings.[111] By contrast, "[a]n interrogation is accusatory," and takes place only when the officer believes the suspect has not told the truth during the interview.[112] The interrogation attempts "to learn the truth" by getting the suspect to admit what he or she has already denied during the interview, and takes place "only when the investigator is reasonably certain of the suspect's guilt."[113]

The Reid Technique begins with the Behavior Analysis Interview, which uses "behavior-provoking questions" to allow the officer both to gather information and to assess the credibility of the suspect.[114] The Behavior Analysis Interview gives officers the opportunity to decide whether or not the suspect has lied or told the truth, because "[r]esearch has demonstrated that innocent subjects tend to respond differently to these specialized [behavior-provoking] questions than do deceptive subjects."[115] Thus the Behavior Analysis Interview revolves around making an assessment of credibility and guilt. Has the subject told the truth, or lied? Is he or she guilty? As cognitive psychologist and law professor Richard Leo puts it, the Reid Technique teaches interrogators that during the Behavior Analysis Interview, "it is their job to act, in effect, as a human polygraph"[116]—to determine the truth. If the officer decides the suspect has lied, based on his or her experience and training, the officer proceeds to the nine-step interrogation process.

The guiding principle of a Reid interrogation is to elicit information that confirms the interrogator's view of the case, so each of the nine steps of the Reid Technique targets that goal: confirmation of guilt through confession. In *Criminal Interrogation and Confessions*, the authors say that interrogation aims only "to learn the truth,"[117] asserting that many people mistakenly believe that "the purpose of an interrogation is to elicit a confession."[118] But this statement is utterly unconvincing. The authors admit that when an interrogation occurs, this "means that the investigator believes that the suspect has not told the truth during [the nonaccusatory Behavior Analysis Interview]"; police proceed to interrogation only when "the investigator is reasonably certain of the suspect's guilt."[119] In other words, the Reid Technique seeks to obtain evidence to support the theory of the case upon which the officer has already decided. Each step in the process serves to obtain that evidence by breaking down the ability of the suspect to resist providing the police with the evidence that they have already determined they need.

Reid-trained interrogators begin by isolating the suspect in a small, private, sparsely furnished room within the police station, equipped with a one-way mirror so that other officers can observe the suspect's behavior.[120] Step 1, "Direct, Positive Confrontation," instructs the interrogator to start "with a direct statement indicating absolute certainty in the suspect's guilt."[121] This exhibits the interrogator's confidence in his or her judgment and knowledge, and demonstrates that denial will accomplish nothing. The interrogator should follow this with a "transition statement" that "offers a reason for the interrogation other than to elicit a confession"—for example, that the police just need to know the truth so they can understand why the suspect committed the crime.[122]

In Step 2, the interrogator introduces the investigation theme. The theme expresses a reason for the commission of the crime that implicitly offers the suspect an excuse for having committed the offense. The theme will blame others for the offense—the victim ("he asked for it") or an accomplice ("it was all your partner's idea, from the looks of it"), or will explain the offense away as the product of a particularly tough circumstance ("a man who's broke has to find a way to feed his family, no matter what").

Step 3 concerns the suspect's denials. All suspects will deny guilt, according to the Reid Technique, and the interrogator cannot allow these protests to stop the momentum or direction of the questioning. Step 3 thus involves brushing aside the suspect's protests and circling back to the excuse of the theme set out in Step 2. Step 4 involves a different kind of denial: dealing with the suspect's stated reasons why he or she would not have committed the crime. The suspect may invoke economic ("I have plenty of money—why would I rob him?"), religious ("I'm observant, so I would never do that"), or even moral ("It's just plain wrong to hit an old lady") rationales. The interrogator should not accept these reasons, because according to the Reid Technique, only the guilty suspect will offer them. The interrogator must not accept these objections, and must press on with the interrogation theme and the excuses already offered: "Whatever, but I think this whole thing was the victim's fault."

When the suspect's denials and objections prove unavailing, the suspect attempts to mentally withdraw. So Step 5 centers around efforts to keep the suspect's attention. The interrogator will keep talking, attempt a tone of utmost sincerity, maintain eye contact, and draw physically closer in an attempt to keep the suspect engaged and to keep the process moving toward an incriminating statement. This may lead into Step 6, in which the interrogator will observe the suspect adopting a passive mood as he or she contemplates the risks and benefits of telling the truth. The interrogator will often recognize this phase by changes to the suspect's behavior, such as crying, slumping over, or looking at the floor.

In Step 7, the interrogator sets up the suspect for the kill by offering the suspect a set of alternative explanations to choose from, one more acceptable than the other. For example, the interrogator may ask, "Was this the only time you did this, or had you done this kind of thing before?" Surely, it seems better if this constitutes the suspect's only transgression. However, any answer traps the suspect. Whichever alternative the suspect chooses, the creators of the Reid Technique say, "amounts to a confession."

In Step 8, the interrogator gets the suspect into the conversation by having him or her talk about the details of the offense, which will establish guilt. Details help; facts confirming guilty action or knowledge (the location of the weapon used or the robbery proceeds) known only to the perpetrator mean the interrogator has struck gold. The more detail, the better. All that remains is Step 9: reducing the confession to writing.

The authors of *Criminal Interrogation and Confessions* take almost two hundred pages to lay out every detail of the nine steps. They cover what kind of reaction to expect from a suspect to virtually everything the interrogator says or does. Yet something is missing: the authors give the reader no evidence that proves their statements. The book contains some footnotes, but they do not substantiate its many recommendations. The authors simply make assertions for the reader to accept, and for decades, most readers did just that.

The Reid Technique's Most Basic Assumption

The Reid Technique assumes that during the Behavior Analysis Interview, investigators can correctly discern truth from lies. Yet as cognitive psychologist and law professor Richard Leo explains, "no physiological or psychological response unique to lying (and never present in truthfulness) has ever been discovered."[123] Thus the theory of the Behavior Analysis Interview remains implausible, especially vulnerable to interpreter bias, and open to doubts about its validity and false positives.[124] Leo also notes that none of the data that allegedly support using the Behavior Analysis Interview to tell truth from lies have ever become publicly available (to allow others to attempt to replicate the results, as is customary in all scientific work). From what anyone can tell from all of the published work of the creators of the Reid Technique, the data seem "to be little more than an accumulation of unsystematic, post-hoc observations intended to verify [their] own preconceptions."[125]

But the problem with the Behavior Analysis Interview goes deeper than the absence of data. For more than ten years, researchers have produced multiple empirical studies that have demonstrated that training in the Reid Technique does not improve one's ability to tell truth from lies; in fact, it actually seems to hurt one's ability to do so. In 1999, Professor Saul Kassin and his coauthor, Professor Christina Fong, studied the ability to detect deception using the Reid Technique and its nine-step method.[126] Subjects watched a video recording of people interviewed using the Reid Technique; the interview concerned whether the people had committed a mock crime. One group of research subjects had received training in the Reid Technique for identifying deception, and the other group had not. All then gave their opinions on the guilt or innocence of the people shown in the recordings, and their level of confidence in their own assessments of guilt and innocence. The results showed that judgment accuracy did not rise above the level of chance for either group; training in the Reid Technique did not make people any better at spotting lies. But Kassin and Fong did identify a distinct down side to using the Reid Technique: those utilizing it were "more self-confident and more articulate about the reasons for their often erroneous judgments." In another study,[127] researchers videotaped male prison inmates giving truthful confessions to the crimes for which juries and judges had convicted them. They also videotaped the inmates confessing to crimes that the researchers had selected that they had not committed. The researchers then had college students and police investigators view the tapes to assess their accuracy at distinguishing true from false confessions. Neither the students nor the trained police officers did particularly well; both groups produced accuracy rates not much different than chance. According to the authors of the study, this tells us that most people cannot distinguish true from false statements with any dependability—and that the training and experience that members of law enforcement have in these matters does not make any difference. Other researchers have replicated these and similar findings on these issues.[128]

How the Interrogation Process Generates False Confessions

In 2004, Steven A. Drizin and Richard A. Leo published a wide-ranging study of false confessions.[129] Unlike previous research, this study examined a large sample of cases that lay at the heart of the issue—"125 recent cases of proven interrogation-induced false confessions (i.e., cases in which indisputably innocent individuals confessed to crimes they did not commit)"—to examine how the criminal justice system dealt with these cases.[130] Drizin and Leo's work shows that these statements from innocent individuals happen as a direct product of police tactics that they observed, which emulate the nine steps of the Reid Technique. The investigator

> usually relies on several well-known interrogation techniques and strategies to persuade the suspect that he is caught and that he is powerless to change his situation. The investigator is likely to accuse the suspect of having committed the crime, cut off the suspect's denials, roll past the suspect's objections, and interrupt or ignore the suspect's assertions of innocence. If the suspect offers an alibi, the interrogator will attack it as inconsistent, contradicted by all of the case evidence, implausible and/or simply impossible—even if none of these assertions is true.[131]

According to the researchers, "The most effective technique used to persuade a suspect that his situation is hopeless is to confront him with seemingly objective and incontrovertible evidence, whether or not any actually exists. American police often confront suspects with fabricated evidence, such as nonexistent eyewitnesses, false fingerprints, make-believe videotapes, fake polygraph results, and so on."[132] People unfamiliar with police tactics often express shock that the law allows police to lie during the interrogations of suspects, but it does; in fact, police deception in interrogation received the U.S. Supreme Court's blessing long ago.[133] The idea of fabricating evidence—for example, telling the suspect that police lifted his fingerprint or found his DNA at the crime scene, or that he failed a polygraph examination, or even manufacturing documents that purport to prove these things—may seem to put police in an ethical no man's land, but the Supreme Court has never ruled these practices out. And make no mistake: the police use them regularly. All of this occurs together with a process that the psychologist Saul Kassin calls "maximization": harsh assertions not only of guilt but of severe consequences should the suspect persist in denying involvement. Failure to confess, the suspect hears repeatedly, will result in the worst possible outcomes: long imprisonment, horrible conditions of confinement—even the death penalty.

Once the suspect becomes convinced by these tactics that no escape exists except through confession, the interrogator offers the suspect an out: an excuse for why the suspect committed the crime. The idea is to give the suspect a moral justification for what the police say he did. The victim "had it coming." The suspect had merely engaged in "legitimate self-defense." The suspect could only have done the crime under the influence of alcohol or drugs or mental illness. And the interrogator portrays all of these excuses as mitigating factors—reasons for the crime that will surely lessen the charges, reduce the punishment, maybe even result in the charges disappearing. They give the suspect a way out. If he will confess to having committed the crime under these circumstances, the interrogator implies, he will receive leniency, favorable consideration, or even escape from confinement. Kassin calls this process "minimization": offering a moral excuse in combination with the implication of favorable treatment as an inducement to escape the situation through confession.

These techniques create a psychological process of great power—strong enough that few can resist, including those who have not committed the crime. According to Drizin and Leo, this creates real danger. "The techniques used to accomplish these manipulations are so effective that if misused they can result in decisions to confess from the guilty and innocent alike," they explain.[134] This means that interrogation-induced false confessions in the American criminal justice system probably occur far more often than previously supposed.[135] According to the data in their study and all of the best recent research, false confessions occur in somewhere between 14 and 25 percent of all wrongful conviction cases.[136] This results in a system askew, untethered to the goal of attaining justice to an extent far more drastic than most people imagine.[137] Worse yet, the confession becomes, for all practical purposes, the end of the investigation.[138] Once police get the defendant to confess, police stop investigating, prosecutors adopt the police theory, and judges and jurors accept the confessions.

The Unrivaled Power of Confessions

Confessions have a singular power to convince judges and juries; the foremost authorities describe confessions as among the most potent types of evidence, with greater impact than other forms of strong proof.[139] Even though people understand that certain types of interrogation tactics create psychological coercion, recent survey research shows that the public does not believe that these tactics could result in false confessions. When researchers examined samples of proven false confessions, the evidence bolstered this point. When defendants who had given confessions proven false decided to plead not guilty and went to trial, the overwhelming number of them suffered convictions; guilty verdicts ranged between 73[140] and 81 percent.[141] Indeed, wrongful conviction cases have shown beyond any dispute that "juries routinely believe false confessions, as do the police and prosecutors" who investigate and prosecute the cases in which false confessions emerge.[142]

Scientists explain the tenacity of our beliefs in confessions, despite evidence to the contrary, as an example of three well-known processes. First, people believe that common sense dictates that one should trust confessions. Confessing to a crime obviously runs counter to the confessor's self-interest. Since it implicates the person in a crime, the confessor may suffer punishment. Thus no one would confess unless the statement represented the truth. Social scientists know this as an example of the fundamental attribution error: observers see behavior and attribute it to the disposition of the actor by taking the behavior at face value. Observers disregard the role that situational factors may play, even though those factors may in fact have everything to do with causing the behavior.[143] Second, as discussed earlier, most people do a poor job of telling truth from deception. Recall the study that compared the ability to judge the truth of people viewing taped confessions from inmates to the actual crimes they committed, and taped confessions to crimes they had not committed.[144] The college student subjects did no better than chance at detecting lies—perhaps not surprising, since they had little experience with this. But trained and experienced police officers did no better than the college students—and yet they endowed their judgments with much greater confidence.[145] Third, many false confessions contain a rich amount of content referring to the details of the circumstances of, and even reasons for, the crime. The confession that includes not just "yes, I did it" but also dramatic details about the scene, the victim, and the way the suspect committed the crime becomes incredibly persuasive. These details make their way into confessions because the high-pressure, leading questioning that forms the heart of the interrogation process will often supply the suspect with considerable information about crucial aspects of the crime, effectively "feeding" the suspect everything he or she needs to produce a highly believable statement. This process is part and parcel of everyday interrogation techniques but does not show up explicitly in the confession itself. Thus the judge or jury never sees how the interrogation process itself introduced these persuasive elements into the interaction between investigator and suspect.[146]

Eyewitness Identifications: Powerful, but Prone to Error

As scientists have learned how traditional police investigative methods have resulted in wrongful convictions, eyewitness identification procedures remain in a class by themselves. First, eyewitness testimony provides one of the most direct links one can imagine between the accused and the crime. The eyewitness to the crime says, in effect, "I saw this person commit the crime with my own eyes; I am here to tell you that it was him." Even a fingerprint discovered in an incriminating place does not have this power; a print found on a murder weapon says, at most, "a person with this fingerprint handled this item at some point," but it does not tell us when this occurred or what the person did with the weapon. Second, eyewitness testimony possesses strong power to persuade. When a witness testifies that she saw the defendant pull the trigger, she got a good look at him, and she will never forget his face, this convinces members of a jury in a way that few things other than a confession can do. Studies show that an eyewitness with no obvious motive to color the truth almost always convinces jurors.[147] Third, however, despite its power to persuade and to link the defendant to the crime, eyewitness identification is uniquely flawed. In the more than 250 cases in which DNA has proved the innocence of the accused, no other single factor contributed more often to miscarriages of justice than mistaken eyewitness identification.[148] Of all of the wrongful convictions that DNA has proven, from the late 1980s through the first half of 2010, eyewitness identification errors show up in an astonishing 75 percent of them[149]—as many as unvalidated or improper forensics (50 percent)[150] and false confessions (25 percent)[151] combined.[152] Moreover, the many wrongful convictions already exposed by DNA "can only be a small fraction of the total number of cases in which people have been convicted because they were mistakenly identified by eyewitnesses," because in the vast majority of criminal cases that depend on eyewitness testimony, there is no biological material left behind to test.[153] Sexual assault cases usually include some trace of fluid or tissue containing DNA, and they therefore make up most of the cases in which exonerations have followed DNA testing. But most robberies, murders, and other offenses that might utilize eyewitness identification do not produce DNA-laden material to test. That means that the cases in which we have DNA-proven mistaken identifications probably represent just the tip of the iceberg of wrongful convictions in which mistaken identifications play a role. All in all, eyewitness identification evidence turns out on close examination to rank among the least reliable types of proof.

Kirk Bloodsworth's case makes an excellent example.[154] Bloodsworth had a clean record when police arrested him for the rape and murder of a nine-year-old girl in 1984. The perpetrator had beaten the victim, raped her, and strangled her. Five eyewitnesses testified that they had seen Bloodsworth with the little girl; the prosecution presented other evidence as well, including statements Bloodsworth had made. Upon conviction, the court sentenced Bloodsworth to death, and he spent two years on death row. An appeals court threw out the other evidence and overturned the verdict, but the eyewitnesses testified in a second trial. The jury convicted him again, and this time the judge gave him two consecutive life sentences. Thankfully, the state had preserved evidence—the victim's underwear—containing the perpetrator's DNA, and when testing of small amounts of biological material became possible in the early 1990s, the results cleared Bloodsworth. He was not the source of the semen, and in 1993 the state released him from prison— the first person ever released on the basis of DNA testing.

Nevertheless, police and prosecutors doubted Bloodsworth, even after his release. The eyewitness testimony seemed so strong that some still believed he had committed this horrible crime; even one of the original prosecutors in the case would not accept the DNA results. Perhaps someone else had contaminated the child's underwear with unknown DNA, they reasoned, and Bloodsworth had actually raped and killed the girl— a theory never mentioned in either of Bloodsworth's trials. In 2003, ten years after Bloodworth's release and nineteen years after he went to death row, something remarkable happened: a computerized DNA search made a hit. Police in another case had entered the real killer's DNA into the system, and it had matched the semen found in the little girl's underwear. The facts finally vindicated Bloodsworth: he had not raped and killed the child; another man definitely had. Bloodsworth's case illustrates just how tenaciously people cling to eyewitness identifications, even in the face of proof through DNA.

The Research on Eyewitness Identification

Pioneers in the field of psychology first published articles and books concerning the science behind eyewitness testimony early in the twentieth century. Hugo Munsterberg's influential 1908 book *On the Witness Stand*[155] and others[156] provided an early glimpse of what psychology might someday achieve. Breakthroughs came in the 1970s, especially with the work of Elizabeth Loftus. Loftus did exacting experiments that proved that laboratory testing "using realistic stimuli" such as pictures "could be used in rigorous scientific experiments that revealed basic phenomena in memory and also had practical utility for understanding eyewitness error."[157] Loftus "legitimized the study of eyewitnesses in the minds of psychological scientists . . . [and] helped spawn a new generation of researchers who have carefully and strategically built an empirical literature that the legal system must contend with."[158] One of these is Gary Wells, whose experiments and research have shaped the agenda of a growing cadre of psychologists who have helped the world understand how the human mind collects, stores, and recalls information that may become eyewitness testimony, and how the actors in the legal system influence the shape of that testimony.[159] Loftus, Wells, and other scientists produced hundreds of studies relevant to eyewitness testimony. Moreover, the identification of suspects by witnesses is an interaction almost perfectly suited to the type of laboratory testing that psychologists know how to do. According to Wells and others,[160] conducting a proper lineup is just like conducting a proper scientific experiment.

> The analogy can be stated as follows: A lineup is like an experiment: the police have a hypothesis (that the suspect is the culprit); they collect materials that could be used to test the hypothesis (e.g., picture of the suspect and filler pictures), they create a design (e.g., placing suspect's picture in a particular position in an array), instruct the subject(s) (eyewitness or eyewitnesses); run the procedure (show the lineup to the eyewitnesses), record the data (identification of the suspect or not); and interpret the hypothesis in light of the data (decide whether the identification decision changes their assessment of whether the suspect is the culprit).[161]

While differences between the real lineups and experiments certainly exist—scientists can bring in as many subjects as needed to rule out chance, whereas police only have as many "subjects" as witnesses who come forward—the analogy helps us to see that the way toward better and more accurate lineups requires doing just what scientists do with experiments: we must take effective measures to eliminate or control whatever variables might interfere with the interpretation of the data.[162] Thus the research helps us identify these "confounding" variables, and the ways in which scientists conduct controlled experiments help us construct ways of eliminating these variables from the lineups—all of which can yield more accurate identification results.

Much of what we can do to improve eyewitness identification starts with relative judgment. Conceptualized by Wells in 1984,[163] the idea of relative judgment articulates a simple but vital idea: witnesses will tend to select the person in the lineup who looks most like their memories of the person they observed commit the crime.[164] When the lineup includes the person whom the witness observed committing the crime, relative judgment creates no problem. But if the actual perpetrator does not appear in the lineup because police mistakenly suspect another person, relative judgment creates real difficulties. Someone in the lineup will always look more like the actual perpetrator than the rest, so the witness is likely to select that person.[165] If the witness selects the person that the police (mistakenly) suspect, the police will find their (mistaken) suspicions confirmed, and that can lead to charges against the mistaken suspect. The following procedures can help control relative judgment.

Pre-Lineup Instructions. Early on in the experimental exploration of how eyewitness identification works, scientists tested the possibility of using pre-lineup instructions for eyewitnesses. The pre-lineup instruction tells the witness that the actual perpetrator might or might not be present in the lineup or array of photos the witness will view. This kind of instruction would effectively tell the witness that the police might or might not have "the right guy"—something that most witnesses would otherwise assume upon a request to view a lineup ("If they didn't have the right guy, why would they have me come in and choose?"), which would of course become an exercise of relative judgment. Roy Malpass and Patricia Devine tested the hypothesis that giving the witness a warning that the lineup might or might not contain the target would dampen the tendency toward relative judgment, and result in fewer mistaken identifications.[166] They showed their subjects lineups with the target and lineups without the target; they gave some subjects the instruction, telling them the perpetrator might or might not be present, and gave other subjects no instructions at all. They found that when their subjects viewed a lineup that contained the target, receiving the instruction did not reduce the rate of correct identifications. When subjects viewed a lineup without the target, receiving the instruction did reduce the rate of mistaken identifications.[167] With the instruction, witnesses did just as well making correct identifications and made fewer false identifications, compared to witnesses who did not get the instruction.[168]

Selection of Lineup Fillers. Fillers are people put in the lineup around the suspect, to fill the lineup with similar-looking individuals. The selection of fillers for lineups can have a critical effect on the possibility that a witness will make a mistaken identification when the lineup does not contain the actual perpetrator. One can imagine two ways to select fillers. First, police might select fillers based on their resemblance to the suspect police already have. The other method would have police select fillers on the basis of their resemblance to the description given by the witness in his or her initial report to the police. Researchers found that selecting fillers according to how much they looked like the prime suspect could result in a lineup in which all members looked like clones.[169] When police used this method, witnesses made fewer accurate identifications and more mistaken ones.[170] On the other hand, selecting fillers on the basis of their resemblance to the initial description given by the witness did not reduce the rate of correct identifications, and it decreased the rate of mistaken identifications[171]—another positive innovation in routine procedures at almost no cost.[172]

Blind Lineups. In a blind experiment, the procedure "blinds" the researcher so that he or she does not know which item—a medicine under testing versus a placebo, for instance—is the actual medicine. Researchers use blinding because of the well-known experimenter-expectancy effect, which tells us that "permitting a person who knows the correct, desired, or expected answer to administer a face-to-face test" introduces subtle communication, intentional or not, that tells the subject to select the answer that the experimenter already knows.[173] In American police work, lineups conducted by the detective on the case, who of course knows which member of the lineup is the suspect, remain absolutely routine. Studies have verified that this failure to use blind procedures in lineups has exactly the effect scientists fear it will. Researchers studying lineups have conducted experiments in which they have a person who is not part of the research team—call him or her the administrator—conduct a mock lineup showing the lineup to an eyewitness. In some of the sessions, the researchers tell the administrator that a particular lineup member (selected at random) is the suspect; in other sessions, the researchers tell the administrator nothing. The researchers never tell the eyewitness viewing the lineup anything. In the sessions in which the researchers tell the administrator which member of the lineup is the "correct" choice, the odds that eyewitnesses (whom the researchers have told nothing) will select this same suspect increase measurably.[174] Additionally, when the eyewitness selects the member of the lineup whom the researchers identified to the administrator, the eyewitness expresses more confidence in the choice.[175] None of these results presumes any bad faith or lack of integrity by a police officer who administers a lineup in his or her own case; it simply demonstrates that, like other human beings, officers who know the "right" choice should not run a lineup.

Fortunately, a simple solution to this problem exists: "The person who administers the lineup should not be aware of which lineup member is the suspect and which members are fillers."[176] This would only disqualify the police officer on the case; any other officer in the department, one from another department, or even a civilian could run the lineup, as long as he or she does not know which member of the lineup is the suspect. In the near future, one can imagine the administration of photographic lineups (sometimes called "photo arrays") via a computer program, which would not, of course, suggest the right answer.[177]

Sequential Lineups. Anyone who has seen a police show on television knows what a lineup looks like. Five or six similar-looking people stand in a line, facing the witness, with their backs to a series of lines that indicate their height. The witness looks at the entire group together and attempts to identify the person whom the witness saw commit the crime. Experts call this traditional arrangement a simultaneous lineup, denoting the fact that the witness sees all members of the lineup together. Contrast this with a new procedure: the sequential lineup. Conceived in the middle 1980s,[178] a sequential lineup uses the same people or photographs, but offers them to the witness one by one. The police tell the witness that he or she will view an unspecified number of people; the witness then decides, as to each one, whether the witness recognizes the person as the perpetrator. The sequential lineup prevents relative judgments because the witness always knows that another lineup member may come along who looks more similar to the perpetrator than any one the witness has seen so far. This forces the witness to focus on the person or photograph in front of him. The witness asks himself not who in the group looks most like the person remembered, but whether the person on view or pictured in the photograph is the one remembered.[179]

Early tests of sequential lineups showed their superiority to simultaneous lineups: mistaken identifications in lineups without the perpetrator present went down, while accurate identifications in lineups including actual perpetrators did not change.[180] But some newer research has raised questions. A 2001 meta-analysis of the combined results of multiple experiments confirmed lower rates of mistaken identification for sequential lineups compared to simultaneous ones, but also found some reduction in accurate identifications of the actual perpetrators present in lineups.[181] (The drop in mistaken identification was larger than the drop in correct identifications.)[182] The sequential lineup procedure produced fewer attempts overall to make identifications; witnesses using sequential lineups seemed to set a higher standard of judgment for themselves, and made fewer guesses.[183] This result—fewer mistaken, and fewer correct, identifications—also correlates with a reduction in relative judgments. According to experts in eyewitness identification, some portion of the correct identifications witnesses make in simultaneous lineups come not from the witness actually recognizing the perpetrator but from making a relative judgment ("which one looks most like the person I saw?") that happens to be correct. If sequential lineups, which combat relative judgments, come into use, it makes sense that witnesses, now shifted away from relative judgments, will make fewer correct identifications; sequential lineups will reduce the portion of "lucky guess" correct identifications that came from relative judgment.[184] The loss of the correct-but-lucky-because-of-relative-judgment identifications still represents a loss of correct identifications, even if they do result from luck. Ultimately, the question will come down to whether or not it seems best to eliminate all identifications based on guesses and luck, even if this includes some number of correct guesses, because eliminating relative judgment has the unquestionably positive effect of eliminating the mistaken identifications that result from relative judgment, which turn into wrongful convictions.[185]

The upshot of all of this is that strong evidence exists proving that sequential lineups provide more protection against selecting an innocent person because of the workings of relative judgment. No scientifically credible evidence supports the proposition that simultaneous lineups do a better job than sequential ones at protecting the innocent. Some credible studies suggest that sequential lineups lower the rate of correct identifications by eliminating lucky guessing that takes place due to relative judgment. Whether the tradeoff between fewer false identifications and fewer correct identifications (though the reduction of correct identifications does not approach the reduction of false identifications) is ultimately a question that policy makers must take on in earnest.

Witness Confidence. Any juror hearing a witness identify a perpetrator in court would want to know how confident the witness feels about that identification; knowing this would tell the juror how much faith to put in the identification. And it would make sense that a juror would put more stock in the identification testimony of a witness who says "I'm absolutely sure of it—I'll never forget that face" than in the testimony of a witness who says, "I think I saw the defendant there—I'm about 60 percent sure." Jurors place heavy reliance on the confidence of eyewitnesses when they decide whether the witness has made an accurate identification.[186] The Supreme Court itself has endorsed the idea that the witness's degree of confidence constitutes a good measurement of the reliability of that identification.[187] Yet the science of eyewitness identification has shown that a high degree of confidence in an identification does not automatically lead to a greater likelihood of an accurate identification. And a variety of external, after-the-fact occurrences can artificially inflate the witness's degree of confidence.

Let us begin with the obvious. Identifying a suspect in a lineup constitutes an interaction between human beings: the witness, the person administering the lineup, and the members of the lineup. For the witness, part of making that choice is deciding whether the recognition the witness feels concerning one of the lineup members reaches some satisfactory threshold of certainty. The witness may feel like lineup member 1 seems somehow familiar, even looks a bit like the perpetrator, but just, well, sort of; looking at lineup members 2, 3, 4, and 6 elicits no feeling of recognition at all. But number 5 looks familiar—more so for sure than number 1, and much more like what the witness remembers from seeing the crime. At that point, the witness interacts with the lineup administrator and might say, "Number 5, I think that's him. Yes, I pick number 5," or "Number 5. It's him. I'm sure of it." These two statements picking out number five differ in important respects; one says "I think" while the other says "I'm sure." The science of lineups has probed into just how important that difference between the two statements actually is.

According to Gary Wells, Amina Memon, and Steven Penrod, twenty-five years of research on the relationship between eyewitness confidence and identification accuracy shows that the association between these two crucial variables is not very strong, and "varies greatly as a function of many other factors."[188] A meta-analysis of multiple studies on this subject produced an estimate of the strength of the correlation between witness confidence and accuracy as .41.[189] To get a sense of what this means, a perfect correlation—the more confident a witness is, the more accurate the witness is always likely to be—would be 1.0. A correlation of .41 is not even as strong as the correlation between height and gender in human beings.[190] Thus the correlation between confidence and accuracy does not seem particularly strong; witness confidence is not "a highly reliable indicator of accuracy. Error rates can be high among even the most confident witnesses."[191] A correlation of .41 between confidence and accuracy is not nothing, but it does not reach the level one would expect, given the heavy reliance that most people—i.e., potential jurors—would usually place on witness confidence.

Further, it turns out that, even if we believe that eyewitness confidence has a positive relationship to accuracy worth considering—far from a sure proposition—the witness's level of confidence can undergo huge distortions between the time when the witness makes the identification and the time when the witness testifies about it. For example, giving a witness positive feedback directly after the witness makes a choice—"Good, you picked the right guy; he has a record for this sort of thing"—can cause distortions in the witness's later testimony.[192] When testifying, a witness given that kind of positive feedback at the time of the identification will later recall himself as more confident in his choice than he actually was when he made it. He may even remember having a better view of the perpetrator and the crime than he actually had, and may recall having paid more attention to the perpetrator's face than he actually did. Psychologists call this the post-identification feedback effect, and many researchers have substantiated its existence.[193] Even worse, the effect inflates the confidence of mistaken witnesses more than it inflates the confidence of witnesses who have made a correct identification.[194]

Fortunately, we can address the confidence-accuracy connection to some degree with a relatively simple fix: witnesses must be asked for a statement of their level of confidence immediately upon choosing a suspect from the lineup, before receiving any feedback. Requiring any choice by a witness to be followed by the question, "how confident would you say you are in your choice?" before anything else happens has an important effect. According to Wells and his colleagues, "if the eyewitness is asked to indicate his or her confidence level before receiving feedback, this tends to inoculate the witness against post-identification feedback effects. . . . Clearly, the most pristine measure of witness confidence is one collected from the witness at the time of the identification and before the contamination influence of these later events."[195]

Summing Up: Science Tells Us Where Forensic Testing, Interrogation Tactics, and Eyewitness Identification Procedures Have Gone Wrong

This chapter has surveyed decades of research on the accuracy of traditional police investigation methods in three central areas: forensic science, interrogation tactics, and eyewitness identifications. In all three, we see that scientific inquiry has produced insights that contradict the received wisdom.

Fingerprint identification, long considered the gold standard in forensic work, sits atop a shaky foundation, with no real scientific backing for what it does, and with a growing suspicion that it has both overstated its power and underplayed its problems. Contrary to what most of us believe, some innocent people who have no mental impairment and who have not experienced physical abuse sometimes do confess to serious crimes they did not commit, and the standard interrogation techniques in use for decades make this more likely, not less. Eyewitness testimony does not, as we have long believed, deserve special reverence as accurate evidence. In fact, it is the leading cause of wrongful convictions, and the ways in which police conduct identification procedures encourage—even create—some of the biggest problems with its accuracy.

What does law enforcement have to say about this new science? Have police and prosecutors incorporated these research findings into what they do? Has this vital new information changed the way they approach the central task of finding the truth? Do they use the new science to enhance the way they prove cases in court?

3

In Their Own Words

Why Police and Prosecutors Say They Resist Science

With the flood of scientific research over the past several decades on foren-sic practices, interrogation of suspects, and eyewitness identification, an observer might guess that proposals for new ways to approach police inves-tigation would receive overwhelming support. Unfortunately, that has not happened. Most police and prosecutors—not all, to be sure, but most—often want nothing to do with what scientists have discovered about the ways in which traditional police investigative techniques should change. DNA evi-dence emerges as the great exception to this resistance: a science-based silver bullet that identifies criminals we would never have caught before. Police love the science and certainty of DNA, except when the results impli-cate someone other than the suspect they have already charged. Prosecutors swear by DNA, except when it clears convicted suspects. At such junctures, even in the face of the best science the modern world can offer, resistance emerges—just as it does to the science on other forensic disciplines, on inter-rogation of suspects, and on eyewitness identification.

What objections do police and prosecutors have? We need not wonder. In reaction to the more than 250 DNA-based exonerations in the last two decades that have undermined confidence in the system and with the release of the National Academy of Sciences' report on forensic sciences, law enforcement has articulated the reasons for its resistance.

Generally speaking, the resistance to the revision of traditional police investigation tactics centers around several central themes: cost, both direct and indirect; the chance that new methods might let the guilty escape; limitations on police autonomy; misunderstanding or undervaluation of science, especially as compared to experience, as the basis for determining the truth; and a fear that science will just become a way for lawyers to help defendants avoid punishment.

Cost

One of the most common arguments made by police and prosecutors concerns the costs of changing basic investigative tactics so that police methods better reflect what modern science teaches. Sometimes these costs come in the form of money for new equipment: for example, adopting a system that requires recording of all police questioning would probably mean purchasing some number of small digital video cameras. These kinds of costs have drawn objections, even in police departments shown to have made grievous errors in interrogations. For example, in New York City, the police department obtained confessions from the young defendants in the notorious Central Park jogger case, which involved a horrific sexual and physical assault on the victim. The confessions, though recanted by the defendants almost immediately after their release from police custody, led to convictions and years of imprisonment. When solid evidence surfaced later pointing to the real perpetrator, who then confessed to committing the crimes alone, the Manhattan District Attorney's Office recommended that the courts vacate the convictions of the defendants. This prompted the introduction of legislation in New York's city council that would require police to record the interrogations of all felony suspects from start to finish.[1] The police department and its allies resisted. Councilman James E. Davis, a former NYPD officer, said that in a time of decreasing resources, the city should not decree that "all of a sudden [the police department must] have enough video cameras and tape recorders to use in all felony cases" because "I don't think there's enough money."[2] And money is a real concern. For example, in departments shifting to a blind sequential lineup procedure using a laptop computer to display photos, the agency must purchase the software and perhaps some hardware, and must also pay for digitizing photos if this has not been done already for other purposes.

Other types of costs take more indirect forms: increased manpower and training expenses, and the costs of logistical changes. A police department moving to adopt the basics of science-backed eyewitness identification will have to train its officers in the new procedures, the way they should work, and what the officers should and should not do. Similarly, a department that has decided to change the fundamentals of how it will interrogate suspects cannot simply set the new procedures down in a departmental policy or rule and proclaim that henceforth all officers will follow it. Changes to something so central to the way police have always done their work would require training for every officer in the department, from the newest recruits to the most grizzled veterans. Moreover, this type of fundamental change to something so basic will almost certainly require periodic monitoring and refresher training. On the question of manpower, consider the example of a police department implementing the use of blind lineups of suspects. This requires that the department have the lineup conducted by someone who does not know which lineup member the police suspect. In large police agencies, having an officer not involved in the case conduct the lineup seems achievable with little disruption. In smaller departments, bringing in an uninvolved officer to administer the lineup could prove more problematic. The unit cost of the action (the cost of having the uninvolved officer drop his or her work and perform the lineup procedure) would be the same in small and large departments, but it might prove disruptive in a small agency with fewer personnel to spare at any given moment. According to the *Chicago Tribune*, blind lineups aimed at improving eyewitness identification "[draw] plenty of resistance from police or prosecutors who worry that suburban or rural police departments with small staffs will have trouble finding someone who is unfamiliar with a case to conduct a lineup."[3] These sorts of personnel and logistical costs are real even if they do not require a payment of money. Thus, "Many police departments resist this [type of] change for a simple reason: it involves more work."[4] For example, in New Jersey, which now requires adoption of some of the most important eyewitness identification reforms, police departments "had to train patrol officers and desk administrators to conduct identification procedures" so that personnel other than detectives involved in cases could perform them. According to Lori Linksey, deputy attorney general of New Jersey, this "was the toughest hurdle to overcome."[5]

Other kinds of indirect costs surface in this discussion as well—sometimes just the cost of implementing changes in practices or procedures. When the American Bar Association endorsed a measure urging law enforcement

agencies around the country to record interrogations of criminal suspects—
an initiative that grew out of the exposure of the false confessions of the
defendants in the Central Park jogger case—the New York Police Department's leadership saw only costly headaches, and no benefits. According to
NYPD commissioner Ray Kelly, the department's 220,000–250,000 arrests
per year made instituting recording of interrogations practically impossible.
"The logistics of [recording confessions] are mind-boggling for an agency
this size," Kelly said.[6]

The cost argument also arises in one unique circumstance that bears men-
tioning. In a number of states, damaging and costly scandals have rocked
the forensic laboratories. These scandals have stemmed from incompetence,
outright dishonesty, and sometimes both combined. For example, in a scandal that arose in West Virginia's crime lab, analyst Fred Zain had an uncanny
ability to produce lab results implicating the person the police had identified
as their suspect, even when other scientists could not. Zain's method: he testified to results of tests he never conducted.[7] Discovery of Zain's misconduct
raised the possibility that hundreds of closed cases would require costly rein-
vestigation. In Montana, Arnold Melnikoff, the former director of the Montana state crime lab, regularly did hair analysis for police in his state, and his
efforts resulted in many convictions. DNA testing conducted later showed
that Melnikoff's hair comparisons, whether based on a lack of truthfulness or
a failure to understand the limitations of his testing, produced three wrongful convictions.[8] After the revelation of these errors, the Innocence Project, joined by five former Montana Supreme Court justices, requested an
audit and retesting of evidence in more than two hundred cases Melnikoff
had handled. No evidence was ever retested, however. As the state's new
lab director said, he simply could not afford to use resources for retesting
when he had a backlog of current cases needing attention. "My biggest nightmare," he said, "is workload."[9] This reaction has become disturbingly common: "the task of reevaluating [so] many cases is so daunting that authorities
have declined to conduct broad audits, despite evidence that analysts have
committed errors or engaged in fraudulent practices."[10] They fear the costs
of doing these audits, as well as the "uncovering of additional problems in a
lab that would spawn lawsuits or unravel an untold number of convictions,"
which would of course add further costs.[11]

In any institutional setting, costs of operation and other aspects of performing the agency's mission constitute an important part of the reality
the institution must face. But the discussion of costs in the context of law
enforcement resistance to using methods that reflect the best scientific
principles seems to gloss over something crucial: any rational analysis of a

problem must consider not only the costs of change but also the costs of failing to change the status quo.

First among the costs of not changing, we must acknowledge that wrongful convictions cost money, too. In some (though not all) states, those freed after wrongful convictions receive compensation. In some instances, these payments have come to substantial amounts of money—in the millions of dollars. Second, when we imprison the wrong person, we stop looking for the right person; the actual perpetrator remains free, able to rob, rape, or kill new victims. The costs to these new victims, and the costs of their injuries to society, are just as real as any others. Researchers who study crime prevention have often made well-accepted, data-based assumptions about the costs of crimes prevented; using the same reasoning, we must acknowledge the costs of crimes permitted when wrongful convictions give the real perpetrators a chance to continue committing crimes.

Third, failure to bring police investigation into line with the best scientific understanding of these processes creates another cost: damage to the reputation and integrity of the whole criminal justice system. When the wrong people suffer conviction and punishment, this destroys the lives of innocent citizens and to a lesser but real extent the lives of their families. When this damage becomes public, as it now has in over 250 cases, it also destroys the confidence that the rest of the public has in every aspect of the system: the individual police officers who performed the investigation and their police departments; the courts; and even the law itself. Public confidence in the criminal justice system acts as the glue that holds our society together, and its loss constitutes a real cost. That this cost comes not in cash but in intangible form makes it no less real or serious.[12]

We must also reckon with one other, largely hidden cost. When a wrongful conviction comes to light, we can see the damage done to the life of the person who suffered the injustice of going to prison for a crime he did not commit. But victims of the crime may also suffer when this happens: they must cope with the idea that they had an important—perhaps *the* important—role in imprisoning an innocent human being. They must also deal with the fact that the actual perpetrator of the crime may still remain at large, due to the mistaken identification of the wrong person. Some prosecutors may also suffer in these situations. Even knowing that they acted in perfect good faith based on the evidence they had, the cost of having imprisoned an innocent human being remains. In Dallas, Texas, which has produced at least twenty wrongful convictions, some of the prosecutors who tried these cases admit to the toll this has taken on them personally.[13] Kim Gilles, who prosecuted now-exonerated defendant David Pope in 1986, still "gets emotional" thinking about the case. When she learned that DNA results did not match Pope, "Talk about walking the floors and crying, that was me," she said. Though she used the evidence in the case properly at the time of the trial, she now calls her involvement "embarrassing."[14] In the case of Gregory Wallis, prosecutor Manny Alvarez, now a judge, used evidence of the defendant's unusual tattoo to convict him. DNA proved that Wallis had not committed the crime after Wallis had served eighteen years in prison. Alvarez was disturbed enough that when Wallis was locked in a holding cell behind a courtroom for his exoneration hearing, Alvarez went to visit Wallis and apologized to him. When Wallis said to him "'Hey, you were just doing your job,'" Alvarez said, "It put me at ease a little bit."[15]

More of the Guilty May Escape Detection, Prosecution, and Punishment

A second objection by police and prosecutors goes to the very heart of the purpose of criminal justice, which is for the police to find the perpetrators of crime and collect evidence against them, and for prosecutors to use the proof collected by police to obtain guilty verdicts. No system of justice that does not put these goals front and center can hope to enjoy public confidence. Thus, police and prosecutors argue that anything that makes this central set of goals more difficult to achieve does not make sense. In their eyes, many of the reforms that science points us toward undermine the efforts of police and prosecutors in exactly this way.

A good example of this thinking comes from William Fitzpatrick, the elected district attorney of Onondaga County, New York, since 1992 and a member of the board of the National District Attorneys Association (NDAA). Concerning the National Academy of Sciences' report on forensic science, Fitzpatrick issues a dire prediction.[16] If the reforms detailed in the report ever become reality, he says, the guilty will go unpunished, perhaps even in the worst cases with the strongest proof.

> You have a Mr. Jones come into your office and he is extremely distraught because a few weeks earlier his daughter has been brutally murdered and police have focused on her ex-stalking boyfriend as the main suspect. And you look at Mr. Jones and say, "You know sir, we did a search warrant on your daughter's boyfriend's house and we recovered a .32 caliber revolver and we ballistically [sic] matched that gun to the bullet that was in your daughter's brain. Also at the scene of her murder we found a fingerprint in blood which we identified as having come from the left hand of her

ex-boyfriend. And finally, we have an eyewitness who was positioned in well-lit surroundings across the street, who saw her ex-boyfriend fleeing the scene. However, we just can't bring this case to the grand jury because the proof is too thin."[17]

According to Fitzpatrick, this is exactly where the National Academy of Sciences' recommendations will lead, because they will interfere with the way police and prosecutors use forensic science. Fitzpatrick does not stand alone in expressing the fear that reforms can do little except allow the guilty to go free. When the California legislature considered legislation to change police investigation procedures to include the electronic recording of interrogations and better eyewitness identification procedures, the California State Sheriffs Association opposed them. The bills would only make it harder to convict the guilty by "creat[ing] loopholes for defendants to get an edge in court on technicalities," the association said.[18] Others have voiced the view that some reforms will result in the collection of less evidence, making it more difficult to convict the guilty. For example, some in law enforcement object to required recording of interrogations on the grounds that recording would stop suspects from giving confessions that they would give in the absence of recording. Detective Thomas Scotto, president of New York's Detective Endowment Association, thinks recording presents special danger to getting confessions. "Some defendants will admit to something. Then when you tell them, 'Well, now we're going to videotape,' they won't respond." There is no evidence to back up any of these claims, but they persist.

For others, the argument comes down to resistance to almost any change in the status quo. For example, when the U.S. Senate Judiciary Committee held hearings on the National Academy of Sciences' 2009 report, they received testimony from Barry Matson, deputy director of the Alabama District Attorneys Association.[19] Matson, it seemed, could not denounce strongly enough the report's conclusions on the shaky foundations of most forensic science. Prosecutors and forensic scientists, Matson said, "do more to free the innocent and safeguard the liberties of our citizens than any defense project or academician will accomplish in a career."[20] The questions raised by the report, he said, constituted nothing more than "agenda driven attacks upon well founded investigative techniques. These same techniques or sciences are used everyday to find the truth in every type of case. As an investigative tool, every discipline of forensic science has not simply led to a conviction, but has delivered the truth. I know the truth, and I sleep very well at night."[21] Thus anything—any questioning of forensic science, any acknowledgment that a particular forensic practice might have a less than rigorous scientific foundation—can mean only that some of the guilty will escape the punishment they deserve, because police and prosecutors will find it harder to prove the truth of the guilt of the accused.

In the end, these arguments stand in stark opposition to the experiences of the small but growing number of police departments and prosecutors' offices that have changed their practices for the better and have not found it more difficult, let alone impossible, to convict the accused (see chapter 6). Moreover, they rest upon a failure to acknowledge that the traditional investigative practices have led to catastrophic failures for the justice system, and that we now know how to do a better job. The argument that "the guilty will escape punishment if we institute these new procedures" also misses an essential point: the criminal justice system exists not only to punish the guilty and to see that victims get a measure of justice but also to protect the innocent. We must balance these goals within the system. Simply insisting on law enforcement's need to do things in the ways they always have constitutes no answer to the problems that have become visible since the advent of DNA testing.

Limits on Autonomy

Few things seem to irritate police more than an outside authority dictating the way officers and detectives should do their jobs. Any such directives—even laws enacted by democratically elected representatives—do not sit well because they encroach on a fundamental aspect of the job: their autonomy in deciding how to fight crime, keep order, and apprehend the guilty.

To an outsider, it does not seem surprising that legislatures and other authorities have begun to make rules that direct police to use some investigative techniques and not others in sensitive areas such as eyewitness identification and suspect interrogations. After all, with the number of DNA-based exonerations exceeding 250 by the end of 2010, and with 75 percent of these cases involving faulty identification procedures, only a handful of police agencies had voluntarily changed their eyewitness identification practices.[22] Thus a few state legislatures have moved into the vacuum and ordered that police agencies change their ways. Understandable as that may seem, police and prosecutors do not want outsiders imposing rules on them. When a bill requiring blind lineups passed in California, the state's Peace Officer Standards and Training Commission urged the governor to veto it. Bob Stresak, the commission's spokesperson, said that the commission did not want the bill to become law because it "limits police in doing their jobs."[23] The International Association of Chiefs of Police (IACP), an organization generally associated with the use of best practices in American policing, does not want to see any limitation of the independence of police chiefs, their departments, or their officers. For example, even though the IACP supports the National Academy of Sciences' call for accreditation and certification for forensic science agencies and personnel, it does not want any requirement for accreditation and certification to have the force of law.[24] Some agencies might find this difficult to afford, and therefore they should not have to accept accreditation and certification as a nonnegotiable priority. Rather, the agencies and their leadership should retain the autonomy to decide what will benefit the agencies most—accreditation and certification, or something else.[25]

For any profession, autonomy in decision making and action is always a cherished perquisite. This holds true for doctors, lawyers, teachers, and especially police officers, who feel that, out on the street, they must have the flexibility to determine their own direction, whether in dealing with a member of the public or investigating a crime. Indeed, police discretion in the nuts and bolts of the way officers perform their work is unavoidable; it is built into the job. For example, in any short drive in a squad car, police witness more driving infractions by more drivers than they could hope to enforce in a week's time, and they do not stop and cite every driver they see violating a traffic law. Even when they do stop a driver, officers do not always give citations; they may instead give a warning. This sort of autonomy goes well beyond traffic enforcement. An officer witnessing a group of young people smoking marijuana may arrest them, may confiscate the drug, may reprimand them, may send them away with instructions to behave differently in the future, or may do nothing. An officer witnessing an angry argument between neighbors may choose to separate and calm the parties, perhaps attempting to clear up whatever triggered the fight, or may elect to arrest the more aggressive neighbor, or may decide to arrest both.

Nevertheless, autonomy and discretion always have limits. A police officer can choose to stop, or not stop, any traffic violator—but an officer who allowed an intoxicated driver to drive home instead of making an arrest would be likely to face disciplinary charges if his or her action became known. An officer could allow two people in a fistfight to go their separate ways with a warning to stay away from each other, but probably would not allow the perpetrator of a serious assault using a weapon to walk away with an admonishment. Further, limits already exist on the way police conduct investigations. They can question suspects, but they cannot use physical force to persuade them to talk, even if this might mean more suspects would confess.[26] Officers cannot threaten to expose suspects to physical harm in order to get them to confess,[27] even if doing so might be a very effective way to obtain truthful statements from suspects. Thus, while police will always have discretion to make enforcement choices, that discretion will always have limits—even when their autonomy remains quite broad overall.

Thus it seems reasonable to limit the discretion of police in other areas in which particular ways of performing investigations might—and in the past, have—brought about disastrous results. Eyewitness identification procedures make a particularly telling example. With incorrect identifications showing up in 75 percent of all of the cases of post-conviction exoneration, and with some proven answers to the question of how to prevent wrongful convictions, such as using blind lineups, saying that the police should retain the right to use nonblinded procedures if they choose is like saying that doctors should have the right to continue to choose a medicine or surgical procedure that has killed some number of patients who need not have died. Police have, and will always have, considerable discretion in the way they do their work, but they should not expect unlimited scope for their choices. When some ways of performing a job—particularly a job that centers on protecting the public—prove risky, and better alternatives emerge, law enforcement should not have the autonomy to tell the public, effectively, to let police and prosecutors decide without interference from outsiders.

The Science Is Too Thin, Too Much the Product of the
Lab, and Divorced from the "Real World" Police Face

Police and prosecutors also resist changes because many do not trust science. They see it as too unsettled to allow police and prosecutors to rely on it, or too contradictory in its results—one study says this, another says that—to serve as the basis for an investigation. Law enforcement also sees these reforms as too laboratory-centric, and therefore too divorced from the real world. Science seems to devalue the lived experience of police officers in the field, especially their capacity to tell whether a suspect has actually told the truth or whether a witness has made an identification solid enough to go forward with a case.

Though these objections have been made to all of the science-based proposals for improvements in investigation techniques, police and prosecutors have directed these criticisms with particular force at proposed changes in eyewitness identification procedures. For example, Joshua Marquis, the district attorney for Clatsup County, Oregon, and a frequent NDAA spokesman, voices tentative support for the use of blind lineups. But he does not believe that legislatures or courts or anyone else should mandate the use of sequential lineups; much of the research supporting reform, he says, is "thin."[28] Tom Needham, the former chief of staff for the Chicago Police Department, joins those who feel research that demonstrates the need for reforms in eyewitness identification procedures may make for a nice scientific debate but does not have enough of a connection to the day-to-day work of police on the street. Needham, who served on the Illinois Governor's Commission on Capital Punishment, said that "[i]t all struck me as theoretical" and not particularly grounded in law enforcement's needs.[29] Rather than having Illinois adopt the commission's recommendations for changes in lineup procedures, including sequential lineups, Needham recommended waiting to see the results when New Jersey adopted many of these procedures.[30]

Calling the research on eyewitness identification "too theoretical" neatly captures the idea that police believe that they have special, experienced-based and intuitive knowledge that those outside their occupational circle neither share nor understand. As they see it, valuing the results of scientific experiments over experience smacks of elitism. The ability of police officers to spot when a suspect is lying, and to recognize when a person on the street is behaving suspiciously and might be involved in crime, is a skill highly prized in law enforcement. Police believe those outside the fraternity cannot match them, and therefore having outsiders telling them how to do something as simple as a lineup rankles. Rick Malone, director of the Prosecuting Attorney's Council of Georgia, criticized efforts to mandate the use of particular eyewitness identification procedures as an unjustified effort to replace the many years of detectives' lived experiences using lineups "with 25 years of studies on human memory." To Malone this makes little sense; research studies simply cannot yield the richness of hard-won experience, and would make for an inadequate substitute. "A clinical study in a research laboratory versus someone walking out of a liquor store who shoots the fellow across the street—those aren't the same conditions."[31] New laws mandating the way police could work with eyewitnesses would, according to many police and prosecutors, "undermine proven techniques detectives use."[32]

Yet in their criticism of scientific elitism, law enforcement reveals an elitism of its own. When a particular scientific experiment validly duplicates the conditions that police face—for example, the ability to recall a face correctly, or the ability to detect when a suspect is lying—this tells us something about the circumstances that the experiment actually and accurately duplicates, whether or not the answers in the experiment rely on a police officer's intuition. It is not a question of wanting to put laboratory techniques to work in the field in place of techniques derived from experience; rather, valid experiments test field-derived experience by successfully duplicating it in the laboratory to see if it actually works the way everyone thinks it does. If the experiments successfully duplicate what police do on the street, and if in doing so they show that the results of these procedures do not measure up as well as other methods would, the results cannot be dismissed as less valuable than street experience; rather, they are a controlled and measured—and therefore tested—version of street experience. Following an experiment, the next step in scientific exploration is review of the results by researcher peers, and then duplication of the experiment by others, to see if the same results emerge. Again, doing these things does not mean that we value abstract science over what police have done with lineups or other procedures for so many years. Instead, the experiments examine and test the very things police have done, in an effort to see whether the assumptions that have always surrounded them actually hold.

Police and prosecutors need to reconsider their claims that scientific research devalues the intuitive and experienced-based skills that police have at telling truth from lies, or at remembering and later recalling faces accurately. As discussed in chapter 2, police often assume that they have superior, experience-based abilities to tell when a suspect has lied to them. In fact, this cherished assumption has become so deeply rooted over so many years that it forms the very basis for the Reid Technique's Behavior Analysis Interview.[33] Recall that this technique, taught to most American police officers, actually rests upon a false premise: police officers do not, in fact, have any greater skill at detecting deception than untrained civilians have. In fact, they actually may not do as well as civilians at detecting deception, because their training and experience orients them toward finding deception, which in some cases is not present.[34]

Police and prosecutors may feel that scientific research on their tactics should not supersede their own well-established understandings; who, after all, would want their expertise and authority questioned? But this does not make the research on police procedures "thin," or "too theoretical." The research is either well constructed and rigorously performed or it is not; the data are either thoroughly and correctly analyzed or not; the results are either accepted by scientific peers and are duplicable or not. Challenging the research because it undermines one's preferred position is not so much an argument as a statement about what one prefers, and should be understood as such.

Science as an Attack on the Integrity of Law
Enforcement, and as a Tool for Defense Attorneys

Others in law enforcement see the scientific work that has revealed the shortcomings of traditional practices in forensic science, eyewitness identification,

and suspect interrogation as an attack on them as police officers and prosecutors. They believe that the science behind the arguments for new and better police investigative procedures is meant to besmirch them professionally
and make them appear less than honest.

In 2007, a state commission on wrongful convictions in Pennsylvania
began to study what had gone wrong in the nine cases in the state in which
DNA had exonerated convicted defendants.[35] By 2009, some law enforcement leaders in the state began to consider implementing some changes
to police procedure to fix the problem. Stephen A. Zappala Jr., the elected
district attorney of Allegheny County, Pennsylvania (which includes Pittsburgh and surrounding areas), who served on the commission, stated that
he would consider instituting some of the "best practices" the commission
had examined, beginning with the use of blind lineups.[36] Allegheny County's police leadership replied quickly and harshly. Howard Burton, chief of
police in Penn Hills, Pennsylvania, and a nine-year member of the Pennsylvania Chiefs of Police Association accreditation committee, said that bringing in blind lineups indicated a real suspicion of the police. "It's suggesting
that police are doing something wrong. It's creating an image of a police
officer that police are corrupt and we'll do anything to get a conviction."[37]
In Northampton, Massachusetts, where procedures now include sequential
lineups, Kenneth Patenaude, a commander in the detective bureau, described
the early resistance to these procedures as a feeling among some officers that
the change "amounted to questioning their integrity."[38] According to Robert
Honecker, who in 2002 served as the chief assistant prosecutor in Monmouth
County, New Jersey, police and prosecutors did not relish hearing that they
must change the way that they had always performed lineups and other identification procedures. "The biggest (objection)," Honecker said, "was that this
meant that we [had been] deliberately doing it wrong."[39] Speaking on behalf
of the National District Attorneys Association at a congressional hearing
on the National Academy of Sciences' report, Matthew Redle, county and
prosecuting attorney of Sheridan County, Wyoming, explained that prosecutors favored improvement in forensic disciplines. But, he said, "opponents
of the current system have gone so far as to indicate the system is 'broken'
and that anyone involved is biased and conducting science in bad faith."[40] In
other words, the National Academy of Sciences' report on forensic science
amounted to an attack on the integrity of forensic scientists working with
prosecutors, and the integrity of prosecutors themselves.

Sometimes, we hear this integrity objection from a slightly different perspective. The science that seems to call for a revised approach constitutes
not just an attack on police and prosecutors; it is also an undeserved benefit

for criminal defense attorneys and their clients. In one of the National District Attorneys Association's responses to the National Academy of Sciences' report, William Fitzpatrick said that the report represents not just an attack on prosecutors but a method for cynical defense lawyers to get guilty defendants off.

> [I]f you haven't had a motion [based on the report] filed yet from some defense lawyer, trust me, you will in the near future. . . . [T]his has to come as an equal shock to you but a number of defense lawyers throughout this country [have] attempted to exploit what they believed the report said to the advantage of their clients.[41]

In New York City, in reaction to a proposal for the videotaping of interrogations after the dismissal of the convictions of the defendants in the Central Park jogger case, police and their allies painted the proposed changes as a big benefit for defense lawyers and their clients. Detective Thomas Scotto of the New York Detective's Endowment Association said that if new rules mandated videotaping of interrogations, legal proceedings would focus on whether the police conducted the taping properly and not on the guilt of the defendant.[42] New York councilman Peter Vallone, a former prosecutor, called required videotaping a problem because it introduces "another technicality in a process that is already overloaded with them. I am very hesitant to have a good confession thrown out for ridiculous reasons" because of such a rule.[43] And Barry Matson, the deputy director of the Alabama District Attorneys Association, who testified at the congressional hearing on the National Academy of Sciences' report, characterized the report and its science-based criticism of the forensic disciplines as "agenda driven attacks upon well founded investigative techniques" by "criminal defense lobbies," and as mere ammunition for "defense lawyers' attacks."[44]

What these points make clear is that police and prosecutors feel quite sensitive about any changes. What seems to underlie this sensitivity may be a misunderstanding of what some of the science actually says, and what it means. Failure to use blind lineup procedures for eyewitness identification in a case does not mean that police *intend* to communicate the right choice to witnesses viewing the lineup; rather, a recommendation that police use blind lineups comes from the fact that all human beings who are showing a person a lineup and who know the right answer will, without knowing it or meaning to do so, communicate subtle cues to the witness about which choice to make. That is the nature of the cognitive biases that much of the science on traditional police investigative procedures has uncovered: these ways of functioning are wired deeply into all of our brains, and are not the product of police or prosecutorial malice. The research results, and initiatives designed to change procedures based on this research, do not attack police or prosecutors but instead attack the methods that have proven to be dangerously flawed, even capable of creating grave injustice, simply because of the way they work.

As for whether defense attorneys would make use of the science that appears to undermine the assumptions of police and prosecution work in convicting defendants, the answer is simple: yes, they will. In fact, they are duty bound to do this. Prosecutors often describe themselves as the only ones in the criminal process with a duty to seek the truth. That is not completely wrong, but it is misleading. According to long-cherished standards of prosecutorial conduct, prosecutors have the duty not just to prove the state's case but also to do justice,[45] which can mean dropping or not pursuing a case if the circumstances indicate that justice requires this. Defense lawyers in the American system do not share this duty. But defense lawyers have another duty, one equally important to the correct functioning of the adversary system: they must zealously represent the defendant within the bounds of the law.[46] This includes, most importantly, challenging the evidence presented by the state by any legitimate, lawful means. Thus calling science nothing but defense attorney spin is grossly inaccurate, and exposes a failure to understand how our system of criminal justice works. Challenging the state's evidence lies at the heart of the defense attorney's task, and it is built into the system in order to counterbalance the government's great power. Painting this as merely the slick and cynical use of science by the defense reveals a shallow understanding of the role of defense counsel in our adversary system of justice.

Deny the DNA

Even if one knows relatively little about science and police investigation, almost everyone knows about DNA and its great power to tell us whether the accused committed the crime. DNA reveals answers in new and old cases, in active investigations and in ones gone cold. It is, without doubt, the single greatest innovation in criminal investigation and evidentiary proof in many decades.

All of this makes the reaction of some prosecutors quite perplexing. They appear to love DNA when it supports their efforts, but they deny its legitimacy when it undermines what they have already decided or done. For some prosecutors, the commitment to a set of charges they have brought or a conviction they have already obtained simply overwhelms the ability to accept compelling DNA evidence that stands against their previously adopted positions.

In Burlington County, New Jersey, a jury convicted Larry Peterson for a 1987 sexual assault and murder.[47] After seventeen years in prison, DNA tests revealed that the skin, hair, and body fluids found at the crime scene had not come from Peterson, as the prosecution had argued at trial, and a judge overturned his conviction. Rather than reopen the investigation to find the true perpetrator, County Prosecutor Robert Bernardi announced that he would try Peterson again: "This office believes that there is sufficient evidence to move forward with a retrial of Mr. Peterson," Bernardi said.[48] Recall also the story of the Norfolk Four, recounted in chapter 2, in which police and prosecutors investigating the rape and murder of Michelle Bosko immediately focused on her neighbor, Danial Williams.[49] After an all-night interrogation by a detective who lied to Williams repeatedly and threatened him with the death penalty, Williams confessed to having committed the crime alone. But when DNA test results revealed that the semen in the victim's body did not belong to Williams, police did not take this to mean that Williams had not committed the crime. They had the right guy with Williams, police concluded; he simply had acted not alone but with another perpetrator, despite the absence of any mention of a confederate in Williams's confession. In other words, the reaction of police was not that they had got it wrong with Williams but that the failure of the DNA test to support their theory of the case meant that Williams had committed the crime but had not done so by himself.[50]

One particularly striking example comes from Illinois. Michael Mermel, chief of the criminal division of the prosecutor's office in Lake County, Illinois, in 2008, has overseen the use of DNA evidence to obtain convictions. But when DNA testing did not support guilt in three cases in which his office had charged or convicted defendants, he decided to pursue the cases anyway, denying that the DNA results settled the facts.[51] In the case of Bernie Starks, convicted of rape in 1986, DNA results contradicted the verdict twice. The first time, DNA testing in 2002 of the semen found on the victim's underwear did not match Starks. In response, Mermel said that the DNA results did not prove Starks' innocence. Only the results from a semen sample taken from inside the victim's body could do that.[52] Three years later, the authorities found a vaginal swab from a rape kit performed on the victim. DNA tests on the swab found that the semen on the swab had not come from Starks; rather, it revealed the same genetic profile as the stain found on the victim's underwear. Mermel still would not drop the case against Starks. Instead, he said that because the samples had come from the same person, this did not mean that Starks had not raped the victim; it meant that, besides the rape, the victim had had consensual sex with someone else. When Mermel's office retries Starks, it will do so in the face of the contrary DNA evidence, and the case will rest on the victim's identification of her attacker and bite mark analysis;[53] both of these types of evidence have generated a long trail of wrongful convictions (see chapter 2). Mermel's other two cases seem even more bewildering, since they involve children, and usually only sexual assault can explain the presence of semen in such cases. The trial of Juan Rivera for the 1992 rape and murder of an eleven-year-old girl ended in a conviction based on a confession; Rivera said he confessed falsely under severe police pressure. DNA testing in 2005 identified a genetic profile from semen that did not match Rivera. A court reversed Rivera's case, but Mermel decided to press ahead. The DNA had no significance, Mermel said, because in his confession Rivera said he did not ejaculate.[54] This answer, of course, does not explain the presence of the semen that originated with someone other than Rivera, but Mermel remained undeterred. "Is it some other killer, contrary to the evidence we have against Mr. Rivera? We say it's not."[55] In another case involving children, Mermel's office charged Jerry Hobbs with killing his eight-year-old daughter and her nine-year-old friend. As in the case against Rivera, prosecutors have relied on a confession, which the defendant has recanted. Attorneys for Hobbs had semen on oral, rectal, and vaginal swabs tested, and the tests turned up a genetic profile that did not match Hobbs. Again, the DNA evidence did not deter Mermel since, he said, prosecutors had not charged Hobbs with a sex crime. Thus the semen and DNA had no relevance.[56] But did the presence of semen inside an eight-year-old victim not show that a sexual assault had occurred? Not at all, according to Mermel; the girl may have picked up the small amount of semen found in her when she played in an area of nearby woods where couples sometimes have sex and where the crime allegedly took place. (The police found the victim there fully clothed.) Mermel does not deny that the tests showed the presence of sperm inside the girl—he could hardly say otherwise—but he told the *Chicago Tribune* that that fact did not mean that the perpetrator had sexually assaulted her. He called it "a goofy logic leap" to assume that "because somewhere in her life she came into contact with a sperm cell it means she was sexually assaulted" and that the person who deposited the sperm in the girl's body on the day she died was also her killer.[57] This is an exceedingly odd statement, given that the presence of semen in a child's body is exactly the kind of evidence that prosecutors use to prove sexual assaults. The only "goofy logic leap" seems to come in assuming that, in a murder in which forensic investigation located semen in the body of an eight-year-old victim, no sexual assault took place. But, as of 2008, Mermel publicly held fast to his theory. "I don't know where everybody gets this idea," he says, that the person who deposited the semen found in the victim's body committed both the murder and a sexual assault.[58] When a November 2011 *New York Times* article showcased Mermel's statements on DNA, Lake County's sheriff and elected prosecutor repudiated what Mermel said (though not anything he had done). Mermel's impending retirement was announced soon after.

What is perhaps the most disturbing aspect of the denial of DNA evidence is that it comes from those who rely on the power of DNA every day. Ronald Eisenberg, who in 2007 served as a deputy district attorney in Philadelphia, attempted to explain this by saying that DNA "often isn't probative of innocence."[59] DNA fragments can survive where deposited for long periods, and may have nothing to do with a crime at all. Moreover, Eisenberg said, the presence of someone's DNA tells us much about a case, but the absence of someone's DNA does not necessarily tell us anything. So charging someone in a crime when his or her DNA shows up makes sense; excluding the person as a suspect when that person's DNA does not show up does not.[60] But Eisenberg's explanation seems unconvincing. The idea that DNA might survive for a long time in an incriminating place but that the absence of DNA means nothing reflects a heads-I-win-tails-you-lose outlook. Even more importantly, in cases like those of Jerry Hobbs or Juan Rivera, in which they are accused but the incriminating DNA left at the scene actually belongs to someone else, the *absence* of DNA that came from Hobbs and Rivera is in fact highly probative. If the theories of the prosecution in these cases—that Rivera and Hobbs, and no one else, killed these children—are correct, we would expect that DNA found inside the victims came from these defendants. The absence of their DNA, and the presence of the DNA of someone else, is so probative that it destroys the prosecution's theory in both cases.

When All Else Fails: There Is No Problem

Beyond all the other ways in which police or prosecutors articulate their resistance to change in investigative procedures driven by scientists' findings over the last decades, one often comes at last to a simple denial: there is no problem. Put another way, the numbers of cases in which problems do arise is so small that they constitute aberrations, and are not representative of systemic or substantial problems.

Sometimes this thinking takes the form of aspirations of those in law enforcement more than an actual reckoning with facts. Peter Modafferi, chief of detectives in the Rockland County, New York, District Attorney's Office, understands this. Modafferi has served as chair of the Police Investigative Operations Committee of the International Association of Chiefs of Police. In that capacity, he wrote an insightful article for *The Police Chief* magazine about the "view from the trenches" of law enforcement concerning changes in eyewitness identification procedures.[61] When he discusses wrongful conviction issues in professional gatherings with his colleagues from departments around the country, "a central attitude is usually present: 'It won't happen on my watch.'" Modafferi correctly notes that this constitutes a noble sentiment, but that it does not really address what the DNA exoneration cases have revealed: "well-trained, educated, determined, and dedicated investigators can make mistakes." Sometimes, even with the best of intentions and acting in good faith, the course of a police investigation can go terribly wrong because of flawed tactics, and at this point we have a pretty good idea of what those flaws are and how they can be fixed.

But from others in law enforcement, one usually hears a minimization of the number of false convictions: these cases just do not happen often enough to constitute any kind of systemic problem. In his congressional testimony on behalf of the National District Attorneys Association, Matthew Redle, the prosecutor in Sheridan County, Wyoming, said that those who saw a systemic problem were just flat wrong. Concerning forensic science, Redle said, "No discipline is infallible; however, the media and opponents of the current system have gone so far as to indicate the system is broken," and the NDAA "strongly disputes this claim. . . . [W]e will not support efforts to label our justice system as broken or proposals that will serve to delay justice under false pretenses of fixing an allegedly broken system."[62] In his congressional testimony in 2002, Paul Logli, then the state's attorney for Winnebago County, Illinois, and chairman of the National District Attorneys Association Capital Litigation Committee, said that mistakes in the criminal justice system concerning guilt and innocence happen only very rarely. "In a very few case[s], mistakenly accused defendants have been freed both before trial and after incarceration."[63] Widespread use of DNA testing, he said, was really not necessary. Paul Cassell, a law professor at the University of Utah and a former federal prosecutor and judge, says that while false confessions sometimes occur, there exists no "pandemic" false confession problem, calling them "extremely rare" and confined to one narrow and vulnerable slice of the population: people with mental impairments.[64] In some cases, law enforcement leaders deny the existence of any problem in need of a solution in the face of cases that seem to say exactly the opposite. In 2001, the *Chicago Tribune* examined thousands of murder cases from the previous ten years in

Cook County, Illinois, in which police closed cases on the basis of confessions.[65] The paper found that in 247 cases—all but eleven of them handled by
the Chicago Police Department—courts threw out the statements as tainted,
or judges or juries acquitted the defendant in spite of the confessions. DNA
evidence proved some of the confessions false; in other cases, records showing that suspects had been incarcerated at the time of the crime proved that
defendants who confessed could not have committed the crimes. In others, the facts related in the confessions did not match with the real facts of
the case, such as when a defendant confessed to stabbing a victim, but the
autopsy revealed no stab wounds, or the case in which two defendants confessed to shooting the victim from across the street but the wounds came
from point-blank shots. Confronted with this evidence, Cook County state's
attorney Dick Devine talked about the steps his office had taken to enhance
the reliability of confessions, but he said he did not in any way believe that
false confessions constituted a systemic problem in his jurisdiction. "[Do]
[m]any people in our system, in this jurisdiction, confess to crimes they
didn't commit? No, I don't believe that." In 2001, a year-long investigation
by the *Washington Post* revealed that in four murder cases, homicide detectives in Prince George's County, Maryland, extracted false confessions from
suspects, and with virtually no other evidence against them, charged each of
them with murder.[66] Prosecutors later dropped the charges in all four cases
when evidence exonerating the defendants came from outsiders: lawyers,
diligent forensic scientists in crime labs, and even detectives from units other
than the homicide squad.[67] But John Farrell, then chief of the county's police
department, denied that any of this showed the existence of a problem. "I'd
say the system worked," he said. In one of the cases, "Another of our investigators did what was supposed to be done. Other information came to light.
It was taken forward . . . and the right thing was done."[68] Similarly, when
new evidence disproved the confessions of all of the original defendants in
the Central Park jogger case, some thought that this illustrated the need for
changes in the way the New York Police Department handled interrogations,
perhaps beginning with a requirement that police record all interrogations.
But Raymond Kelly, then the commissioner of police in New York, did not
agree. "I don't see a need, quite frankly," he said.[69]

For those like Professor Paul Cassell, who look at the numbers and declare
that the exoneration cases represent very minor aberrations rather than a
systemic problem, meeting their numbers with numbers seems fair. And the
basic data are available for all to see. Of the more than 250 exonerations now
on record, 25 percent involved "innocent defendants who made incriminating statements, delivered outright confessions, or pled guilty."[70] (A guilty plea

requires an admission of guilt by the defendant in open court—another form of confession—before a judge can accept it.) Recall that DNA evidence—the basis for nearly all of the exonerations to date—is available only in a fraction of all criminal cases; experts estimate that police recover testable biological evidence in only 5 to 10 percent of all cases.[71] This means, of course, that in 90 to 95 percent of all cases, DNA cannot prove or disprove guilt; DNA testing cannot occur. But in these other 90 to 95 percent of cases, we have no reason to think that interrogation tactics work any differently, or any better, than in cases in which police recover DNA evidence. Thus, if false statements by suspects appear in 25 percent of the DNA-testable cases, we should expect a similar percentage in the other 90 to 95 percent of cases. Put another way, if there is no reason to think that the DNA-based exoneration cases differ from others in the system, they provide us with a window into the whole criminal justice system. And that means that the problem we see—the 25 percent of the DNA cases in which false statements occur—represents the tip of the proverbial iceberg, and rational, conservative assumptions would lead us to believe that we should expect to see false confessions and statements by defendants in 25 percent of *all* cases.

Perhaps 25 percent does not seem large to some observers, but what if 25 percent of all airplane flights ended in crashes, or 25 percent of all vehicles had defects that injured drivers? Think of the outcry. Perhaps the DNA cases might seem more prone to have errors show up, since a high percentage of them contain rape and murder charges, thus upping the pressure on police to solve these cases, and therefore leading to more errors. But even if we scale back the estimate to account for this—even cutting it in half, from 25 to 12.5 percent—the problem still affects a large number of people, who may end up in prison for something they did not do, and leaves the real criminals out on the street.

The Reasons Given May Hold No Water

None of the reasons law enforcement has given for resisting science can justify the failure to adopt proven, better methods; none of the claims police and prosecutors make hold up under close examination. Something else is at work here, and we explore the answer in the next two chapters. It turns out that the resistance of law enforcement to science originates from two sources: cognitive barriers (chapter 4) and institutional and political barriers (chapter 5).

4

The Real Reasons for Resistance

Cognitive Barriers

As we have seen in the previous chapters, scientists in multiple fields have done rigorous, peer-reviewed work that casts doubt on some of the most common procedures in police investigation: suspect interrogation, eyewitness identification, and most forensic science methods. Just as important, the same science also tells us how to correct many of these procedures to produce better, more reliable evidence that will not result in wrongful convictions. Yet most police and prosecutors have tended to resist much of what science seems to say on these questions. New procedures would cost too much, some say. This research and scientific work does not reflect what we know from our years of work on the street, say others; these "results" just reflect lab experiments, not the day-to-day realities police face. For some, the very mention of better ways to handle basic police investigation smacks of disrespect for law enforcement, or a general accusation of corruption and dishonesty. And for others, no problem exists. DNA-based exonerations represent a vanishingly small percentage of cases, they say, and besides, the mere fact that the DNA sometimes does not match does not mean that the defendant did not do the crime.

As we saw in the last chapter, none of these explanations constitutes a convincing reason to resist years, even decades, of accumulated scientific proof that points toward better, more accurate police investigation. Nevertheless, the resistance of police and prosecutors to better practices remains quite real. Thus we circle back to the same question: Why? What makes key actors in law enforcement reluctant to the point of refusal to reexamine how they do what they do? Why the hesitancy to grab hold of better, more accurate investigative tools?

Some legal scholars and commentators have suggested that at least when it comes to prosecutors, the resistance reflects a deficiency in values. According to this view, prosecutors share a culture of overzealousness that pushes them away from ethical practices in pursuit of convictions and long sentences.[1] Others see a lack of "moral courage"[2] among prosecutors, or their failure to fulfill their duty to act not just as advocates for the state but as "minister[s] of justice,"[3] as the norms of the profession require. Still others have concluded that the willingness among prosecutors to break the rules in the pursuit of guilty verdicts runs both wide and deep.[4]

None of these explanations seems any more convincing than what law enforcement itself says. No evidence exists to prove that prosecutors have less in the way of ethical scruples than other lawyers. While plenty of cases in reported legal opinions do contain examples of prosecutorial misconduct of one kind or another, this does not explain the general resistance to change. In order to understand why prosecutors and police resist the pull of science toward better investigative practices, we must understand two other sets of forces. One concerns the enormous institutional and political hurdles to change, the subject of chapter 5. In this chapter, we will explore the other forces: significant cognitive barriers that obstruct the ability of police and prosecutors to turn toward the improved investigative tactics to which modern science points us. These cognitive barriers are not peculiar to those in law enforcement; rather, they exist in every person, whatever he or she does for a living. To one degree or another, they interfere with our ability to come to rational conclusions concerning our own knowledge, actions, or plans. Thus the answer lies not in the fact that police or prosecutors are especially unethical or immoral, or particularly inclined toward misconduct. Rather, it is that they are human beings. And human beings share a number of important thought processes that distort their attitudes, reasoning, and decision making. Professor Alafair Burke of Hofstra Law School puts it well when she says that prosecutors "sometimes fail to make decisions that rationally further justice, not because they fail to value justice, but because they are, in fact, irrational. They make irrational decisions because they are human and all human decision makers share a common set of information processing tendencies that depart from perfect rationality."[5] Even the most excellent and principled prosecutors can fall into cognitive missteps.[6] The common cognitive errors that help us account for the resistance of police and prosecutors to new science-based improvements in police investigation include cognitive dissonance, loss aversion, group polarization, fear and anxiety over loss of the status quo, and challenges to the special status of police and prosecutors.

Cognitive Dissonance

If one had to select the single strongest psychological or cognitive explanation for why police and prosecutors resist the scientific evidence on investigative techniques, one would choose cognitive dissonance.

The theory of cognitive dissonance emerged from the work of the American psychologist Leon Festinger in the late 1950s. In his seminal book, *A Theory of Cognitive Dissonance*,[7] Festinger said that a person holding two inconsistent cognitions (points of knowledge or belief)[8] in her mind experiences an uncomfortable tension.[9] The tension may arise because the person holds two inconsistent beliefs, or holds a belief inconsistent with knowledge of her own behavior.[10] Festinger called this tension cognitive dissonance, and explained that those experiencing cognitive dissonance feel a strong internal drive to ease this dissonance.[11] Elliot Aronson, now one of the foremost experts on cognitive dissonance, came to Stanford University in 1956 as a graduate student, the same year that Festinger began work there as a professor, and the two began collaborative work on the idea of cognitive dissonance. In a 2007 book, Aronson and coauthor Carol Tavris use a classic example to explain the concept.

> Cognitive dissonance is a state of tension that occurs whenever a person holds two cognitions (ideas, attitudes, beliefs, opinions) that are psychologically inconsistent, such as "Smoking is a dumb thing to do because it could kill me" and "I smoke two packs a day." Dissonance produces mental discomfort, ranging from minor pangs to deep anguish; people don't rest easy until they find a way to reduce it. In this example, the most direct way for a smoker to reduce dissonance is by quitting. But if she has tried to quit and failed, now she must reduce dissonance by convincing herself that smoking isn't really so harmful, or that smoking is worth the risk because it helps her relax or prevents her from gaining weight (after all, obesity is a health risk, too) and so on. Most smokers manage to reduce dissonance in many such ingenious, if self deluding, ways.[12]

This explanation illuminates the power of cognitive dissonance very well. The smoker knows that smoking constitutes a real health hazard; the accumulation of years of evidence, well known to the public, looms large. On the other hand, another thought anchors firmly in her mind: she smokes. These two inconsistent thoughts cannot coexist without giving rise to tension, and any normal person will seek relief from that discomfort, if not by quitting then by reworking her beliefs. These reworked beliefs aim to bring the two dissonant cognitions into harmony, even if these new beliefs take the form of deluding rationalizations. Explaining this process, Elliot Aronson says it shows that we should not view "people as rational beings [but rather] as rationalizing beings."[13]

To get an idea of how cognitive dissonance can make a difference in an individual police investigation—the role it can play in the course of a single case—think back to the Norfolk Four, the rape and murder case discussed in chapters 2 and 3. Recall that detectives quickly focused on Danial Williams, a neighbor of the victim. Police detained and questioned Williams overnight, pressuring him ever more harshly, asserting with perfect certainty that they knew he had done it, even manufacturing apparently indisputable evidence of his guilt. Williams then gave police a confession. These facts form the first cognition for the police: Williams killed the victim; case closed. But, just a short time later, the detectives received the autopsy report and discovered that the confession contained major errors that made it inconsistent with the physical evidence. This forms the second cognition: the confession, which police had already accepted, included numerous statements that conflicted with basic physical facts and evidence. This resulted in dissonance, of course, creating considerable tension that had to find some resolution. Detectives could conclude that they got it wrong with their first cognition: Williams had not committed the crime, and had only confessed (incorrectly) to escape multiple hours of harsh questioning. Despite the glaring differences between the confession and the physical evidence, the detectives could not bring themselves to think that they had gotten things so wrong. Instead, they chose a different route: extract another confession from Williams, the details of which agreed with the evidence from the autopsy. This seemed preferable to admitting their own mistake. The police had not gotten it wrong; Williams had killed the victim, they said, but had also lied about the details. This resolved the dissonance: Williams's second confession squared with the evidence. All of this held until, some weeks later, the DNA results show that Williams's confession did not actually comport with the evidence; the DNA actually belonged to someone else. Dissonance arose again: this time in the form of tension between "we know Williams did it because he confessed" and "the DNA does not belong to Williams; if Williams had confessed truthfully, the test would have revealed his DNA." Resolution: not reconsideration of Williams's guilt but a third new confession, stating (for the first time) that Williams committed the crime with someone else, who must have left the DNA. Again, dissonance resolved.[14]

Cognitive dissonance can also play a role in institutional beliefs and behaviors. Andrew McClurg has supplied a useful example in his work on perjury by police officers. Observers of the criminal justice system have long known, and sometimes expressed, a usually unspoken truth: some police officers lie under oath in court in order to assure that evidence does not get thrown out of court for violations of constitutional rights. In 1961, the U.S. Supreme Court announced that when police violated the Fourth Amendment's rules against illegal searches and seizures, state prosecutors could not use this illegally gathered evidence even if the evidence absolutely proved guilt.[15] This exclusionary rule proved instantly and wildly unpopular with police. Many flouted the law and continued to conduct searches as they always had, but adopted the habit of lying in court hearings. They testified that they had gathered the evidence in accordance with the Fourth Amendment, when they had not.[16] In a magazine article in 1967, Irving Younger, a brilliant lawyer and law professor who also served as a judge, prosecutor, and defense attorney during his career, explained that in drug cases in New York courts, "policemen are committing perjury in some of [these cases], and perhaps in nearly all of them."[17] Professor Alan Dershowitz of Harvard Law School made the same claim in 1982, when he said in one of his books that "[a]lmost all police lie about whether they violated the Constitution in order to convict guilty defendants."[18] When he repeated and even elaborated on this idea on a national television program fifteen years later, telling the interviewer that "police departments tell their detectives it's OK to lie, they learn it in the academy,"[19] his comments ignited a firestorm of criticism.[20] Dershowitz may have spoken brazenly, in a way that offended a good many in law enforcement. But the evidence on this issue proves that even if Dershowitz did offend, he was not completely wrong. New York's Mollen Commission, created in the early 1990s to investigate a corruption scandal among a small group of NYPD officers, delivered an unexpected conclusion in its final report.[21] Certainly, the type of corruption the commission had been created to investigate (beating and robbing drug dealers and reselling confiscated illegal drugs taken from the dealers) constituted a deadly serious stain on the NYPD. But the commission found that another type of corruption was far more widespread and even accepted within the department: lying under oath in court at hearings on Fourth Amendment search and seizure violations. Indeed, "testilying"—the name coined for this practice by NYPD officers themselves—was "probably the most common form of police corruption facing the criminal justice system."[22]

Andrew McClurg's analysis of police perjury makes use of the concept of cognitive dissonance to explain what goes on in a police department that would allow for this to happen. He begins with two propositions. "Proposition 1. Most police officers are honorable, moral persons. Proposition 2. Many of these same police officers lie in the course of their official duties."[23] McClurg observes that "many people" believe Proposition 1; more importantly, "many police officers hold this view."[24] But Proposition 2 is also true, and police officers who behave this way know it. This means that "these propositions are irreconcilably in conflict. . . . Honorable, moral police officers do not lie, particularly under oath, in situations where the life or liberty of another human being is at stake. . . . Lying under oath is perjury, a felony punishable by a lengthy term of imprisonment."[25] Thus, cognitive dissonance arises between the ideas "I am a police officer, and a good, moral person" and "I lie under oath, an immoral and criminal act." How do police officers—indeed, how does the culture of a police department—resolve the tension between these cognitions? Rather than ceasing to commit perjury, or changing the belief in their own moral goodness, they change the cognition concerning lying under oath. The ends justify the means: the ends of locking up guilty defendants justify the means of falsifying the facts regarding the way police gathered the evidence. Thus, lying (Proposition 2) carries no moral down side because the lies keep "the system" from allowing guilty criminals to avoid punishment on "legal technicalities."[26] In the words of the Mollen Commission, "despite the devastating consequences of police falsifications, there is a persistent belief among many officers that [lying under oath] is necessary and justified, even if unlawful."[27] This explains one officer's pithy description of "testilying" in order to convict the guilty: "Doing God's work."[28] This makes for a tidy resolution of the tension caused by cognitive dissonance: "I, a police officer, am a good and moral person" now pairs with "I am doing God's work when I testify in court, and nothing could be better and more moral than that."

Cognitive dissonance plays a huge role in the persistent resistance of police and prosecutors to science-based evidence that inaccurate investigative procedures, which have resulted in hundreds or perhaps thousands of wrongful convictions, must undergo substantial change. The basic problem emerges from two conflicting cognitions in the minds of officers and prosecutors. The first is, we, police officers and prosecutors, are the instruments of right, truth, and justice in the system. The second is, we used traditional, accepted investigative procedures to investigate and prosecute, and by doing so, we have sometimes gotten it wrong.

As to the first cognition, no one should doubt the strength with which police and prosecutors believe that they occupy the side of justice and righteousness. They are "the thin blue line" that separates and protects law-abiding citizens from the criminal element that would, left unchecked, rob, rape, kill, and pillage without mercy.[29] They see themselves as the good guys, with a strong moral compass and a real sense of right and wrong, which they act upon every day, in contrast to the bad guys, who would do whatever they could to whomever they wanted were it not for the good guys. And what matters is catching the bad guys and assuring that they receive the punishment they deserve.[30] If anything, prosecutors feel the same way, and then some. They see themselves as the champions of justice in the courtrooms of America, locked in a struggle with the forces of darkness. Testifying before the U.S. Senate Judiciary Committee in 2009, Barry Matson, deputy director of the Alabama District Attorneys Association, described prosecutors as the crusading knights of justice in the system, facing daunting challenges "with integrity, a strong work ethic, and a deep seeded [sic] passion to protect the public and to do justice. . . . [Prosecutors], and no one else, are the only person [sic] in the criminal justice system charged with the responsibility of seeking justice."[31] In a video statement on the website of the National District Attorneys Association, William Fitzpatrick, a member of the organization's national board, says that on "every single day of our professional lives," prosecutors do everything they can "to get to our ultimate goal, which is truth and justice."[32]

It is important to understand why these self-conceptions matter. I am not saying that police are not honest and moral; on the contrary, I believe most are. And I am not saying that prosecutors do not try to pursue justice by convicting the guilty and protecting the innocent; most do. Rather, the crucial idea here is that these descriptions constitute their strongly held views of themselves—and thus the primary cognition we must understand. As Andrew McClurg said in his study of lying by police, many police officers hold to the belief that they are honorable, moral persons,[33] and my point here is quite similar: police officers and prosecutors, both individually and collectively, believe that they are moral people doing the right thing in the justice system. And they don't need scientists to tell them the right way to do a job that they know better than anyone.

Over the last twenty years, since Kirk Bloodsworth became the first person to walk out of prison on the basis of DNA evidence in 1989, a new cognition has developed: some terrible mistakes have occurred in the criminal justice system. Police have pursued, and prosecutors have tried, innocent people. Law enforcement has not done this intentionally, but it has happened, and it has done enormous damage. As a result of these disastrous mistakes, innocent people have served many years of prison time, sometimes even on death row, for crimes that we now know, definitively, they did not commit. This has happened more than 250 times that we know of; many experts believe that this number represents only the tip of the iceberg. And this has happened because police gathered, and prosecutors used, evidence obtained through traditional law enforcement procedures now revealed to be unreliabled.

Now think of the two cognitions at issue here:

Cognition 1: We police officers and prosecutors are "the good guys" in the criminal justice system, convicting the guilty and protecting the helpless and the innocent against the predators among us.

Cognition 2: We police officers and prosecutors have performed investigations and tried cases resulting in the convictions of factually innocent people for the worst crimes imaginable. This has happened as a result of using procedures that, while generally accepted at the time, science now shows to have been likely to generate mistaken evidence. Our actions have landed innocent people in prison, often for long periods.

Cognition 1 constitutes a positive view of two professional groups serving the highest purposes. Cognition 2 describes a set of mistakes—horrible ones, even if completely unintentional—that constitute a crushing blow to the view that police and prosecutors always do the right thing.

Looked at this way, the profession-wide resistance to moving away from inferior investigative techniques, and toward best practices validated by science, becomes easier to understand. The tension of cognitive dissonance must find a resolution, and one way to resolve it would be to change the way police gather evidence, in the ways described in chapters 2 and 6. But this would require significant shifts in the way police and prosecutors think and act, as well as an admission, at least at some level, that catastrophic mistakes have occurred and that some basic aspects of traditional investigation caused these legal horrors. Thus it becomes far easier to resolve the tension through adjustments to the second cognition. So we see William Fitzpatrick of the National District Attorneys Association tell his fellow prosecutors that of the well over 250 DNA-based exonerations, "when you look at the actual statistics regarding those reports, only four of them, only four, are cited within the last ten years"[34]—in other words, this stuff may have happened before, but it's a tiny problem and growing steadily smaller. Prosecutor Paul Logli, also speaking for the NDAA, also minimizes the problem. "In a very few case[s], mistakenly accused defendants have been freed both before trial and after incarceration."[35] Barry Matson, deputy director of the Alabama District Attorneys Association, says, "Have regrettable incidences [sic] occurred in the forensic setting? Yes. Is it to the level that some entities and special projects would have us believe? Absolutely not."[36] In Pinellas County, Florida, witnesses misidentified a dozen defendants; sheriff's deputies arrested two-thirds of them.[37] The defendants were later cleared—some had actually been in jail at the time of the crimes. But Pinellas County sheriff Everett Rice saw no problem and no need to change police procedures. The fact that the errors came to light showed the system worked. "Fortunately, these cases were discovered and corrected," Sheriff Rice said. When mistakes occur, "it's the defendant's attorney's job to find these things out." In Georgia, even in the face of five exonerations based on DNA in her state,[38] all based in whole or in part on eyewitness misidentification, District Attorney Gwendolyn Keyes Fleming of DeKalb County resisted the need for any legislation requiring better eyewitness identification procedures. No need existed for better procedures, she said; individual jurisdictions in the state should have the discretion to decide what to do.[39]

When law enforcement leaders like these look out at the post-DNA world and see no problem of wrongful convictions generated by unscientific procedures and disproven investigative methods, cognition 2 disappears, or at the very least has little or no traction. Dissonance resolved; problem remedied.

Group Polarization

When we speak about police departments or prosecutors' offices, we refer to groups of people. In all but the smallest towns, concerned citizens call the police *department*, not an individual, and even the most rural areas are likely to have a prosecutor's office consisting of a small staff of lawyers. And both police officers and prosecutors have numerous professional organizations. For police, there are police officers' benevolent associations and national organizations like the National Sheriffs Association, the International Association of Chiefs of Police, and the Major Cities Chiefs. In addition, most states and counties have their own police associations, even specialized ones: the California Police Chiefs Association, the Florida Police Chiefs Association, and the Allegheny County (Pennsylvania) Chiefs of Police Association. Prosecutors have a similar set of organizations. The most prominent, the National District Attorneys Association, has members across the country, and statewide organizations for prosecutors exist as well: the Alabama

District Attorneys Association, the Ohio Prosecuting Attorneys Association, the California District Attorneys Association, and so forth. All of these groups have governing boards that deliberate and promulgate rules and policies. They respond to public controversies or proposals for change in the law or in government that may affect their members. They take positions on government policies, proposed legislation, and the like.

But beyond these observable organizations, both police and prosecutors belong to occupational sets that exhibit strong group identities. This is especially true of police. As I have written elsewhere,[40] the strength of police cohesiveness fully justifies speaking of a police culture. Officers tend to feel that only those within their own group can truly understand the job they do and the life they lead; they believe that outsiders to policing can never truly grasp the risks they take and what they put up with day to day. For most police, outsiders possess no insight—indeed, they have no standing—that would allow them to criticize, or even give advice to, police. The bonds among officers form early in their careers, and remain unshakable. They depend on each other for their physical safety in the event that they need help, and they rely on each other to never say anything against another officer to an outsider—the so-called "blue wall of silence." Police culture often coalesces around a simple idea: "it's us" (police officers) "versus them" (everyone else). Consider a statement by a police officer speaking to an interviewer concerning his belief in the law and the Constitution. "If we're going to catch these [bad] guys," the officer said, "fuck the Constitution, fuck the Bill of Rights, fuck them, fuck you, fuck everybody. The only ones I care about are my partners."[41]

Prosecutors may have less of an absolute conception of their group identity than police officers do; they are, after all, also anchored in the larger legal culture as lawyers. But within prosecutors' offices and organizations, a strong sense of solidarity exists. Recall the thrust of the statements (quoted earlier in this chapter) by William Fitzpatrick, Barry Matson, and others on behalf of their professional organizations: prosecutors, and only prosecutors, shoulder the responsibility of seeking justice in the American criminal justice system. This is a strong statement, and in a limited way a true one: the norms of the legal profession actually impose the obligation to seek justice on the prosecutor. The prosecutor does not act only as the advocate for the position of the state, seeking convictions, but also in the interest of justice, even when something other than a conviction (for example, dropping the charges) best serves justice. But surely this does not mean that no other actor in the system is interested in justice. The judge acts in the interest of justice when she makes rulings on evidence, or instructs the jury on the applicable law, or imposes a sentence upon a convicted defendant. While the defense law-yer's obligation is only to zealously defend his client, the profession puts this duty and no other on the defense attorney precisely because of the interest of justice. Having a strong advocate totally dedicated to the defendant is a requirement for justice in our adversary system, because without the ability to challenge the prosecution, the entire system, based as it is on opposing presentations of evidence, would cease to function. Yet little of this surfaces in the rhetoric of the prosecuting groups; instead, they wave the obligation to pursue justice as a flag of both superiority and solidarity, symbolizing the forces of light (them) against darkness (everyone else). Prosecutors are cru-saders, this thinking goes; they are warriors for justice, and those in other roles do not aspire to the same ideals. Professor Alafair Burke, herself a for-mer prosecutor, captures this well: prosecutors, she says, "see themselves as warriors in a fight between the good and the guilty."[42]

Set against this background, the phenomenon of group polarization becomes quite important. This idea, first described as group-induced atti-tude polarization in a 1969 study,[43] seeks to explain what happens to atti-tudes when groups of people deliberate or discuss items. According to Daniel Isenberg, group polarization occurs "when an initial tendency of individual group members toward a given direction is enhanced following group discussion."[44] In a more recent explanation, Cass Sunstein says that "group polarization means that members of a deliberating group predict-ably move toward a more extreme point in the direction indicated by the members' predeliberation tendencies."[45] Thus if members of a group whose individuals all share attitudes on a given point come together in any formal or informal context and discuss the issue or share thoughts about it, they will probably move toward a more extreme position, becoming more firmly committed to the idea than the average beliefs of all of the individual group members before the discussion. Additionally, groups that have in common what Sunstein calls "a salient shared identity" will see even greater shifts toward extremes.[46] Thus we would expect to see that police, in any group dis-cussion—training sessions, roll calls, squad car chat with patrol partners, or after-work bull sessions—would become more extreme in their beliefs, and all the more so because of their strong group identities. Prosecutors, as the "warriors" for good against evil in the criminal justice system, would experi-ence group polarization as well.

For groups that already know that they represent the cause of justice and righteousness against all others, and who have a strong stake in criminal investigation practices as they now stand, the new scientific information on improvement of the criminal investigation, coming from those outside the

brotherhood, would never get a warm welcome. And when police or prosecutors gather, it seems even less surprising that both their rhetoric and their
actions can seem extreme from the outside: resist at all costs. These people—the scientists, the academics, the defense attorneys—have no idea what
they're talking about. We will not give in to their ivory tower, bleeding-heart,
self-interested meddling.

Behavioral Economics: Prospect Theory, Loss Aversion, Endowment Effect, and Status Quo Bias

Another set of key insights concerning the reasons for law enforcement resistance to scientific findings comes from the relatively new field of behavioral
economics. For many years, classical economics supplied one of the leading theories of human behavior. But for most experts interested in the way
people make judgments and decisions, that focus has shifted over the last
two-plus decades; at the very least, some new assumptions have come into
the picture. Without these new insights, we risk proceeding without a full
understanding of the ways in which people actually behave, and why.

Start with the conventional economic theory of human behavior. In his
book *The Economic Approach to Human Behavior,* Nobel laureate Gary S.
Becker describes the principles of standard economics and their relationship to behavior this way: "[A]ll human behavior can be viewed as involving participants who (1) maximize their utility (2) form a stable set of preferences and (3) accumulate an optimal amount of information and other
inputs in a variety of markets."[47] Becker's description captures the modern
building blocks of our heretofore-solid beliefs about the economic behavior
of modern human beings and our society. Using this theory, economists predicted that people would make rational choices: as rational utility maximiz-
ers, they "compute any action's likely effect on their total wealth, and choose
accordingly."[48] In other words, people, as rational actors, will maximize what
they have of a desired good; they will do this by choosing among goals and
courses of action dictated by their own preferences, which will only vary
on the basis of relevant information, which they will accumulate as needed.
Others have described the theory as "the concept of rational choice," in which
"economists believe that economic agents—individuals, managers, government regulators—should (and in large part do) choose among alternatives
in accordance with well-defined preferences. . . . [Under] the rational choice
model . . . only preference relevant features of the alternatives influence the
individual's decision."[49] These theories portray a neat, rational, and understandable world, in which a logical mind can quantify finite inputs and goals

and can predict the choices of the rational beings acting within it. Given the great appeal of this theory to economists, it "has dominated the analysis of decision making under risk. . . . Thus, it is assumed that all reasonable people would wish to obey the axioms of the theory, and that most people actually do, most of the time."[50]

But some began to question the model because, under empirical examination, it actually did not predict human behavior very well. The assumptions about human beings it relied upon did not reflect the way human beings operated in the world; more importantly, the theory's predictions did not hold. As Milton Friedman, another Nobel laureate in economics, once said, people should judge the power of economics not according to the quality of its assumptions but according to the quality of its predictions.[51] And in the last several decades, a new set of theories, broadly called "behavioral economics," has shown that the predictions of classical economics simply cannot explain some very important aspects of human judgment and decision making.

Much of the earliest and most important work that built the foundations for what has become behavioral economics originated with Daniel Kahneman and Amos Tversky. Of greatest importance to our discussion, their 1979 article "Prospect Theory: An Analysis of Decision under Risk"[52] discussed their empirical testing of the economic utility theory. They challenged this then-dominant economic approach to human behavior because it did not hold up under actual testing. Kahneman and Tversky's experiments produced results contrary to what the utility maximizing theory predicted. In their experiments, they gave subjects various choices that included some level of uncertainty, and asked for their preferences. Their results established a number of surprising new things. Kahneman and Tversky found key differences between what their "prospect theory" and the expected utility theory would have predicted, with prospect theory significantly more accurate at predicting the results. First, people give more weight to certainty among prospective choices than those choices actually deserve when looked at rationally; this tends to promote risk aversion with regard to possible gains that might result from a choice, and risk seeking with regard to possible losses.[53] Second, the carrier of utility—in other words, what decision makers actually value in a possible result—comes from changes in wealth or welfare relative to a starting point, not from the decision maker's expected final total of assets (including the wealth or welfare with which the decision maker began).[54] This idea—that people choose not on the basis of rationally maximizing their total wealth or utility but on the basis of how much the decision changes those things relative to some starting point—is "the cornerstone" of prospect theory.[55] Accordingly, decision making under uncertainty will always be about the reference point from which we start. Our decisions will not come from expectations of the absolute magnitude of what we have in the end, but from "the evaluation of changes or differences."[56] This, Kahneman and Tversky point out, mirrors the way that basic principles of judgment and perception actually work: "an object at a given temperature may be experienced as hot or cold to the touch depending on the temperature to which one has adapted."[57] (To check this for yourself, think of stepping outside a building into a temperature of 50 degrees Fahrenheit. If this happens in mid-July in the northern hemisphere, the thought "cold!" comes to mind immediately; but if it takes place in February, in the dead of winter, you may think, "At last, a warm day!")

This leads Kahneman and Tversky to the important principle of loss aversion: "A salient characteristic of attitudes to changes in welfare is that losses loom larger than gains."[58] Put another way, "A loss of a given size generates more pain than an equally large gain yields pleasure."[59] In many instances, the same transaction can carry the label of either a loss or a gain; for example, a business might give its customers the choice of paying with a credit card or receiving a "cash discount" of 5 percent. Alternatively, the exact same choice could be described as a 5 percent surcharge for using a credit card. Consumers making purchasing decisions will react very differently to these choices, but under rational choice theory, they should not; both choices represent exactly the same alternatives. Since consumers, like all other people, will exhibit loss aversion, they will react negatively to the surcharge, but not to the discount. Thus prospect theory and loss aversion explain some things about the world that classical economics and rational choice theory do not.

Richard Thaler built upon this idea of loss aversion in describing what happened in experiments in which half of the subjects received a small item of value—in this case, a coffee mug.[60] Those who had received the mugs could sell them, and those without mugs could buy them from those who had them. Those students given the mugs proved quite reluctant to sell them, and they generally asked more than twice as much for their mugs as those without them would willingly pay. (Only 15 percent of the mugs actually sold as a result.)[61] Thaler called this the endowment effect: those endowed with something, even something of relatively small value, consider it much more valuable than any rational market would, because they experience loss aversion—they would feel the loss of the good (from selling it or otherwise giving it up) more keenly than they would feel whatever they might gain for this.[62]

Both loss aversion and the endowment effect lead to consideration of another important idea of behavioral economics: status quo bias. William

Samuelson and Richard Zeckhauser's seminal work on status quo bias[63] describes the concept as "a general experimental finding—consistent with, but not solely prompted by, loss aversion."[64] And certainly the concept is both general and broad: people making decisions automatically carry a bias that causes them to favor the status quo alternative over other choices. Under the rational choice model, Samuelson and Zeckhauser say, only features of the alternatives relevant to the decision should make a difference in any decision.[65] Yet this does not reflect real life, where "alternatives often come with influential labels. Indeed one alternative inevitably carries the label status quo,"[66] and this turns out to make a strong, measurable difference in the way people choose when they make decisions. The main finding of their work "is that decision makers exhibit a significant status quo bias."[67] Framing a choice as the status quo had "predictable and significant effects on subjects' decision making. Individuals exhibited a significant status quo bias across a range of decisions."[68] Samuelson and Zeckhauser's experiments found that the status quo bias did not represent a mistake that subjects might easily correct; rather, it would probably persist, usually unrecognized, in most decision making.[69] And given the usual circumstances of everyday life, most individuals, policy makers, and institutions would probably have considerable psychological and sunk-cost investment in the status quo, making it that much more difficult to resist in any given situation.[70]

Loss aversion, endowment effect, and status quo bias can tell us a lot about why police and prosecutors and their organizations and agencies resist the possibility of change toward the better practices in police investigation toward which science points. The individuals who lead these agencies, who make up their membership, and who band together in professional organizations all experience the results of these forces on their behavior, and they act accordingly. Think first about loss aversion and the endowment effect, and about the law enforcement establishment confronting the fact that some of its traditional investigation practices have produced grave injustices. Add to this that scientists in multiple fields have shown that we can avoid many of these mistakes by adopting changes in these practices that produce more accurate results. These new approaches spell out the possibilities of gains for any police department or prosecutor's office that adopts them. They will have verdicts that are less likely to suffer from the types of errors and mistakes exposed in DNA exoneration cases over the years. At the very least, appeals based on using discredited practices will decrease in number, and they will enjoy greater certainty of winning the appeals based on claims of the insufficiency of the evidence that convicted defendants often file. And not least, they can personally feel greater certainty that the suspects they do arrest and prosecute are the actual guilty parties. This, of course, has a hugely important complementary benefit: they can feel more assured that the real criminal does not remain on the street. But against all of these potential gains, consider the possibility of loss as well. It seems easy to imagine that police or prosecutors who feel that no real problem exists (see chapter 3) would not accept that accuracy would increase with new procedures; in fact, they might believe that since what they do now works fine, changing their practice would inevitably mean that they might not solve some cases with the new procedures that they do solve now with traditional methods. Taken together with any evidence (or even anecdotes) indicating that the proposed new procedures might carry costs, this would build the fear of real loss incurred for switching tactics. For example, as noted in chapter 2, considerable scientific work, especially the work of Gary Wells, shows that substituting sequential lineups for traditional simultaneous lineups will decrease the use of relative judgment in making identifications, and will produce considerably fewer incorrect identifications. But some work by others also shows that sequential lineups may also decrease the number of correct identifications. This small decrease does not compare to the magnitude of the decrease in incorrect identifications, and probably follows from the elimination of lucky guesses that come from relative judgments by witnesses.[71] Nevertheless, law enforcement will undoubtedly see the loss of these correct identifications, accidental though they might be, as a loss. And any similar uncertainties in the way that newer procedures work will probably appear as a potential loss to law enforcement as well. These losses will, as Kahneman and Tversky predicted, loom large; they'll seem greater and more important to avoid than whatever potential gains new procedures might provide.

Think also about how police and prosecutors probably see the ways that they have always investigated criminal cases. These very basic methods of operating—how one first evaluates and then questions a suspect, how to construct and use a lineup, what to expect from forensic testing—come to police officers in their academy training, their in-service training, and most importantly in their on-the-job training and socialization by senior officers and detectives. They are not just lessons from books; they are, rather, the wisdom received from the initiated members of the profession, the combined lessons of experience handed down from generation to generation of police officers. They constitute, in every sense, the special inheritance of every police officer, the revered customs and secrets of the tribe. While prosecutors work at one remove from the actual police investigation itself, they are also believers in and consumers of the same set of practices. We investigate cases this way, a member of the police or prosecutorial forces might say, because it works, we know it works, we've always known it, and those that came before us knew it, too.

If we can think of the coffee mugs Richard Thaler gave his experimental subjects as an endowment with which those subjects would part only reluctantly, at an unrealistically high price, think how much greater the unwillingness to give up the endowment would be when it consists of the received and (until recently) unquestioned wisdom of the profession. Law enforcement would probably not give this up unless made to do so; the unwillingness to part with the endowment handed down from one's trainers, supervisors, and authority figures over so many years would probably be an extraordinary impediment to change.

The application of the status quo bias to the adoption of new police investigative procedures practically explains itself. Simply put, all of the now-discredited practices in police investigation—from the Reid Technique for interrogation to the use of nonblind lineups to the continued use of evidence such as fingerprint identification and tool mark analysis—all of these constitute the status quo. These methods now enjoy wide use and confidence among police and prosecutors, and have for years; one can still find contemporary cases using methods like bite mark identification, which has produced astounding incorrect convictions. Despite the considerable and mounting evidence that these methods result in unreliable proof, the status quo bias predicts that removing these methods from law enforcement's arsenal will prove difficult indeed. This is, of course, just what we see. And perhaps this should not surprise us, because, as Samuelson and Zeckhauser explain, the status quo bias only becomes stronger given the realities of prior emotional, psychological, and physical investment in the status quo.

> [A] decision maker in the real world may have a considerable commitment to, or psychological investment in, the status quo option. . . . His or her past choice may have become known to others and . . . he or she may have lived with the status quo choice for some time. Moreover, many real-world decisions are made by a person acting as part of an organization or group, which may exert additional pressures for status quo choices.[72]

Thus the resistance of police and prosecutors to ways to improve the accuracy of investigation and prosecution does not seem so illogical or irrational. Even knowing that they may gain something from switching to better ways of doing things, they may also perceive potential losses from change, and those losses will appear larger than the gains, perhaps stifling any possibility for change. Few in law enforcement will want to give up their special inheritance for something new; at the very least, they will be likely to over-value what they have, and thus resist all the more strongly giving it up. And thus change from the established ways of doing things will always remain difficult.

Status Challenges

In the context of our ability to understand the resistance of police and pros-ecutors to better, science-based investigative procedures, we need to under-stand how social status—and perhaps more importantly, loss of that status—might prove threatening enough to cause that resistance. In lay terms, social status means the standing, esteem, or prestige that a person holds within a given society or social group. People have status depending on numerous factors, including occupation, education, ownership of property or other wealth, and family background. When sociologists conceptualize status, they often break the concept into two general categories: ascribed status and achieved status. Ascribed status comes from birth into a high-status family or group, or may come later in life through the assumption of such a posi-tion. Achieved status describes a social position that a person attains vol-untarily, usually through deliberate effort. This type of status is achieved by dint of hard work, development and cultivation of special talents, or demon-strated achievement of occupational, educational, or personal goals. Exam-ples of this kind of status might include becoming a doctor, attorney, pro-fessional athlete, or teacher—and, of course, a police officer.[73] Those having special talents enjoy enhanced social status by virtue of these gifts; members of the group who have them perceive themselves, and may be perceived by others, as having greater status than those who do not have them. Certainly, monetary rewards may flow from these specialized types of expertise, but the more important concept for our purposes is the enhanced social status that comes with these kinds of positions.

Think now about police officers. They certainly constitute an identifi-able social group within society. Policing has its culture, with its own norms, ways of acting, and beliefs. Within this culture, police officers believe that they have special talents that uninitiated lay people lack. And they believe that these talents set them apart, giving them the ability to see and under-stand things that most people cannot. And this enhanced status carries over to other members of society, who also see police as having special, higher status. Thus being a police officer confers a strong positive status on offi-cers in the eyes of the public (contrary to the expectations of police officers themselves).[74]

Interrogation of suspects makes a good example. The Reid Technique (see chapter 2), the dominant method of interrogation in American police work for decades, taught to literally generations of police officers, proceeds in two stages. First, having identified a suspect, the police officer makes an evaluation of the suspect's truthfulness and guilt or innocence. Second, if the detective concludes that the suspect is not telling the truth and is guilty, he or she then moves on to the interrogation, with the goal of extracting a confession that will prove the suspect's guilt. Everything about this process centers upon one important assumption: the trained, savvy detective, instructed in the Reid Technique and sharpened by years of experience, has a well-honed ability to tell truth from lies and guilt from guiltlessness that the rest of us lack. Most of us probably believe that we'd score no better than chance at figuring out if a person has told the truth, and research confirms this. The trained detective, on the other hand, possesses a superior set of skills for this task.

We can also see these special abilities when we consider the subject of forensic sciences. Forensic science operates in ways that expose the invisible and heretofore unknowable. This is the literal truth of some of the forensic disciplines: specks of human tissue or fluid, tested in high-tech labs, reveal the guilt of the real perpetrator and even exclude virtually all other human beings as possibilities; fingerprints, invisible to the naked eye, make for foolproof identification of perpetrators; the tiny marks on a bullet casing allow the ballistics expert to say whether or not the shell came from a particular firearm. Interpretation of the results of such testing and investigation leads us to the critical question prosecutors must address to prove a case: Did the defendant commit the crime? Thus both police and prosecutors come, over time, to repose an enormous amount of trust and confidence in the results of forensic testing. These tests may operate at so technical a level that to the untrained, forensic science might seem like magic. But this magic plays a vital role in securing convictions. And the magicians—the forensic scientists—become members of the law enforcement team in the eyes of police and prosecutors, and their special "powers" enhance the abilities, and thus the status and prestige, of law enforcement generally.

Now consider the new, science-based evidence concerning how to conduct a lineup, how to interrogate witnesses, or which disciplines of forensic science actually work meaningfully and which do not. We make a mistake if we see this new information as just information—simply new knowledge that we should take into account. Viewed through the eyes of a police officer, much of this new information comes across as something more: a direct challenge to the specialized knowledge that has given them increased social status for decades. And as with any other individuals, status has value for police officers, and we cannot expect them to give it up any more willingly than anyone else would. For example, think about the special ability of police to sift truth from lies in order to home in on the right suspects and to conduct traditional interrogation using the ubiquitous Reid Technique. It certainly seems plausible that "professional lie detectors, whose work may depend upon their ability to detect deceit, ought to be more successful at this task" than untrained, inexperienced lay people. As explained in chapter 3, lay people have no special ability to detect the truth—not surprising, because they have no special training or experience. But professional lie detectors, like police officers, customs officers, and federal polygraph operators, actually do no better. As one team of researchers put it, "Officers' fairly poor accuracy in assessing the credibility" of suspects "has been well documented."[75] Officers lack an accurate sense of the importance and meaning of eye contact and the relative scarcity of body movements, mistaking what they see as clues showing deception when, actually, these "clues" show the exact opposite.[76] Thus news of studies and research proving that police performed no better than the general public on this central task would not just surprise police and prosecutors; it would undercut their belief in their own special abilities, and therefore undermine their claims to higher status. The same thing would no doubt follow from the release of the National Academy of Sciences' 2009 report. As discussed in chapter 3, the report discusses at some length the shortcomings of many forensic disciplines, especially forensic odontology (bite mark analysis) and hair and fiber analysis, and even takes on such venerable disciplines as fingerprint and firearms identifications. The report creates real doubt about how well these methods work, and whether they actually produce valuable, accurate evidence. Throwing forensic science into question hits law enforcement hard: when the National Academy of Sciences' report questions the basics of forensic science, it strikes at the heart of the special abilities the forensic disciplines give police to crack cases and convict the guilty. And that, of course, cuts into the special social status of police and prosecutors generally.

To be sure, not all of the science-driven evidence on police investigation challenges what police do. If anything, the National Academy of Sciences' report on forensic science burnishes the reputation of DNA; it does not diminish it. But much of the new science does have a direct bearing on what has given law enforcement special status. Viewed this way, it does not seem surprising to find police officials and prosecutors actively resisting the science that indicates that some of their supposed special talents really do not exist. These new ideas directly challenge the status of police officers and law enforcement institutions as special and uniquely valuable in carrying out their mission. And, as with any status challenges, those who see themselves confronted this way are likely to resist any change that might undermine the status they see as rightfully theirs. This therefore breeds resistance as surely as night follows day.

The Real Reasons for Resistance Emerge

Thus we can see that there is something more than what law enforcement says, and something very important to understand, as we explore the real reasons for police and prosecutorial resistance to the new knowledge we have concerning suspect interrogation, eyewitness testimony, and forensic science. It is not simply a matter of cost, or of there being no problem, as we often hear from those in the field. Rather, considerable evidence suggests that issues of cognition and thinking lie behind what we see. Cognitive bias keeps us well rationalized and thus fortified against any change. Fear of loss and a desire to maintain the status quo press hard in the direction of avoiding change. And challenges to their status keep law enforcement professionals reluctant and defensive, since admitting any of this new information to one's thinking would result in a decrease in status. These concepts help us understand why the resistance is there and what to do about it. In the next chapter, we explore another array of forces that might explain the resistance to the new things known now about how to improve police investigation: institutional and political issues.

5

The Real Reasons for Resistance

Institutional and Political Barriers

In chapter 4, we saw that much of the resistance to better methods of police investigative practice comes from cognitive barriers to change, such as cognitive dissonance, loss aversion, and status quo bias, the polarization of groups, and challenges to status. These explanations help us understand why police officers, prosecutors, their agencies, and their professional organizations resist the implementation of new methods, despite a strong scientific consensus on the benefits of virtually all of the changes that follow from the research. In this chapter, we explore another group of reasons for resistance: institutional and political barriers to change, which have a long reach in our political system. If one could read the message of chapter 4's discussion of cognitive barriers as "police officers and prosecutors are people, and they suffer from the same cognitive shortcomings and limitations as the rest of us," this chapter contains a different message: police and prosecutors are people acting within institutions and political frameworks. Police officers act as agents of the state, and as members of a government agency; the police department functions as the institution for the delivery of police services to fight crime, ensure public order, and attend to emergencies. Similarly, prosecutors try cases on behalf of the state against persons accused of crime. The political barriers involved have an unambiguous and forceful effect in this context. The overwhelming number of head prosecutors in counties around the country stand for election—the prototypically political act, one might say—making them, their institutions, and perhaps even their employees subject to political pressures, expectations, and accountability. In policing, this rings true for county sheriffs, since almost all of them run for election as well. For state and local police departments, elected officials almost always choose the police department's leader. The governor or mayor of the jurisdiction appoints the state police commissioner or the city police chief, and the commissioner or chief serves at the elected official's pleasure, subject to immediate dismissal for any reason, ensuring the leader of the agency's accountability to the appointing official.

Institutional and political barriers take many forms; all focus on the way people within institutions, and the institutions themselves, react to the changes taking place in the environment that we call the criminal justice system. We should think first about institutional incentives: What goals and benchmarks pull police and prosecutors along in their roles, and what effects does this produce? The second institutional barrier involves the highly insular, distrustful nature of police culture, referred to briefly in the last chapter but explored in greater depth here. Third, political ambition may play a powerful role for prosecutors. Fourth, police unions and professional organizations have had a strong impact on the way the resistance to scientifically proven improvements in investigative techniques has played out. Fifth, media coverage of criminal justice issues and crime generally has become crucial in determining how well or poorly the public and political leaders respond to suggestions for reform. Last, our legislative bodies, and the degree to which they really are representative, have much to do with whether or not the desire for change will take concrete form in new law.

Institutional Incentives: The Imperatives of Arrest and Conviction

For any job, employers value certain outcomes over others. To move employees toward achieving those results, jobs have incentives. The clearest example comes from sales work, in which salespeople earn commissions. Their earnings depend directly on how much they sell; the more they sell, the more they make. In other types of work, employers can offer the incentive of better pay for better performance, and can offer other types of incentives, too, including promotions, more desirable assignments, greater responsibility, and status-enhancing titles or privileges.

In law enforcement, these rules hold just as they do elsewhere. While neither police officers nor prosecutors receive cash bounties for getting the bad guys, the other types of incentives—promotions, raises, better assignments, and the like—surely form part of the occupational landscape. And beyond just denoting the types of behavior that bosses want, these incentives remain tightly interwoven with the culture of police and prosecutorial agencies. In other words, police and prosecutors do these things not just for personal advancement but because the cultures of these agencies consider these outcomes the highest and most valued achievements. Thus achieving them will gain the respect of one's peers. For police, the institutional imperative is making arrests; an officer earns rewards by closing cases with arrests. For prosecutors, the institutional drive is to get convictions. The higher the conviction rate, the more one advances.

Police: "Case Closed by Arrest"

For police offices, the institutional Holy Grail has always remained the same: solving cases by arresting perpetrators. Police officers who make a lot of arrests become known as proactive, resourceful, take-charge officers—the ones who go out on the street and make things happen. An aggressive attitude toward making arrests earns them accolades from fellow officers, commanders, and others. They become known, in the parlance of the stationhouse, as "cop's cops." And the numbers of arrests they make sit at the core of what makes them the most admired, promoted, and rewarded members of the police departments in which they serve. Bob Stewart, who retired as a captain from the Washington, DC, police force and who has also served as chief in other police departments, works as an independent consultant and trainer for police departments all over the United States and the world. Stewart understands the central importance of arrests. "The way in which you get recognized and rewarded is to make arrests. It's a prerequisite to transfer or promotion to [desirable positions]. It's embedded into the police culture."[1] According to Samuel Serio, a lawyer and former police officer who represented the Fraternal Order of Police (one of the main police labor unions) for seventeen years, what makes for success in police work has little to do with the niceties of suspect interrogation or other legal requirements. What matters comes in a phrase known by police everywhere: "case closed by arrest." Serio says, "The stats are, 'Did you close the case,' not 'Was justice done.' That's not even on the [police report]."[2]

Those who study police have long understood the central importance of arrests to the culture of police departments, and the vital role that arrests play in determining how well, and how quickly, any individual officer progresses up the ladder within his or her department. The more arrests an officer makes, and the more serious the crimes involved, the better the officer's career. In 1978, Peter K. Manning wrote about the difficulties of the police officer's job. In a classic statement about the dilemmas faced by officers, Manning said that police departments tended to increase the difficulties because they rewarded not protection of the public welfare but arrests. "Most police departments promote [officers to] . . . more desirable duty, for 'good pinches'—arrests that are most likely to result in convictions." As a result, the public demands ever more arrests, and arrests have thus become "an index for measuring how well the police accomplish their mandate."[3] Writing in 1986, William F. Walsh observed that for at least thirty-five years, criminologists and other scholars of police in the United States had identified making arrests for felonies as "one of the more important standards of professional excellence in policing."[4] In the New York Police Department, the subject of his study, Walsh found that the patrol supervisors he interviewed viewed the officers under their commands much differently depending on the number of felony arrests they made each year. Supervisors felt that an officer who made nine such arrests per year met only the minimum standard, while they saw an officer who made twenty-four or more felony arrests a year as "a superior performer."[5] As one NYPD officer told Walsh, the officers he considered "hot-shots" made the most arrests, as a way of trying to get recognized and promoted.[6] This same attitude has long pervaded almost all police departments.

While the imperative of arrest certainly predates the war on drugs, the efforts of police to control the use, distribution, and sale of illegal narcotics has become a huge stimulant to the existing incentives to make arrests. The public and political leaders demand that the police do something about drugs; drug use and sale remain common throughout American society, despite years of laws and police pressure aimed at curtailing it; and, in some areas of towns and cities, trafficking takes place outside, in open-air drug markets, putting abundant suspects within relatively easy reach of police. Thus drug arrests rank high on the list of preferred police activities. According to one group of researchers, "Arrest statistics are the metric by which police departments everywhere increasingly judge officer productivity and often supervisor productivity; when arrest numbers are high, many within the police department benefit. Misdemeanor arrests, especially drug possession misdemeanor arrests, are easy to make and, compared to other police work, they are relatively safe." These arrests result in lucrative overtime pay for officers and "also count toward promotions and choice assignments."[7] Given the pressure from political leaders and the public, these arrests make perfect sense for the police to pursue, and as long as the incentives remain and officers perceive that they will receive rewards for making drug arrests, the swelling numbers of drug arrests will continue. In a study of more than four hundred police officers in twenty-three police departments in the Cincinnati, Ohio, metropolitan area, officers understood the arrangement perfectly well: when an officer sees that his or her department rewards drug arrests, the officer makes more of them.[8] Thus, it does not matter that the desire to address drug use and addiction could take multiple approaches—universal access to treatment, needle exchange programs, decriminalization of some drugs, or any number of other avenues. It also does not matter that the unabated flood of arrests for drugs for many decades has not really dented drug use or the drug trade. The wish to act against the drug problem has taken exactly the form one would predict given what we know about the imperative of arrest: ever more arrests.

Michael McNulty, a former NYPD commander, frames the issue correctly: "everybody knows that the active cops were the ones who were ultimately getting the more enviable positions, the good details, being considered for detective designation and so forth."[9] In the law enforcement culture, police officers understand what to do to get ahead; they know how to find the rewards. In the words of Thomas Reppetto, a former Chicago Police Department commander and later president of the Citizens Crime Commission, "workers are workers everywhere," including police officers.[10]

Prosecutors: The Imperative of Convictions

According to the norms of the legal profession, prosecutors have two roles in criminal cases. First, they serve as the lawyer for the state, gathering, marshaling, and presenting the evidence. Second, the prosecutor also carries the role of minister of justice, and with it the duty to do what serves justice even when this dictates not pursuing certain cases or even dropping them midstream.

This, in any case, is the theory. In practice, things often work differently, because for many prosecutors, what matters is not how many cases you dismiss before trial in the interests of justice. It is how many you win: your conviction rate or "batting average." For prosecutors, this stems at least in part from a basic fact about their work: very few ways exist to measure their overall performance on the job, but we can measure convictions. Thus

supervisors in prosecutors' offices compare the lawyers under their authority using this readily quantifiable number,[11] since other aspects of the prosecutor's job performance do not lend themselves to easy measurement, or
any measurement at all.[12] Therefore, prosecutors' careers advance according to their conviction rates. The higher the rate, the better they do. In this
culture, better numbers bring higher prestige within the office and the profession, and may help secure the path to political office or a lucrative private practice.[13] According to Professor Daniel Medwed of the University
of Utah, "Prosecutors with the highest conviction rates (and, thus, reputations as the best performers) stand the greatest chance for advancement
internally." Even without explicit financial incentives, "the inducements are
implicit in a system where promotions are contingent on one's ability to
garner convictions."[14] This puts a premium on winning, both office-wide
and for individual prosecutors; prosecutors must do everything they can
to win each and every case.[15] According to Barbara O'Brien, prosecutors'
offices have "an incentive structure that encourages prosecutors to seek
convictions at all costs," with very little in the way of effective limits.[16]

All of this can lead a prosecutor's office into what some have called a "conviction psychology"[17]—a worldview that values convictions above all else,
and in which other concerns, such as the idea that the prosecutor has an
obligation to do justice, disappear. The conviction psychology changes the
prosecutor's attitudes with regard to the defendant, the judicial process,
and even his or her role as an advocate. According to George Felkenes, who
wrote about this phenomenon in 1975, a prosecutor with a conviction psychology "thinks of the defendant as guilty, and reasons that an innocent person would not be introduced into the system. . . . The result of these attitudes
is a deterioration of the ideal purpose of the prosecutor—to seek justice."[18]
And given the crucial role of the prosecutor, all of this leads to real and con-
sequential distortions—of purpose, of focus, and of results—across the entire
criminal justice system.

The Consequences of the Imperatives of Arrest and Conviction

Where does this lead our police and prosecutors? The imperatives of arrest
and conviction become self-sustaining, because they form the basis for
career advancement and the accumulation of status within police departments and prosecutors' offices. Arrests (for police) and convictions (for prosecutors) may become not means of doing justice, but ends in themselves.
When the means become the ends for the actors on the ground, views can

become all too easily distorted, bent to the institutional imperative instead of to the overall purpose.

How does this affect the willingness to embrace new investigative methods? When new procedures or innovations or proposed changes come along in policing or prosecutorial work, those who have a stake in the existing order will scrutinize the new approaches with extreme skepticism, to see how they might affect the ability to attain the imperatives of making arrests or gaining convictions. Anything that appears to create obstacles to arrests or convictions will, without a doubt, encounter resistance. So if the work of scientists shows that simultaneous lineups will reduce the number of false identifications, but could also cause a slight drop in the number of correct identifications (because, as discussed earlier, simultaneous lineups will eliminate a small number of lucky relative guesses), the improvement that the innovation will bring will often seem trivial to actors in the system who will fear the loss of those few correct (even if luck-based) arrests and convictions. Similarly, many in law enforcement seem to feel (despite evidence to the contrary—see chapter 6) that recording the interrogations of suspects will cause the suspects to refuse to speak to police. This would threaten the ability to arrest and ultimately the ability to convict, and therefore will, like other innovations, engender resistance.

Police Culture: The Insular World of "Us versus Them"

Those who serve in police departments and those who study them would probably agree on one thing: police departments have a strong, insular police culture, with "commonly held norms, social practices, expectations, and assumptions" that favor particular goals, behaviors, and beliefs.[19] For example, one influential study described police culture as typified by autonomy, bravery, secrecy, isolation, and solidarity with fellow officers.[20] Another commentator included loyalty among members, suspiciousness of both the public and newcomers to the organization, and a strong degree of both overall social isolation and loyalty to their own group.[21] These unique aspects of police culture stem from the efforts of officers to cope with the occupational and organizational environments in which they find themselves. Occupationally, they confront potential and real violence, directed toward them and fellow officers, and have the power to use force in their dealings with the public. Organizationally, officers must endure regular scrutiny by supervisors, and they feel that they operate under rules that sometimes seem capricious, opaque, less than sensible, and always imposed on them from on high. This means discipline may seem random and undeserved, and they seldom hear praise.[22] All of this has major downsides for the routine functioning of police officers and their departments, including the so-called blue wall of silence (one officer will never reveal another officer's wrongdoing), and it poses major obstacles to efforts to reform police and ensure police accountability to the public.[23]

These influences, and the attitudes that they engender, lead to an unfortunate feeling among police that "it's us" (our fellow police officers) "versus them" (the public, the bosses—really, everyone else). As a kind of sum total of negative police attitudes, the "us versus them" streak in American police culture is important to understand. In their book *Beyond 911: A New Era for Policing*, Malcolm K. Sparrow, Mark H. Moore, and David M. Kennedy quote a police officer who, perhaps without realizing it, gives as lucid a description as one could want of the us-versus-them attitude:

> No one else understands the real nature of police work. That is, no one outside the police service—academics, politicians, and lawyers in particular—can comprehend what we have to do. The public is generally naïve about police work. . . . Members of the public are basically unsupportive and unreasonably demanding. They all seem to think they know our job better than we do. They only want us when they need something done.[24]

The officer's alienation and isolation from the general public, as well as his loyalty only to his peers, jumps off the page: "No one else understands," he says. In his work on morality in law enforcement, Steve Herbert echoes this view. Only police officers, he says, "understand their particular mission, and hence they are isolated from the rest of the misguided populace."[25] Even *The Police Chief* magazine ("The Professional Voice of Law Enforcement"), published by the International Association of Chiefs of Police, acknowledges the us-versus-them phenomenon, though it does not use the phrase.

> [T]he individuals who make up the thin blue line . . . think of themselves as set apart from normal society. . . . [T]hey usually belong only to each other. They are their own social group . . . [and they] tend to associate only with other law enforcement officers and their immediate families. . . . The result is a unique societal group with its own norms and practices.[26]

With the suspicion of anything imposed on them from outside, the feeling that no one outside the group understands what they do, and the undeniable difficulties of the job, it becomes hard to imagine any reform that police officers might welcome. The us-versus-them mindset of police culture stacks the deck against the acceptance of change.

If resistance to any change is almost a given, the us-versus-them mindset will resist all the more strongly the kinds of reforms suggested by scientific work on traditional police investigative practices. For example, police have always showed all the people in a lineup to the witness simultaneously, and they—the officers involved in the investigation—have conducted the lineups themselves. Along comes a group of, not police officers, not even former police officers, but social scientists—psychologists—who tell law enforcement that the way they have done this basic task forever violates certain basic scientific principles. These outsiders say that using the traditional method has resulted in wrongful convictions, and that new methods are needed for this simple task, including taking themselves out of the process and inserting someone who does not know the case, so as to assure that the procedure comports with principles of blind testing. Along with the psychologists, lawyers stand among those pushing these new ideas at police; police think of lawyers not just as outsiders, but as among the people they like the least.[27] Since, in the police view, psychologists and lawyers have no more understanding of what police do than the general public does, they have no standing to make suggestions about the ins and outs of conducting lineups, especially when the traditional methods have worked just fine (with a tiny number of exceptions, in their view) for decades upon decades.

Add to this that the reforms proposed—changes in the use of lineups, in suspect interrogation, and in the utility of certain well-accepted types of forensic testing—will be seen not just as coming from outside of law enforcement, but perhaps as helpful to the enemy: suspects and defendants and convicts. These new methods would, perhaps, make it harder to obtain convictions and would definitely keep police from using tried-and-true methods to pressure suspects to speak in the interrogation room. That helps *them*— and there exists no group of *them* police despise more than the suspects they arrest.[28] And if these reforms help *them,* they inevitably hurt *us.* Thus, to one degree or another, police opposition to these reforms will almost inevitably arise; with "us versus them" in the air, attempts to find a middle ground or compromise position will have a tough time getting traction.

Penetrating the us-versus-them divide will take persistence, and a great degree of trust. Among some prosecutors, however, another force looms large: ambition. When the ambition is political in nature, anything that stands in the way will get shunted aside.

Political Ambitions

In his 1920 book, *The American Credo: A Contribution to the Interpretation of the National Mind*, H. L. Mencken (and coauthor George Jean Nathan) focused on government misuse of the law during World War I, especially the trials of so-called dissidents. These events, Mencken said, served as entertainment designed to stir up the populace, just as criminal trials do during peacetime. And prosecutors interested in beginning, or in furthering, political careers, Mencken said, should attempt to "play a leading part in a prosecution which attracts public notice." Many of the era's great public figures had risen in just this way, he said. "Every district attorney in America prays nightly that God will deliver into his hands some [well-known defendant], that he may get upon the front pages and so become a governor, a United States senator, or a justice of the United States Supreme Court."[29]

Mencken's statement hit the bull's eye. Working as a prosecutor has long been an excellent springboard for a career in public office or on the bench. In 2010, *The Economist* saw the same tendencies in American prosecutors that Mencken commented on long ago. "For many aspiring politicians, the position of prosecutor has become a stepping stone to higher office. As a result, fair-minded justice has often been sacrificed for tough-on-crime posturing, which tends to create a more politically salable reputation for an aspiring politician or judge."[30] Voters like politicians who can boast a conviction-after-conviction record; "[a] reputation for 'fair-mindedness,' not to say 'merciful,' just doesn't have the same appeal."[31] Discussing the rape case against a group of Duke University lacrosse players in 2007, in which prosecutor Michael Nifong went ahead with the charges despite exculpatory evidence, one commentator tried to account for why a prosecutor would do something like this. One reason, she said, was political ambition: "the DA's job can be a stepping stone to higher political office for a prosecutor with a high conviction record or high-profile cases that draw media attention." Nifong, she noted, pursued the case in the midst of a "hotly contested" election for the post of district attorney.[32] This kind of political agenda in a prosecutor's efforts poisons the very role of seeking justice that supposedly characterizes prosecutorial decision making.

Since the great majority of chief prosecutors in the United States are local elected officials, and because even the top appointed federal prosecutors—United States attorneys—must have political connections to achieve their positions, lawyers joining prosecutorial staffs can become part of a strong political network as well. Those hired as assistant prosecutors can become something akin to protégés of the elected prosecutor almost by default; the networks of local politics and the legal community that intersect in the prosecutor's office can help anyone with political ambitions and a reasonable level of competence to become part of that web, enhancing chances for a political or judicial candidacy down the road.

Considerable evidence exists that the prosecutorial path helps the politically ambitious lawyer attain his or her goal of election to higher office or ascension to a judgeship. For judges, the statistics are strong. Sheldon Goldman, professor of political science at the University of Massachusetts at Amherst, has spent decades studying the careers, backgrounds, and demographics of the men and women who have become federal judges going back at least four decades. In a 2009 study examining the judicial legacy of President George W. Bush, Goldman and his colleagues compared Bush's judicial appointees to those of the Carter, Reagan, George H. W. Bush, and Clinton administrations.[33] They examined everything from occupation at time of appointment to experience, undergraduate and law school institutions attended, ethnicity and race, gender, political identification, age, and net worth. They split the results to examine separately appointees to U.S. district courts (federal trial judges) and appointees to circuit courts of appeal (judges who heard only appeals). Goldman and his fellow researchers found that for all five presidents, roughly 50 percent of district court appointees had served on another court (perhaps on a state court or as a federal magistrate) before selection.[34] For courts of appeal, the average was close to 60 percent.[35] Only one other type of occupational background was relatively common: prosecutorial experience. Roughly 40 percent of all of the appointees to the U.S. district courts under each of the past five presidents had experience as prosecutors.[36] For those picked to serve on the courts of appeal, about 30 percent had prior prosecutorial experience.[37] None of the other law practice categories represented in the study came close: private practice backgrounds of various types ranked lower than either judicial or prosecutorial experience, and public defender and criminal defense work among appointees apparently did not come up often enough to merit a separate mention. This pattern held true for both traditional (i.e., white male) and nontraditional (African American, female, etc.) appointees.[38]

Federal judges gain the bench, of course, through presidential nomination and Senate confirmation, not through election, as happens in most states. But this does not make the idea of prosecutorial political ambition any less powerful. Susan Rozelle, professor of law at Florida's Stetson University, has said that regardless of whether they serve in federal or state court, "judges are political animals," and they must have political support if they want to become judges. Most judges must run for the office, and even among those appointed, "those who wish to wear the robe someday have to come to the (favorable) attention of those members of the nominating commission 'composed of members of the bar and the public' who do the appointing. And the public [whether voting in an election or serving on a selection commission] is leery of criminal defendants and their so-called constitutional rights."[39]

Does Rozelle's prediction hold when one looks at state courts? The data we have on state courts does show that prosecutors seem to have an edge in seeking judicial office. For example, in Cook County, Illinois, thirty-six judges at the main courthouse at Twenty-Sixth Street and California Avenue in Chicago hear the great bulk of all felony criminal cases in the county.[40] Of all of the judges hearing felonies at "Twenty-Sixth and Cal," fully 75 percent had served as prosecutors; most of these judges had *only* served as prosecutors in their careers, never holding any other type of legal job before becoming judges. Other state-level courthouses may not have quite as high a percentage of former prosecutors on the bench, but the pattern does not vary.

One sees similar patterns among elected officials, though few studies have focused on this. A study of elected prosecutors in Indiana revealed that many harbored political ambitions, and viewed their offices as stepping stones to further political office.[41] More than half of the prosecutors planned to seek further public offices in the future; 83 percent of them thought that holding the office of prosecutor would help them realize that ambition.[42] Three-quarters of the prosecutors who harbored further political ambitions believed that the office had, in fact, propelled many political careers, as it would theirs.[43] Data going back to 1900 showed that, for the office of congressperson, the prosecutors' beliefs had a solid basis; a quarter of all members of Congress from Indiana during that period had served as county prosecutor.[44] Only those who had held no prior public office exceeded the number of former prosecutors.[45]

We see prosecutors elected to the U.S. Congress as well. For the 111th session of Congress, covering the years 2009 and 2010, approximately 8 percent of the members of the House of Representatives were former prosecutors. For the Senate, nine of the one hundred senators had served as prosecutors.[46]

Naturally, lawyers in prosecutor's offices know what will help them get ahead, and the politically ambitious among them act accordingly. For these lawyers, building a resume through a strong record of convictions, particularly (though not only) in high-profile cases, is the best way to create and enhance a type of capital crucial for a run for office. Thus many prosecutors will see any changes that might stand in the way of obtaining convictions as at best undesirable, and at worst something to oppose at all costs. For example, changes in presenting witnesses in lineups may, as discussed earlier, result in greatly reduced levels of false identifications, but may also reduce, even if only slightly, the levels of correct identifications, because simultaneous lineups will probably eliminate correct identifications obtained through lucky guesses. Regardless of the fact that the new method seems to result in a net gain—a small number of correct identifications obtained through guesswork would seem a worthwhile price for a substantial reduction in incorrect identifications—prosecutors will perceive the elimination of the correct-through-luck identifications as a loss. They will not have the opportunity to use these correct (lucky guess) identifications to bolster their crime-fighting credentials. And that will inevitably engender resistance to these new methods. This constitutes another significant barrier to the adoption of better, science-based practices for investigation of crimes and the gathering of evidence. For the politically ambitious, only one thing counts: winning, and preserving the resulting convictions no matter what evidence of innocence might come up later. This goes for admitting an error in any particular case, but it applies just as strongly to admitting that police or prosecutorial practices in general— especially those that have served prosecutors so well for so long in their quest for advancement—have not always produced justice, and in fact need a complete overhaul. Thus we should not expect that moving toward better and more evidence-based approaches for gathering evidence will come easily. Rather, since it threatens the ability of politically ambitious people to attain their goals, it will happen only with considerable difficulty.

Media Coverage of Law-and-Order Issues

Television, newspapers, and radio (and by extension the internet, which aggregates news stories reported by so-called old media) seem to understand the significance of exonerations of the wrongfully convicted. These cases get reported every time one occurs. At least implicitly, each case carries the message that police methods involving eyewitness testimony, suspect interrogations, and forensic testing must change, in order to avoid the catastrophe of convicting the innocent. But while the exoneration cases present a twist on the usual crime story, after twenty years they have lost their novelty and, sadly, the power to shock. We now take it as a given that these things happen. They also come along less frequently than they did in the mid-1990s, which saw the peak numbers of these cases.

But more important, the stories of exonerations caused by faulty identifications, interrogations, and forensic testing come as exceptions to the general rules concerning reporting on criminal justice issues in the media, especially (though not only) on television. While a story on a DNA-based claim of innocence may come along once a year in large jurisdictions, reporting on crime—the *commission* of crimes, especially violent crime—has long served as an everyday staple for local news. The flow of these stories in the media, especially on local television news, dwarfs everything else, and no doubt dampens the effect of reporting on the no-longer-new stories of the exonerations of innocent people. This may create considerable obstacles to the possibilities for criminal justice reform.

According to a 2006 study, one source of information accounts for the great bulk of where Americans get their news: local television news broadcasts. Almost two-thirds of those surveyed—65.5 percent—named local TV news as their source; this was more than twice the percentage reported for local newspapers, and almost six times the figure of those reporting that they turned to the internet for news.[47] The Pew Research Center for the People and the Press, in its own study going back more than ten years, found that more people watch local TV news—54 percent—than any other news programming on television, almost doubling the audience for network TV's nightly news programming (28 percent).[48] In short, network newscasts and newspapers may cover the bigger stories of national and international importance, but local television newscasts around the country remain the audience champion in almost every community.

If local TV broadcasts dominate news for most Americans, one subject clearly dominates those local newscasts: crime. Nothing else, it seems, attracts viewers and produces ratings the way crime does, and the more lurid, sensational, and violent the crime, the more likely that the incident will top the newscast.

In an unusual and insightful book called *If It Bleeds, It Leads: An Anatomy of Television News*,[49] Matthew Kerbel, a former television news writer turned professor of political science at Villanova University, examined hours of broadcast television, including local television news, from all of the stations in several large television markets. Kerbel's fundamental rule of television is simple: "It is a pretend medium."[50] And news of crime plays a major role in helping this pretend medium keep our attention, with its drama, built-in fear, and pictures of crime scenes surrounded by police tape and squad cars and their riot of lights in the night. Crime gets ratings. It comes as no surprise, then, that the so-called sweeps months of November, February, and May, when the Nielson ratings establish advertising rates based on viewership, the "pretend medium" seems to come alive with crime—sensational, bloody, violent crime. "You've probably seen statistics that say violent crime is declining in the major U.S. cities. These statistics do not take the Nielson ratings into account. Nielson statistics suggest that violent crime is declining in most major U.S. cities nine months of the year, with dramatic peaks in November, February, and May."[51]

Looked at across the nation, the amount of local news coverage devoted to stories on crime towers over these newscasts, completely overshadowing the coverage of any other subject. In the Pew Research Center's Project for Excellence in Journalism's 2006 "State of the News Media" report, stories about crime made up an average of 42 percent of news by topic, far outpacing domestic issues (14 percent), government and elections (11 percent), and "lifestyle" (10 percent). All other story topics showed up in single digits.[52] According to Fairness and Accuracy in Reporting (FAIR), a media watchdog group, the amount of crime reporting in local news reporting had reached 30 percent.[53]

Do these trends still hold in today's hyperaccelerated, cable-oriented, internet-savvy world? The answer is yes. In a 2010 study for the Annenberg School for Communications and Journalism at the University of Southern California, Professors Martin Kaplan and Matthew Hale described their initial findings concerning "all local TV news broadcast in the Los Angeles media market—the country's second largest—on 14 randomly selected days," covering eight stations.[54] Noting that "more people—68%—say they get [their] news from local television station than from any other source,"[55] the researchers said that, just as in 1995, and in 2006, "The most common topic [of local news stories] by far was crime. . . . Nearly half of those were about murder, robbery, assault, kidnapping, property crime, traffic crime and other common crime."[56] As for the old newsroom saying that "if it bleeds, it leads," the tradition of trying to hook viewers right at the top of the broadcast with juicy, violent crime stories continues, and shows no sign of flagging. In the Los Angeles market, fully one-third of stories leading the newscasts concerned crime; as in the past, no other topic came close.[57] Crime, it seems, remains king of the local television news mountain, and local television news still dominates news consumption in the United States.

We might consider this nothing more than a hardy if unattractive tendency in our media landscape: simply "giving the people what they want," or feeding viewers the thing most likely to keep their attention. But more hangs on all of this crime reporting than simply a matter of what interests the public or a coarsening of the public dialogue. This begins to become clear when we juxtapose this constant media bombardment of crime news with some real facts about crime, and add data on public attitudes toward crime.

First, by any authoritative measure, crime in the United States has fallen steadily for at least fifteen years.[58] Despite an aberrational one-year increase in violent crime in 2005,[59] the long-term trend remains unmistakable: crime of every type has dropped, to the point that, as these words are written, the occurrence of all kinds of crime in the United States has reached historic lows not seen since the 1960s.[60] Second, even as crime has dropped, regularly and significantly, for a decade and a half, we can also observe a contrasting related phenomenon. Despite the downward trend in crime, high-quality polling data taken over the same stretch of time indicates that the fear of crime, and the percentage of people seriously concerned about it, has not fallen with the crime rate. On the contrary, fear of crime has generally *increased* during the last ten years—occasionally holding steady, but usually trending upward. The Gallup organization, among the most respected polling concerns in the world, has noted that this attitude, out of sync with reality, remained the same in 2006,[61] 2007,[62] and 2008.[63] In 2009, the most recent year for which Gallup has data, with crime at record low levels, 74 percent of Americans told Gallup that "there is more crime in the United States than there was a year ago."[64] Obviously, the occurrence of criminal activity itself cannot account for these consistently high and generally increasing numbers; the statistics concerning crime show a steady downward trend, even as these measurements of the public's beliefs and fears about crime climb just as steadily. What, then, might explain this disconnect?

The answer may have much to do with the idea with which we began this section: media coverage matters, and much of this coverage, especially that seen on local television news, gives us an unrealistic, inaccurate view of the prevalence of crime, especially violent crime. We know, for example, that media coverage of crime gives outsized play to the worst and most violent crimes, especially murders. A study by Joseph Sheley and Cindy Ashkins funded by the National Institute of Justice showed, as other researchers had, little relationship between media coverage of crime and actual crime statistics. More important, local television news distorted the seriousness of the crime that did occur by devoting a huge percentage of their coverage to homicide. In New Orleans, the location of the study, only .4 percent of all crimes were homicides; yet 46 to 50 percent of all crimes stories on local television newscasts concerned homicides.[65] In another study, Allen Liska and William Baccaglini used data from the National Crime Survey to examine twenty-six cities and the fear of crime. Actual crime rates, they said, had no effect on media coverage. Homicide stories, which had the biggest impact on the fear of crime, made up only .2 percent of the crime in the study, but almost 30 percent of all crime stories in the media.[66] Small wonder, then, that for decades, researchers have found strong positive relationships between media coverage of violent crime and citizens' perceptions of the amount of violent crime. And among all news sources, television news coverage of crime matters. Garrett O'Keefe and Kathleen Reid-Nash examined how the public's attention to crime news on television and in the newspaper affected perceptions and attitudes. The more attention one paid to crime news on television, the more one exhibited fear and concern over crime, even engaging in "avoidance activity" designed to address that fear. Attention to crime stories on television news programs had a much greater effect than attention to similar stories in newspapers.[67]

Along with increased fear of and concern about crime, media and especially television news coverage of crime has a powerful effect on setting the public agenda: not so much what to think, as what to think *about*.[68] In other words, media coverage has much to do with putting an issue on the public agenda and determining the level of importance the public gives it. In a study concerning this agenda-setting power and the public's fear of crime, Dennis Lowry and his colleagues examined the public perception of crime as the most important problem facing the nation, which inexplicably jumped from 5 percent in March 1992 polling to 52 percent in August of 1994.[69] They compared (1) FBI crime statistics and (2) the amount of television news coverage of crime, in order to measure the impact of both on the public's belief that crime was the most important problem facing the country. The results "provided strong confirmation for earlier studies that have also found positive statistical relations between crime news coverage and public perceptions about crime." Television crime news certainly proved much more successful "in telling many more people what to think about crime" than actual experience with crime or accurate information about crime did.[70] In short, "TV news variables accounted for almost four times the amount of variance in people's perception of crime as the most important problem facing the country than did the actual crime rates."[71]

This aspect of the media landscape and its impact on public perception of crime and its importance has real consequences for our nation, and for the prospect of improving our criminal justice system. Television and other media constantly pump up crime news, especially news about violence and murder, in their quest for ratings success; the picture television presents to the public has little to do with the falling crime rates and the success of police work against crime that has shown up in statistics on crime for roughly fifteen years. This bleak (though inaccurate) picture of crime in our society correlates strongly with years of careful measurement of public opinion, all of which indicates that public attitudes and beliefs about crime show growing fear and a false perception that crime continues to increase. Wrongful convictions and releases of prisoners because of new DNA evidence receive coverage when these things happen, but they happen only occasionally and not as often as they once did. In contrast, the drumbeat of news of violent crime remains constant, unflagging, and does not disappear with the end or resolution of one case or incident. Rather, each night, images of a new shooting or robbery or murder replace the images of the shooting or robbery or murder shown on the news the night before. Small wonder, then, that this generates the "law-and-order" climate in public opinion that we see reflected in the polling data year after year.

Of course, this makes for a very unfavorable political atmosphere in which to try to attempt criminal justice reforms. Members of our legislative bodies and holders of executive branch offices tend to gravitate more toward the public's wishes for tough justice and harsh punishment than they do toward making sure that the system performs in a fair and just way. With crime, as with any other politically salient issue, political expediency will always triumph, and political courage will remain in short supply. This means it will remain easy to tar an opponent with the broad brush of being "soft on crime." Few politicians on any level will want to face this if it represents any significant political risk. Thus it will take some guts for a legislator to stand up and say, "We need to change our investigative methods, because sometimes they lead to injustice, and because we know how to do these things better than we used to." When the public believes—even if incorrectly—that crime continues to grow and presents a real threat, champions of change will find new methods a tough sell when opponents can so easily portray these new measures as handcuffing our police officers or favoring defendants.

The Opposition of Police Unions to Reform

A number of police labor unions have opposed many of the proposals for reform of eyewitness identification methods, interrogation tactics, and forensic science. This has given police labor organizations an outsized impact on the course of police reform over the last four and one-half decades in the United States. Because police unions are the organizations representing most rank-and-file police officers in many American law enforcement agencies, their opposition has had a negative impact on the issue of better police investigation tactics.

The story begins in the 1960s. In that decade, the civil rights movement came fully into its own, and police misconduct and abuse ranked high among the issues of greatest concern to members of the black community. Rioting took place in many major cities in the United States in that decade; deadly police-citizen encounters provided the spark for a number of the worst conflagrations.[72] In response, President Lyndon Johnson appointed the National Advisory Commission on Civil Disorders, headed by Illinois Governor Otto Kerner.[73] The Kerner Commission (as most people called it) found, among other things, that chronic problems existed in relations between police and minority communities,[74] often exacerbated by the utter failure of police departments to treat complaints of abusive treatment by officers with any seriousness.[75] The commission recommended the establishment of government bodies independent of police departments to conduct "external review" of citizen complaints against police and to review police department policies more generally.[76] Following on the heels of the establishment of civilian police review boards in Philadelphia, New York, and some other cities,[77] the recommendation of external oversight of police by the Kerner Commission seemed to promise needed change in police-community relations.

But that did not happen. Instead, these tentative steps toward the imposition of efforts to address police misconduct, racism, and abuse became the rallying point for backlash against reform, and this occurred largely through the efforts of police unions.

From the first calls for civilian oversight and review of complaints against officers, police unions became uncompromising foes of the idea. In fact, the fledgling movement toward civilian oversight and complaint review brought police unions to the fore in a new and powerful way. The idea of outsiders passing upon the correctness of police actions personified the worst nightmare of law enforcement's us-versus-them culture: civilians who know nothing about policing telling police what to do and second guessing them. Unions vowed to fight this. According to distinguished scholar of American policing Samuel Walker of the University of Nebraska, "The most significant and lasting impact of the oversight movement was to foster the creation of what would prove to be its major opposition: police unions." Civilian oversight "galvanized rank-and-file officers and spurred the creation of local police unions. Recognized police unions existed in a few major cities in the early 1960s; ten years later, they were virtually universal in cities outside the southeast."[78] Surely, other factors also help explain the rapid rise and growth of police unions: poor relations between officers and departmental leadership; low pay; and a general feeling that society at large did not respect police, among others. But in many places, the threat (as officers saw it) of civilian oversight crystallized all of these grievances and helped organize unions where this had not happened before.[79] In 1966, the Patrolman's Benevolent Association (PBA) in New York City led a campaign against the Civilian

Complaint Review Board that culminated in the board's outright abolition.[80] According to Walker, this struggle "left a lasting scar on city politics" in New York, and the PBA "remained an implacable foe of any form of civilian oversight" ever after.[81] Thus the first attempts at civilian oversight died in most places with the 1960s.

But the idea of civilian oversight of police revived again in the 1970s, in the wake of the Watergate scandal and the increased skepticism of government institutions those events created. Interest also resurfaced because of increased black political power that began to emerge as a result of the passage of the Voting Rights Act a decade before.[82] This led to the creation of civilian police oversight agencies in the 1970s in Berkeley, California, Detroit, Michigan, and other places; in the 1980s and 1990s, cities as diverse as San Francisco, Portland, Oregon, Minneapolis, Los Angeles, Albuquerque, and Seattle established oversight bodies that took different forms.[83] But as American policing entered the twenty-first century, with civilian oversight bodies increasingly common in cities across the country, many unions have remained, in Walker's turn of phrase, "implacable opponent[s]" of this form of accountability.[84]

Now, as we begin the second decade of the new century, the police unions are playing lead roles in opposition to another type of reform: changes in the ways police conduct lineups, interrogate suspects, and make use of forensic science. And their opposition to change bears an uncanny resemblance to their opposition to civilian oversight of decades past. A typical example tells the story.

In Illinois, lawmakers reinstituted capital punishment in 1977. Between 1977 and 2000, the state executed twelve people. During that same period, thirteen people convicted and sentenced to death in Illinois were exonerated; new evidence (often DNA) proved their innocence. Many of these exonerated men had, according to police, given full confessions of guilt, which the DNA and other new evidence proved absolutely false; the police had coerced the defendants into confessing. This incredible run of occurrences convinced Governor George Ryan, a Republican and a supporter of the death penalty, to declare a moratorium on executions in 2000. "I have grave concerns about our state's shameful record of convicting innocent people and putting them on Death Row," Ryan said. "I cannot support a system, which, in its administration, has proven to be so fraught with error and has come so close to the ultimate nightmare, the state's taking of innocent life."[85] Ryan announced that he would appoint a commission to study the administration of the death penalty in the state, and that the moratorium would remain in place at least until the completion of the commission's report.[86] That report, delivered to

Ryan in April of 2002, took a comprehensive look at the system, and recommended many far-reaching reforms; most important for purposes of this
discussion, the commission recommended a requirement that, in homicide
cases, police must videotape the entire interrogation of the suspect at the
police station.[87] The report stated, "Custodial interrogations of a suspect in a
homicide case occurring at a police facility should be videotaped. Videotaping should not include merely the statement made by the suspect after interrogation, but the entire interrogation process."[88]

The recommendation that police must record all homicide interrogations came against the backdrop not just of the numerous death penalty
exonerations in Illinois, many featuring false confessions, but also of a
case involving false confessions by two young boys to a rape and murder
they did not commit.[89] In the words of attorney and Innocence Project
cofounder Peter Neufeld, Chicago had earned the title of "the Cooperstown
of false confessions."[90] Thus if any place, at any time, might have seemed
ripe for the imposition of legal requirements for recording interrogations,
it would have been Illinois, in the wake of these and other revelations about
false confessions. But there was strong resistance to the recording proposals, and it came most prominently from police unions. When legislators
eventually considered a package of reforms, it included the requirement
for taping homicide interrogations; it allowed for audio recording when
police could not use video, but it made recording of some kind mandatory, not optional. At first, the Fraternal Order of Police in Chicago, which
represents 17,500 active and retired officers in the city, opposed any recording requirement of any kind. As the proposed legislation inched closer to
passage, the union attempted to disguise continued opposition beneath
a more moderate tone, focusing on giving police the discretion to decide
when to record. But in reality, the FOP's position remained unchanged.
Michael Donahue, the FOP president in Chicago, continued to say that
"his organization oppose[d] mandatory recording." They did not want the
recording requirement put into law because he and his members saw it
"as unnecessary meddling in their operations." Instead, he said, the homicide team on the case "should have discretion on when to tape."[91] Donahue
told the *New York Times* that the FOP is "not in favor of the mandatory
provision. We would prefer that it be voluntary."[92] Of course, a voluntary
standard for recording interrogations would amount to no standard at all;
with the choice remaining within the discretion of the officers involved,
recording would occur, if ever, only if it served the interests of police. In
fact, police had discretion already to record interrogations, since no law or
regulation prohibited recording. Nevertheless, they almost never recorded

interrogations in Chicago, so no reason existed to think they would suddenly begin to do it "voluntarily."

As the premiere labor union in the nation for rank-and-file police officers, the Fraternal Order of Police has an outsized voice on all matters of law enforcement policies and methods that the government might address. The organization has long been deeply woven into the fiber of law enforcement policy making at the highest levels.[93] Since the FOP represents rank-and-file officers, its members do not create policy for police organizations; they carry it out. But that does not mean that the FOP does not take part in all of the discussions and debates at the national level on any and all law enforcement issues of the day, including proposals and ideas for reforming interrogation practices, eyewitness identification methods, and forensic practices. On these issues and virtually all others that concern police practices and policy, the FOP is always present at any meeting at the Department of Justice, the White House, the Department of Homeland Security, or on Capitol Hill; policy makers always ask them for their views on national policy and trends in law enforcement, and also for a perspective on specific incidents.[94] For state and local legislative proposals, the national FOP typically defers to its local or state lodges. The national organization backs the local groups up with whatever assistance or guidance they might need, but they leave it to the local organizations to formulate positions and fight for them in the state legislative or executive branches.[95] And all of the FOP's forty-three state and local lodges have the capability, willingness, and experience to work closely with legislatures and other government bodies to make their positions known; office holders regularly consult them, and they are often successful in arguing for their legislative priorities.[96]

Chicago's FOP unit does not stand alone in taking the stance that reforms that seem needed to address problems with police investigation are not necessary at best, and at worst might even prove harmful. For example, police unions in California helped to defeat proposals aimed at securing the criminal justice system against the dangers of false confessions and lying jailhouse snitches making up testimony in order to reduce their own sentences. The Los Angeles Police Protective League told the California Commission on the Fair Administration of Justice that several legislative proposals the commission had sponsored went too far. For example, the union said, it could not support a bill mandating recording of interrogations. The bill seemed relatively even handed, taking account of the interests of law enforcement; it only applied to homicide cases and contained numerous exceptions (it required no recording when there was no access to equipment, when the defendant refused to talk while being recorded, or when good faith attempts to record failed, for example).[97] Nevertheless, the union opposed the bill because, if a police officer failed to record a homicide interrogation and none of the exceptions applied, it allowed the judge to tell the jury that the jury should regard the defendant's statement with skepticism. "We cannot," said Robert Baker, president of the union's board of directors, "support the prejudicial jury instruction as required as part of this bill."[98] In Texas, two bills—one that would have required the recording of the entire interrogation, and another that would have required improved procedures for police lineups and photo spreads—came before the legislature. In its publication *Badge & Gun*, the Houston Police Officers Union claimed credit for killing both bills. The union had "successfully killed" the recording measure, it said. On the bill to improve lineups and photo spreads, it "opposed the bill all the way to the end of the session" along with its allies in the legislature, and its efforts "resulted in the measure meeting its much-needed death."[99] In Suffolk County, New York, twenty years after a false unrecorded confession put seventeen-year-old Martin Tankleff in prison for the murders of his own parents, Suffolk County police still did not require that police record full interrogations. Despite Tankleff's release after almost two decades in prison for a crime that he did not commit,[100] the police union in the county saw no reason to require recording of the interrogation of the defendant. "There's a fine line in an interrogation," Jeff Frayler, president of the Suffolk Patrolmen's Benevolent Association told *Newsday*. "Do you really want to videotape it and put that into the jury's brain that [the defendant was] duped into [confessing]?"[101] And, even after the reversal of convictions in the Central Park jogger case, one of the highest-profile cases of false confessions ever seen, the detective's union in New York City remained opposed to recording. According to Detective Thomas Scotto, president on the Detective's Endowment Association, recording of interrogations may result in fewer confessions. "Some defendants will admit to something. Then when you tell them, 'Well, now we're going to videotape,' they won't respond." Even worse, a recording requirement would turn into a bonanza for sharp defense lawyers, who will use the law to gain advantage for their clients. The ins and outs of recording, Scotto said, "will tie up the courts endlessly with the technical aspects of the issue rather than the crime itself."

These are only a few examples of police unions moving beyond traditional labor issues of working conditions, wages, and benefits, and moving aggressively to stifle much-needed reform of police investigative tactics. Note that almost all of these examples here focus on just one proposed reform: recording of interrogations. In many others examples, union objections focus on one of the other proposals, such as better lineup methods or forensics. One thing remains constant: the steady drumbeat of objections from these labor groups. This has the effect one would expect: change becomes more difficult, if not impossible, even though the evidence in favor of better practices comes from sound science, and even from the experience of other police officers.

Battles in the Legislatures: The Strong Influence
of Police Professional Organizations

For the most part, the battles for and against reform of traditional police practices based on science take place not in the U.S. Congress but in state legislatures. After all, the vast majority of criminal cases arise not under federal law but in the states: fully 96 percent of all felony prosecutions and 99 percent of all misdemeanor prosecutions occur in state jurisdictions.[102] This means that the action concerning criminal justice issues occurs in state legislatures; almost all prospective reform on eyewitness identification, suspect interrogation, or forensic practices must come through those bodies.[103] This will tend to make reform and change difficult, because the voices that tend to oppose it have ample representation in legislative debates, while those who might support change in these areas of law have a comparatively small presence.

On one side of these issues, police departments, police officers, and prosecutors will want to have their say; changes in these practices would impact what they do and how they do it. On the other side, the answer seems less clear. The parties affected by less-than-accurate practices on these questions would be defendants in criminal cases. These people would be mostly poor, disproportionately members of racial and ethnic minority groups, and for the most part politically unorganized, disengaged, and even disenfranchised. More to the point, these people would either be passing through the system as current defendants, or those already incarcerated and pursuing appeals or post-appellate claims of innocence. For either current or past defendants, reform of the system as a whole would rank far below the importance of their own active cases, appeals, or other types of relief; with the rare exception of persons already exonerated who have become reform advocates, most would use whatever limited resources they have to pursue their own more personal and immediate interests, not systemic reform. This means that advocacy groups with an interest in criminal justice reform will almost certainly be the only ones to take up these issues. And the law enforcement voices clearly have a stronger, more consistent presence in these legislative debates. Thus their points of view predominate, stopping or at least slowing the pace toward reform in most places.

As we have seen on the law enforcement side, local police unions constitute a constant presence on these issues, but they do not always have the loudest voices. That distinction goes to police professional associations: organizations that represent law enforcement not on issues of labor or working conditions but rather on a broader array of law enforcement policy issues. Some represent police leadership (chiefs, command officers, and middle management), and others represent rank-and-file police officers.[104] At least thirty-one states have professional organizations like state chiefs of police associations, state peace officer associations, or police officer alliances that track legislative proposals, lobby for or against these initiatives, testify in committee hearings on these bills, and urge their memberships to support or stop particular pieces of proposed legislation.[105] At least twenty states have a separate, politically active statewide sheriff's association that works for or against proposed legislation. These organizations represent the interests of elected sheriffs and their deputies; these interests sometimes differ from those of police chiefs and their departments.[106] At least fourteen states have *both* a statewide police chiefs, peace officers, or police officers association *and* a statewide sheriffs association that work for and against legislation on criminal justice issues.[107] All of these organizations would typically take positions on bills that would impose reforms on traditional police practices; usually—though not always—they oppose this type of legislation. All of this, of course, adds to the voices already present through the police unions.

On the other side of the debate, a few organizations work on criminal justice reform at the state legislative level, but their presence in the debate seems much spottier. The American Civil Liberties Union (ACLU) has fifty-three affiliates (e.g., ACLU of Pennsylvania) in the United States. Most affiliates cover an entire state; a few cover regions of larger states (ACLU of Southern California) or more than one state (ACLU of Western Missouri and Kansas).[108] Twenty-three of these affiliates have a staff member who works full-time lobbying state legislatures. These people work on bills and proposals covering the entire gamut of civil liberties issues; criminal justice concerns would constitute just one portion of the ACLU affiliates' interests. In the affiliates without full-time staff to do legislative work, the affiliate's executive director or legal director or another staff person will take on this task along with the other responsibilities he or she carries. In a few states, the affiliate may hire a lobbyist on contract to work for the organization during all or part of the legislative session; sometimes these contractors work on just one set of issues as part of a grant received by the affiliate. For example, the grant may fund the efforts of a lobbyist focusing on reproductive rights or press freedom, confining the lobbyist's work to that area. Thus, in most states, the ACLU affiliate has some presence in the legislature, though the scope of that presence varies.[109] Rachel Bloom, advocacy and policy strategist for the national ACLU, who has studied the organization's state-level efforts, says that in many legislatures, the ACLU constitutes the only organized group that might oppose or support bills on criminal justice issues, including bills designed to reform police methods. Most of the energy expended by the affiliates goes not into crafting or supporting new proposals to improve or reform the system but into beating back law enforcement initiatives that, in Bloom's view, would make things worse in the areas of criminal justice or civil liberties generally.[110] And even in the states with a full-time person to work with the state legislature, their efforts get stretched thin, given all of the concerns outside criminal justice that they must also address. According to one ACLU affiliate's state legislative coordinator, his organization has long remained the only one concerned with criminal justice issues that has a daily presence in his state capitol, and he also covers all other civil liberties issues as well, not just reform of eyewitness identification and the other issues discussed here. Organizations other than the ACLU make occasional lobbying forays in his state, sometimes on criminal justice issues, but not consistently and certainly not daily. In contrast, in the state in which he operates, law enforcement organizations have "a heavy hammer at the capitol" and the state's "[House of Representatives], especially the House Judiciary Committee, hangs on [the state prosecutors organization's] every word."[111] The state legislative coordinator agrees with Rachel Bloom: in the state legislatures, law enforcement advocates have a significant edge in every respect.[112]

The Innocence Project, a national organization based in New York that focuses on the exoneration of the innocent and actively works for the reform of police investigation methods, has affiliated organizations based in forty-three states. Collectively called the Innocence Network, these state-level groups focus primarily on litigation and advocacy for allegedly innocent clients in individual cases. Some of these state organizations have, from time to time, worked to initiate, support, and encourage reform efforts on these issues, but very few have staff members who work full-time with the legislatures of their respective states. Rather, their efforts depend on staff members who devote the great bulk of their time and effort to working on cases for individual defendants, not on systemic reform in the legislature.[113] In some states, Innocence Network member organizations have become involved in crafting and supporting reform legislation, along with other interested organizations. For example, the Ohio Innocence Project, based at the University of Cincinnati College of Law, played a central role in the passage of legislation that addressed the recording of interrogations, improved eyewitness identification practices, made changes in procedures for the handling and collection of DNA, and mandated the preservation of biological evidence.[114] Mark Godsey, professor of law and director of the Lois and Richard Rosenthal Institute for Justice and the Ohio Innocence Project at the College of Law, and his coworkers at the Ohio Innocence Project, did much during a six-year effort to shape, advance, and advocate for the legislation.[115] Godsey and his coworkers at the project (along with University of Cincinnati law students) do the bulk of the project's advocacy work in individual cases; no member of the project's staff works full- or even part-time as a legislative advocate or liaison. Instead, Godsey and others fit the legislative work into their already substantial workload.[116] This ad hoc approach to legislative efforts reflects the way that most Innocence Network organizations around the country handle work in legislatures aimed at creating reforms, with only a few of these organizations having personnel dedicated to legislative work.[117] The efforts of the Ohio Innocence Project and its allies have proven very successful, but Godsey says that in struggles for criminal justice reform in the legislature in general, law enforcement and prosecutorial groups easily overmatch the resources and manpower that groups like his can muster, making successful reform elusive and rare.[118] According to Stephen Saloom, policy director for the Innocence Project, somebody within virtually every Innocence Network organization has responsibility for policy matters (which include legislative efforts), but almost always this same person carries other responsibilities, too—in some cases a considerable load of other responsibilities. He agrees with Mark Godsey that just a few of these organizations might have a staff person solely dedicated to working with the legislatures of their respective states. Given this, Saloom says, reforms supported by the Innocence Project have succeeded remarkably often.[119]

The National Association of Criminal Defense Lawyers (NACDL) also has an ongoing interest in moving police and prosecutorial agencies toward better, science-based methods for eyewitness testimony, interrogation, and forensic science. As one would guess from the organization's name, NACDL focuses itself on issues of interest to the criminal defense bar, and issues of innocence and exoneration have become central to their concerns over the last twenty years. NACDL's magazine, *The Champion*, has published a number of articles on these subjects over the years, and has discussed the issues in its conferences and seminars. But even though NACDL has a national organization and local affiliates, the size and scope of these state organizations means that they are not always able to play a regular role in state legislative debates on criminal justice reform. According to Angelyn Frazer, director of state legislative affairs for NACDL, the state affiliates do a great job given their resources and the opposition they face. In many states, members of the state affiliates, most of whom are attorneys with their own practices and some of whom are activists, work as volunteers to advocate the organization's positions on key issues in various state legislative forums—visiting legislators' offices and giving testimony at hearings, for example. Occasionally, a state affiliate organization might pay for the services of a lobbyist for this purpose, but this remains rare, and in any case the national organization does not fund that activity. The national organization runs a listserve for those volunteers at the state level who do some work with their legislatures, but Frazer says that there are no staff members dedicated to the job of legislative affairs.[120]

Thus the legislative struggles at the state level over these issues, when they occur, will almost always begin with law enforcement groups stronger, better organized, and therefore far ahead of reformers. Law enforcement professional groups have experience with the process, are well known to members of the legislature and their staffs, and are outfitted with personnel whose jobs either consist of or include legislative advocacy on behalf of their interests. They usually join with partners from police labor unions, who have many of the same advantages. In contrast, they may face opposition from a few advocacy groups, only one of which (ACLU) has full-time legislative advocates on its roster, and only in fewer than half its state-level organizations. The Innocence Network organizations have had some legislative successes, but these groups understandably gear themselves mostly toward advocating in courts on individual cases, not advocacy in legislatures. All in all, winning reforms of traditional police methods on the basis of science seems like a long shot under these circumstances, unlikely to succeed. This makes those few successful reform efforts that have come out of state legislatures rare and remarkable victories.

Caution dictates that we not assume that law enforcement and prosecution advocates would always oppose reforms of eyewitness, interrogation, and forensic methods; occasionally, they have joined with advocates for reform, making the success of these efforts possible. Nevertheless, the fact that police and prosecutor organizations of every type so overmatch those who might advocate for reform means that any effort at reform that law enforcement does oppose will face, at best, an uphill climb. And most of the time, the state chiefs of police association, the sheriffs' organization, the labor unions, and the state prosecutors' association do in fact line up against reform initiatives. And that usually means that reform efforts end in stalemate or outright defeat.

The Next Question

All in all, institutional and political barriers hobble efforts to move law enforcement toward the better investigative practices created by science. Institutional incentives for police officers and prosecutors, as well as political ambition, tilt the whole field toward preserving the status quo. The drumbeat of violent crime news takes away any appetite for reform and instead creates a climate of fear that disfavors change. And the opposition of unions and police professional organizations makes political success difficult.

Chapters 2 and 3 sketched out the problem for us; chapters 4 (cognitive barriers) and 5 (institutional and political barriers) explained why the resistance to science-based solutions persists. The next question, then, is what we do about it. What must change? And, in this difficult political and institutional environment, how do we make those things happen? That is the subject of chapter 6.

6

What Must Be Done and How to Make It Happen

We now have a clear picture of the problem. Law enforcement has fully embraced DNA as an investigative tool and continues to use most forensic methods. But despite the appearance of science-driven police and prosecution work that emerges in both the press (the near-constant drumbeat of DNA-based convictions) and in popular entertainment (*CSI ad nauseum*), law enforcement generally does not wish to adopt the best practices toward which science points. Instead, most police and prosecutors—not all, but most—resist. And we see now that this resistance involves cognitive, professional, and institutional barriers.

This brings us to some difficult questions. If science points toward change, what, specifically, should those changes look like? What should those concerned with fairness and just outcomes in the criminal process strive to obtain, given what science tells us, and given the political climate in which we now find ourselves? And, once we know what we should work toward, we must ask an even harder question: How do we get there in light of law enforcement resistance? How do we reach an acceptable solution that respects *both* the role and culture of law enforcement *and* what science has to offer?

Fortunately, the scientific findings on eyewitness identification, suspect interrogation, and forensic work present us with not just criticism of the present but also guidance toward the future. Almost all of this work tells us not only what goes wrong when we use traditional methods but also how to do a more accurate job of finding the correct culprit, with lower risks of identifying the wrong person. Chapters 6 and 7 will give us a path that can enable us to persuade more of the dedicated professionals in law enforcement to join in these efforts to improve the system.

What Must Be Done
A Preliminary Word: A Modest Approach and a Modest Goal

There already exist a large number of well-documented possibilities for reform of traditional investigative methods, all based on sound science. But not all of the alternatives appear among the proposals that follow. Two considerations animate the changes I believe we should seek now.

First, we need to accept that all of these proposals for change become part of the highly contentious debate over science and law enforcement explored in the previous chapters. Many voices in the argument, including some of the loudest, do not accept that any need for change exists; they do not agree that we have a problem of wrongful convictions of any significant magnitude. Given this reality, a modest approach to change, one that may not attempt to fix all the problems we know about but that moves toward the strongest ideas around which we find the greatest consensus, seems right. The question at the top of this chapter—"What Must Be Done"—focuses the discussion, and forces us into the real world of making choices among alternatives. Reformers must confront the question of what they can realistically expect to obtain. The alternatives I espouse here reflect this realistic and practical point of view. They do not constitute a complete list of all the best practices one might adopt if given unlimited power to remake the world to the highest standard. Rather, they reflect a set of changes about which there exist both a strong scientific consensus and a budding acceptance in the professions of policing, prosecution, and the law as a whole.

Second, the goal of the process is not perfection. No one can expect that police investigations will always get the right person, or that prosecutors will always convict the truly guilty party. Since human beings created and run the criminal justice system, it contains all of the usual human flaws and the shortcomings of all human institutions. Therefore, our goal should not be the perfection of the police investigation process but rather implementation of procedures that give us the best chance of coming to accurate conclusions in the greatest number of investigations. When we have wide agreement on which methods or procedures actually give us the best odds of doing this, there is no excuse for not putting these methods in place as standard ways of operating. Further, we will want practices that eliminate—and, if that does not seem realistic, at least reduce—the possibility of harms that our current methods of investigation seem to cause. If we know that using a particular method of interrogation contains within it the seeds of error as a routine matter—not because the method has been misused in some particular instance but because it systematically produces errors—that practice should cease, and we should replace it with something else.

Eyewitness Identification: Four Basic Changes to Make, and One More to Consider

As discussed throughout this book, errors of eyewitness identification occur more often than any other single type of mistake in the cases of the wrongfully convicted. Of the more than 250 cases of exonerated people released from jail at this writing, eyewitness errors occurred in 75 percent of them.[1] The science explaining these errors and demonstrating better ways to accomplish the identification of perpetrators has existed for years, some of it for nearly four decades. A small but growing number of law enforcement agencies, prosecutors, courts, and legislative bodies have begun to embrace these reforms. This will give similar agencies that have not yet made these changes the confidence that they can do so successfully, without endangering their core missions.

In 1998, a group of the best researchers in the field of eyewitness identification and human cognition came together and produced a white paper called *Eyewitness Identification Procedures: Recommendations for Lineups and Photospreads*.[2] This groundbreaking paper, drafted as a set of "good practice guidelines" for the American Psychology/Law Society, has been vetted and accepted by the governing body of the organization and named an official "Scientific Review Paper."[3] The next year, in 1999, the National Institute of Justice of the U.S. Department of Justice and its Technical Working Group for Eyewitness Evidence (TWGEYEE) published its own handbook, *Eyewitness Evidence: A Guide for Law Enforcement*.[4] The Technical Working Group included several of the researchers who had published the *Eyewitness Identification Procedures* white paper, in addition to officials from police agencies and prosecutors' offices across the nation.[5] What immediately jumps out in a comparison of the *Eyewitness Identification Procedures*, written entirely by social scientists, and the TWGEYEE handbook, put together by a group dominated by law enforcement professionals, is that most suggestions that appear in one document appear in the other as well. With that degree of consensus, we can feel comfortable beginning the process of reform with these changes. And since the United States Supreme Court passed up its opportunity for eyewitness identification reform in 2012, change from either source is more important now than ever.

Recommendation 1: The person who conducts the identification procedure should not know which member of the lineup is the suspected culprit. In conducting behavioral experiments, scientists have long understood the experimenter-expectancy effect (chapter 2). Recall that this means that anytime a person conducting an experiment knows the correct or expected result, he or she may send subtle signals to the subject indicating the "right" choice, without any awareness that it is happening. This is particularly true when physical proximity between experimenter and subject allows for eye contact, visible facial expressions, and verbal exchanges."[6]

Administering a lineup constitutes just such an interpersonal interaction. In the course of a traditional investigation, the officer or detective involved in the case helps assemble the lineup, puts the suspect among similar-looking "fillers," and then brings the witness into the viewing room and tells the witness what to do. The witness and the officer usually stand near each other, close enough to talk, with their faces and gestures clearly visible to one another. This makes a traditional lineup a perfect example of what a sloppy scientific experimenter might do, and it subjects the identification procedure to the same danger that one would see in an experiment conducted this way: the witness may receive subtle but unmistakable nonverbal (or even verbal) signals from the police officer indicating the correct answer. None of this implies any deliberate or bad-faith action by police; on the contrary, the officer typically has no idea that this phenomenon takes place. It occurs not because police officers or detectives are bad people but simply because they *are* people.

The answer lies in doing exactly what experimenters do to secure their work from this naturally occurring, unwanted cognitive bias. Scientists use a blind administrator in their experiments; police should use a blind administrator when they conduct lineups. This goes for lineups of live people or photographs. Blind lineup procedures work. According to Gary Wells and his coauthors on the white paper *Eyewitness Identification Procedures*, "This simple use of procedures in which the person collecting the evidence is unaware of the 'correct' answer is an effective prevention for this powerful phenomenon."[7]

Recommendation 2: The administrator of the lineup should tell the eyewitness that he or she does not know who the "correct" choice is and that the person who committed the crime might not be in the lineup at all, so that the witness feels no obligation to make a choice. The first part of this recommendation aims at sealing off the possibility of experimenter-expectancy bias. If using a blind procedure assures us that the person conducting the lineup cannot send the witness any unintentional signals indicating the right choice, telling the eyewitness that the person running the lineup does not know the correct choice tells the eyewitness not to expect any cues.[8] This provides an extra margin of security against the hazards of experimenter-expectancy effect.

The second part of this recommendation leads us back to the idea of relative judgment: the inclination of the eyewitness to look at the group of photos or persons and decide which of them looks the most like the person who did the crime. When the witness assumes the police believe they have the correct suspect, he or she has a powerful desire to make an identification. This elevates the risk of an incorrect identification if the correct person does not appear in the lineup, but someone who looks like him does; in such a case, the eyewitness chooses the member of the lineup who looks most like the perpetrator. Gary Wells and his coauthors of *Eyewitness Identification Procedures* explain that empirical data have shown that "instructions [that the witness might not appear in the lineup] reduce the rate of incorrect identifications in culprit-absent lineups but these same instructions produce no appreciable reduction of accurate identifications in culprit-present lineups."[9]

If the correct suspect always appeared in every lineup, we would not need this recommendation. However, we have lineups precisely because the identity of the perpetrator is not yet certain. That makes the lineup very much like an experiment designed to test a hypothesis, and it should be conducted like a proper experiment, with witnesses being told by administrators that they should not assume that the correct suspect appears.[10]

Recommendation 3: The filler members of the lineup should appear similar to the eyewitness's original description of the perpetrator. Fillers should also share any special distinguishing features of the suspect that might draw extra attention to the suspect's appearance. When police construct a lineup, they must attempt to match the fillers to the verbal description that the witness gave to the police at the time of the event. If this does not occur—i.e., if the police pick fillers instead on the basis of resemblance to the person they suspect—this biases the lineup in favor of selecting the suspect.

This recommendation goes against common practice. In many law enforcement settings, police choose the fillers in the lineup according to how closely they resemble the suspect they have identified, instead of how closely they resemble the original description of the suspect. This undesirable practice can cause the whole lineup to look like a group of clones. This challenges the ability of eyewitnesses to make accurate choices in that it interferes with recognition of the real perpetrator.[11] Having each of the fillers fit the description given by the eyewitness does not do this, and therefore does not interfere with the making of accurate selections, and at the same time does not create the risk that an innocent suspect will stand out as the only one who has an appearance that the witness describes.

If the suspect has any special distinguishing features—tattoos, visible scars, an especially noticeable hair color—the fillers selected should share these as much as possible, so that the suspect does not stand out in an obvious way. Similarly, in a lineup of photographs, the suspect's photos should not stand out from the others used. If the suspect's photos are color, the photos of the fillers should be too; the photos should share the same camera angles, such as front and profile mug shot formats across the group.[12]

Recommendation 4: Immediately after the eyewitness makes a selection, the police should obtain a statement of confidence from the witness before giving the witness any feedback of any kind on his or her choice. Researchers have found that jurors believe that more confident witnesses produce more accurate identifications. According to Gary Wells, a witness's confidence "is the most powerful single determinant of whether or not observers of the testimony will believe that the eyewitness made an accurate identification."[13] All of this collides with a disturbing fact, also well established by the research: eyewitness confidence *does not* predict accuracy very well. Eyewitnesses who express a high degree of confidence in their identifications are probably no more likely to make accurate identifications than witnesses who express less confidence.[14] This combination of a strong tendency by jurors to rely on witness confidence, and the fact that confidence does not predict accuracy, means that police must exercise extra caution when they ask witnesses who have made identifications how confident they feel in their selections. Anything that might artificially bolster witness confidence would obviously present a danger of inflating the value of the witness's testimony later in court.

A considerable amount of scientific evidence indicates that events that occur after the identification can have a dramatic impact on the witness's confidence in his or her choice. And one can imagine few things more likely to bolster a witness's confidence than a statement by the officer involved like "good job—you've identified the right man" or "that's the guy we arrested." This kind of statement by the police officer would cause an eyewitness to feel supremely confident in his or her choice; the person in charge, telling the witness "you're right," could not help but influence confidence. It would actually be shocking if a witness were not influenced by such a statement.[15]

Therefore, the eyewitness should be asked, right after an identification occurs, "How confident are you in your choice?" Nothing else should be said in the meantime, because of the likelihood of interference with the process. As the NIJ *Guide* says, "If an identification is made, avoid reporting to the witness any information regarding the individual he/she has selected prior to obtaining the witness's statement of certainty."[16]

(Optional) Recommendation 5: Sequential, as opposed to simultaneous, lineups should be used. This recommendation should remain an option for now. As discussed in chapter 2, research tells us that using a sequential identification procedure—showing the eyewitness one person or one photograph at a time (as opposed to the more common simultaneous lineup, in which the witness views all persons or photographs together) yields markedly fewer inaccurate identifications. This happens because the simultaneous lineup procedure lends itself perfectly to the exercise of relative judgment. The implicit question in a simultaneous lineup is "which of these people looks most like the person who committed the crime?" A sequential lineup, by contrast, forces the witness to ask herself, for each person or photograph, "Is that the person I saw?" This turns out to make a measurable difference; an eyewitness makes fewer incorrect choices using the sequential procedure.

However, some evidence exists that the sequential procedure produces another effect: it reduces the number of accurate identifications. The magnitude of the reduction does not match that of the reduction in inaccurate choices; the effect on inaccurate choices is much stronger. Nevertheless, the effect on accurate choices cannot be dismissed out of hand; it appears to be real. Some researchers explain this reduction in accurate identifications as the elimination of lucky guesses that happen as a result of relative judgment (see chapter 2). Using relative judgment ("which one looks most like the guy I saw?") yields some number of correct guesses—that is, choices based on an eyewitness saying not "that's him" but rather "that looks the most like him."

The lucky guess theory may explain this result. Nevertheless, these lucky guess choices are correct. Whether or not to obtain a (great) reduction in inaccurate identifications at the expense of a (smaller) reduction in accurate identifications ultimately comes down to a policy choice; one answer cannot claim absolute superiority over another though the effect on inaccurate identifications is stronger. Thus, despite the science that shows that the sequential method does a good job of reducing mistakes, this should remain optional.

Interrogation of Suspects: Five Changes Needed to
Minimize the Chances of False Confessions

In many ways, the problem of false confessions presents the most difficult idea for law enforcement to swallow in the discussion of the flaws in traditional methods of investigation. People have begun to understand, at some level, that eyewitnesses do not always get identifications right, and that some incorrect identifications result in miscarriages of justice. They also know, to some extent, that not all of forensic science works as well as DNA identification does. But it remains difficult for most of us to come to grips with the idea that innocent people might confess to a crime they did not commit. We fall prey to the fundamental attribution error: observers make dispositional attributions (assumptions about someone's attitude and motivation) for a person's actions by taking those actions at face value; they do not consider the role of situational factors or context that might induce the person to take those actions.[17] If a person confesses to a crime, we attribute this action to the fact that she in fact did the crime. We do not consider what aspects of her situation might have influenced her decision to confess: Was she held and questioned for fifteen or twenty straight hours? Is she now or was she then mentally impaired? Was she threatened, or promised leniency?

Moreover, people generally cannot detect deception well, and this includes those with law enforcement training or experience; police do not detect lying any better than civilians.[18] This inability to tell truth from falsity, which police and civilians share, can become even worse for officers, because police training pushes them toward using behavioral cues—e.g., gaze aversion, posture, and particular gestures—that actually have no statistical correlation with deception.[19] Finally, confessions to police often contain specific information—sometimes vivid facts and even feelings about the crime that the perpetrator would have experienced—that seem so particular that only the guilty party could know, making these confessions even more believable.[20] These facts often originate not with the confessing suspect but with the police, who, often inadvertently, feed this information to the suspect during the interrogation. This results in a confession that seems so tellingly detailed that only someone involved could make it, and thus so powerfully incriminating that no innocent person would ever utter it.

According to Professor Brandon Garrett of the University of Virginia School of Law, of the more than 250 DNA-based exonerations now documented, forty involved cases in which the defendant had confessed falsely in cases of rape and murder.[21] "As a result," Garrett says, it can no longer be denied that "innocent people falsely confess."[22] As with the problems involved in eyewitness testimony, scientists have produced a considerable amount of work that gives us a good idea of what factors might enhance the probability that people might confess falsely, even to serious crimes. Their work also tells us what will help to remedy these problems in a concrete way. And, as with the scientific work involved in eyewitness identification, this work has not appeared suddenly in the last couple of years; on the contrary, scientists have conducted studies in this area for decades—long enough for thorough reviews and duplication of results by peers. In short, we have strong evidence concerning what police techniques raise the risk of false confessions, and guidance on what to do to keep this from happening.[23]

Recommendation 6: Every interrogation or interview of suspects in police custody in a place of detention should be recorded electronically, from the beginning of the suspect's in-custody conversation with officers to the end of the statement. The video should show both the interrogator and the suspect equally. Many in law enforcement strongly oppose a requirement that police record interrogations. But recording of interrogations now has many champions as well, a surprising number of them within police departments and prosecutor's offices. These people probably have the most persuasive message of all for their law enforcement colleagues: recording interrogations assists police and prosecutors, even as it makes for a better, more complete record that helps to root out other bad practices.

Alaska (in 1985) and Minnesota (in 1994) became the first two American jurisdictions to mandate electronic recording of statements, when their state supreme courts ordered police to record.[24] More recent laws or court decisions in seven other jurisdictions now require recording in some circumstances.[25] Massachusetts does not require recording, but a decision by the state's Supreme Judicial Court from 2004 says that when police do not record an interrogation without an acceptable reason for failing to do so, defendants can request a jury instruction telling jurors that they should consider unrecorded confessions with care.[26] In studies in 2004[27] and 2008,[28] Thomas Sullivan and his colleagues found that hundreds of police agencies in jurisdictions that did not require recording had adopted the practice voluntarily, to one degree or another. While the number of departments recording voluntarily is small relative to the seventeen thousand police departments in the United States, law enforcement now has a substantial body of experience with electronic recording of confessions, built up over many years.

Despite the growth in recording interrogations, critics continue to raise objections to the practice. Recording will cost agencies scarce resources, some say, and will make the taking of confessions logistically difficult. Suspects will "clam up," refusing to talk when cameras intimidate them, or worse yet they will refuse to confess because they know about the recording, which will definitively incriminate them. Others fear that the cameras and their presence will interfere with detectives' efforts to "build rapport" with suspects in order to get them to confess.[29] With the field-based know-how that law enforcement now has, we can evaluate these objections against real facts.

One rarely finds complete consensus on difficult issues in criminal justice and law enforcement, which makes Thomas Sullivan's finding all the more striking. In the police departments he investigated that record interrogations, he found virtually unanimous positive reactions among law enforcement agencies that regularly recorded interrogations. Officials in these departments "enthusiastically favored the practice."[30] Sullivan listed the benefits of recording that officers mentioned in their comments.[31]

- Recording gave officers the ability to listen to and watch the defendant carefully, instead of focusing on copious note taking.
- Recording protected officers from bogus claims of police misconduct or abuse, such as failing to give *Miranda* warnings, committing physical abuse, or the like.
- Recording captures fleeting reactions, subtle indications of emotion or lack of it, and other nuances that later testimony or dry reports cannot reproduce.
- Some defendants confess more easily when recorded than when faced with the task of writing out a statement or reading and agreeing to one written for them.
- Some recording equipment allows officers not in the interrogation room to view the interaction in real time and even to relay questions to the officer doing the questioning.
- Recording of interrogations results in fewer motions to suppress, because the record regarding whether *Miranda* warnings were given or whether the statement was voluntary is virtually incontestable.
- Recording of interrogations increases the number of guilty pleas, resulting in savings of resources by eliminating contested motions and trials.
- When cases do go to trial, the number of guilty verdicts increases, because the recordings eliminate avenues for the defense to attack the confessions.
- Recordings allow detectives to go back after the conclusion of the interrogation and look for clues they missed, and to observe how they can improve their own techniques.
- Recordings help to increase public trust in the police, because they show that police conduct themselves legally and properly, and have nothing to hide.

What about the original impetus for recording: reform of police practices and curbing of abuse in interrogation rooms? Sullivan reports that recording

interrogations "deter[s] improper police conduct during custodial interviews
. . . [I]f detectives have conducted themselves in a manner that goes outside
the law, and impinge on the rights or overcome the willpower of the suspect,
the judge and jury will have a first-hand look and the advantage shifts to the
defense." This is, of course, as it should be, and police officers in jurisdictions
that record know it. Thus recording becomes a direct deterrent of the abuses
and problems that have produced false confessions in the first place.

Despite all the advantages recording produces for law enforcement and
the benefits to the integrity of the interrogation process as well, resistance to
recording continues, largely from police officers and prosecutors who have
not tried recording statements.[32] This is especially true of federal agents and
prosecutors—which is odd, because they use recording technology often for
their own purposes.[33] According to Thomas Sullivan, "Although they have
no experience with this superior method of capturing what occurred during custodial interviews, many expound dire predictions of serious negative
consequences that they believe will inevitably result if they are required to
record." Sullivan calls these predictions "speculations" that ignore the "glow-
ing descriptions of benefits" of recording interrogations that he and his colleagues heard during the course of his study.[34] The International Association of Chiefs of Police, one of the leading law enforcement organizations in
both the United States and the world, now has a model policy for electronic
recording of interrogations and confessions[35] and has also produced a "Concepts and Issues Paper"[36] to provide background information and supporting
documentation to law enforcement executives who wish to fashion recording policies for their departments. The "Concepts and Issues Paper" notes
that "[v]ideo technology has become widely accepted among law enforcement agencies and today is used routinely for a variety of purposes" in "both
large and small jurisdictions."[37] This makes it important to prepare agencies
to adapt to this new world correctly.

Given all of the benefits, and the growing acceptance of recording, why
the continued resistance? Sullivan identifies one objection expressed by some
opponents: they are afraid that "judges and juries may disapprove of the
[interrogation] tactics used."[38] A related objection may be that officers may
simply prefer not to record because this gives them the ability to hide the
methods used, the exact words used, or even the actual events that occurred
during the interrogation, all of which the recording would reveal. Sullivan
calls these objections inappropriate because they rest on the premise that
"the testifying officer should be able to avoid revealing what occurred during
the custodial interview, despite the obligation to report the session fully and
objectively and to testify to the whole truth."[39] He calls it "an embarrassment"

that several federal agencies raised this very argument in opposition to a proposal to record interrogations. Nevertheless, objections continue, with some arguing that requiring officers to record constitutes "an unwarranted slap at their integrity."[40] But again, this does not ring true for officers who have actually used recording. Overwhelmingly, they say that recording interrogations supports their integrity and helps build trust and confidence in the police "by eliminating unrecorded, closed-door stationhouse interrogations and placing all interrogations on the record, literally."[41]

The mechanics of the process of recording would require some underlying understandings. First, a recording requirement should apply at least to all Part I Crimes: the crimes that the FBI deems the most serious. These crimes—murder and nonnegligent manslaughter, rape, robbery, aggravated assault, burglary, larceny-theft, motor vehicle theft, and arson—set the standard for the study of major criminal activity, and the FBI focuses on them first and foremost in its periodic Uniform Crime Reporting statistics.[42] Simply saying that police should record interrogations in all serious crimes is too vague and would undoubtedly require litigation. Limiting recording to felonies[43] would sweep in crimes that are felonies simply because they cross an arbitrary statutory line—for example, theft of property worth $1,000 (felony) versus property worth $999 (misdemeanor).[44] Second, recordings should include video and audio, but if video recording is shown to have been impossible in the circumstances, audio would do. Third, the recording requirement should apply whenever the defendant is in police custody in a place of detention: a police station, a county jail, or a holding facility of any kind. While recording of statements in police vehicles or on the street might be possible in some circumstances, it should not be required. Fourth, the recording should begin at the start of the interrogation session—typically, with the administration of *Miranda* warnings—and should include the entire interrogation. It should not simply recap the part of the interrogation in which the suspect admits to the crime. Recording only a recap of the juicy parts of the questioning leaves the police open to charges that they used illegal and abusive tactics to elicit the confession that they have hidden from the judge and jury through a failure to record. Recaps also fail to record all of the nuances, the give and take, and the full responses of both interrogator and suspect, and constitute a selective, incomplete, and probably misleading picture, and the defense at any hearing or trial will use this against the prosecution.[45] Last, video recordings should utilize a perspective that includes both interrogator and suspect equally. This guards against bias that can seep in when a suspect becomes the camera's sole focus, and it also captures the full scope of the interaction.

What if, after a requirement became law, an officer did not record an inter-rogation? If the officer did not record inadvertently, or recording just was not possible under the circumstances—accidental improper camera operation, no equipment available at the time, a technical failure, or a refusal of the sus-pect to talk except with the recording equipment turned off, for example—the recording requirement should allow for the use of the officer's testimony about what the suspect said. If the judge hears evidence that convinces her that the failure did not come from deliberate avoidance of recording in a bad faith effort to skirt the requirement, the officer should testify to the statement made, either from written notes or from memory. A number of states that require recording have provisions in their rules that allow the use of officer testimony about statements gathered in such situations.[46]

But if the officer does not record when he or she could have, the law could automatically exclude any testimony about the defendant's statements. Alter-natively, the law could create a presumption that the statement will not come in if not recorded, absent evidence that comes from an independent (i.e., nonpolice) source that the statement was given voluntarily and without coer-cion, that it is reliable, and that it is necessary that it be admitted to avoid an injustice. Further, the law could create a requirement that the judge or jury must presume that the content of an unrecorded statement would favor the defendant's version of the interrogation. Finally, the law could instruct judges or juries that, because a statement was not electronically recorded, they should "weigh evidence of the defendant's alleged statement with great caution and care."[47]

It seems too harsh to mandate that courts should always exclude evidence in the event of a failure to follow the recording requirements. While a cat-egorical rule would have the virtue of clarity, it would have too little flexibil-ity to meet the unexpected situations that constantly arise in life, and would exact the loss of key evidence as the price for failure—a solution that has long antagonized critics of the Fourth Amendment's exclusionary rule.[48] On the other end of the spectrum, a simple instruction to the jury that they should view the unrecorded confession evidence with care seems unlikely to have a strong effect, given the way that juries disregard or fail to listen to instruc-tions courts give them.[49] A better balance would be struck by either the sec-ond or third alternative above.

In the end, police officers who have actually used electronic record-ing know the most about it. As they see it, recording is a tool that works—period. Neil Nelson, a former police commander in St. Paul, Minnesota, who is now a law enforcement consultant, says recording interrogations "is the best tool ever forced down our throats."[50] Washington, DC, metropolitan police detective James Trainum has a similar take. "When videotaping was first forced upon us by the D.C. City Council, we fought it tooth and nail." But now, "we would not do it any other way."[51]

Recommendation 7: Interrogations should continue for more than two hours only with the express and informed consent of the interrogating officer's supervisor, based on a factual justification; all interrogations should be discontinued after four hours, absent a compelling reason based on the interest of justice or a general public safety emergency. To conduct an interrogation, police place the suspect in a room in the police station, usually without windows, with very little furniture or other contents, and they lock the door. The interrogation takes place in this relative isolation, without contact with family, friends, or an attorney (unless the suspects make a specific request for counsel, and most do not). When the interrogation extends for a long period of time, this prolonged isolation combines with the tension inherent in the questioning process itself to cause significant psychological stress. This is exacerbated by the individual's inability to meet his own needs for food, sleep, the use of a restroom, and other basic functions; all of these are under the control of the police during custodial interrogation.[52] All of this adds up to accumulating mental pressures that sharply increase the suspect's desire to do anything to escape the situation—even confess falsely, as long as it gets him out of that room.

Most interrogations last between thirty minutes and two hours;[53] extended interrogations greatly increase the odds of something going wrong. In cases in which defendants have given false confessions, interrogations "lasted an average of 16.3 hours."[54] Fred Inbau, who wrote police interrogation manuals for decades, warned that interrogations usually should not exceed four hours.[55] It is probably more important to recognize that extending interrogations to great lengths can contribute to false confessions than it is to pin down when, exactly, that point arrives. After all, it will be likely to come at a different point for each suspect. Therefore the rules for interrogation should allow situational flexibility. Any time an interrogation will exceed two hours—the point at which the great majority of them conclude—the officer conducting the questioning should get the permission of his or her supervisor to continue, and should have to justify the request on the basis of concrete facts, not just hope that more time and pressure will get the suspect talking. After four hours—Inbau's own cut-off point—questioning should not continue without a compelling reason that follows from the interest of justice, such as the need to get the final details of a crime that will allow police to rescue a hostage. There is no magic in two and four hours; they are drawn from the average experience of interrogation, as recognized by experts in the field.

One could also probably select two hours and six hours as defensible limits. The point is less what the limits are than to have some reasonable limits and controls in place.

Recommendation 8: Even though the law allows police to use deception while questioning suspects, interrogation should not include fabrication of forensic evidence or test results, falsified records, or falsified polygraph results. In *Frazier v. Cupp,*[56] a 1969 case, the suspect told police that he had been with his cousin; the police lied to the suspect and told him that his cousin had confessed, which prompted an immediate confession from the suspect. The U.S. Supreme Court did not find anything wrong with using lies to try to induce confessions; nothing in the Constitution condemned deception as a police tactic.[57]

There may be nothing wrong with using a lie to catch a criminal; after all, much of what criminals do includes deceit. The problem, as the DNA-based exonerations tell us so plainly, is that not all suspects are guilty. Police deception has a profound effect on the innocent. Saul Kassin and his colleagues tell us that the scientific and social science literature strongly supports the idea that "outright lies can put innocents at risk to confess by leading them to feel trapped by the inevitability of the evidence against them," because they literally see no other plausible way to react.[58] More than one hundred years of study "proves without equivocation that misinformation can substantially alter people's visual perceptions, beliefs, motivations, emotions, attitudes, memories, self-assessments, and even certain psychological outcomes,"[59] and we should not expect this to be different just because the setting is an interrogation room.

Thus police deception can pose real danger. And the biggest danger comes from fabricated scientific and forensic evidence: nonexistent DNA "found" on the defendant's shoes, a polygraph test that the suspect "fails," fingerprints "found" on the victim's clothing. The case of Michael Crowe makes a good example. An assailant killed Michael's sister Stephanie, stabbing her to death in her bedroom. Crowe, a fourteen-year-old boy, underwent multiple interrogation sessions, during which police confronted him with the fact that he had failed a lie detector test and that Stephanie's blood and hair were linked directly to him. None of these facts was true, but they were enough to convince Michael that he must have killed his sister, even though he had no recollection of having done so. The interrogation convinced him that he had a "split personality" and that "bad Michael" killed Stephanie out of jealousy and "good Michael" blocked the incident from his memory. Michael's fundamental view of himself, his personality, his actions, and his memory were altered, and he became convinced that he was his sister's murderer: "I'm not sure how I did it," he told police, "All I know is I did it."[60]

Falsified scientific and forensic evidence seem qualitatively different from simple made-up statements, such as "your cousin just said it was you." These kinds of deceptions can easily be challenged: "Oh yeah? Let me talk to my cousin." Scientific or forensic evidence—fingerprints, polygraphs, DNA—is seen as unassailable by most people. Thus the pressure created by forensic and scientific fabrication is much greater and is likely to have a considerably stronger effect. Therefore, while we might choose to outlaw all types of deception at some point, we should at least begin reform of the interrogation process by banning scientific and forensic deception.

Recommendation 9: Police must not make promises or offers of help in exchange for a statement by the suspect, and must not use tactics that minimize legal (as opposed to moral or psychological) guilt. Promises of help in exchange for making a statement, and methods that minimize the suspect's guilt as a way to get him or her to talk, have a strong similarity to each other. This section treats them together.

Under the Constitution, the prosecution must always establish that a confession given by a defendant came voluntarily: the defendant made a free choice to speak. A confession becomes involuntary, and therefore not usable in court, if the defendant spoke because of coercion—actual or threatened use of force, infliction of pain, or the like. A confession also becomes unavailable to the prosecution if the defendant talked because he or she received a promise of some benefit in exchange for the confession. This "no promises" rule comes from the venerable Supreme Court decision of *Bram v. U.S.*, decided in 1897, which declared that no voluntary confession could be "extracted by any sort of threats or violence, nor obtained by any direct or implied promises, however slight."[61]

The *Bram* rule against promises is old, but it reflects perfectly what we see in the scientific work of researchers who study interrogation. Promises of leniency, better treatment, or the like push suspects toward complying with the interrogator's desire for a confession. For innocent suspects, the promise of help or leniency may represent the only way out of the excruciating dilemma in which they find themselves: keep denying guilt, which seems to achieve nothing because the interrogator will not accept these statements as true, or confess and receive help, including perhaps escape from the interrogation room.

The rule of the *Bram* case against "any direct or implied promises, however slight" would address these problems quite effectively, but in the modern era, *Bram* has been vastly diluted and weakened. Today, police can come very close to making promises; they can even articulate what sounds like a promise in every way to any legally untrained ear; they can even use the word "promise"—and the courts will find a way to decide that what police said did not promise anything. In *Miller v. Fenton*,[62] a U.S. Court of Appeals case decided in 1986, Detective Boyce interrogated Miller, a suspect in a murder, in an attempt to get him to confess. Miller continued to deny his guilt, and Boyce began to tell Miller that the person who had committed the crime must have been mentally ill—the killer "had mental problems and was desperately in need of psychological treatment."[63] The detective repeated this idea several times, indicating that such a mental illness would mean that the killer was not legally responsible for his actions: the killer was "not a criminal who should be punished, but a sick individual who should receive help."[64] According to a transcript of the interrogation, Boyce told Miller,"I mean really, you need help, you need proper help, and you know it, my God. . . . You are not a criminal, you are not a criminal."[65] After telling Miller repeatedly that he bore no responsibility for the crime because of mental illness, Detective Boyce made what any fair reading would call a promise. "Okay, listen Frank. If I promise to, you know, do all I can with the psychiatrist and everything, and we get the proper help for you, and get the proper help for you, will you talk to me about it?"[66] To most people, this violation of the *Bram* rule—no promises, direct or implied, however slight, in exchange for a statement—seems clear, but, incredibly, the majority of the court of appeals did not agree. Boyce did not say that Miller would not be prosecuted or that he could mount a successful insanity defense; the statements to Miller that he was "not a criminal" and "not responsible" should not be understood for what they seemed to be in this legal never-never land. Rather, these statements just expressed the detective's personal opinion: "I don't think you're personally responsible." None of this promised leniency, the court said. "Miller's confession may have been made in the hope of leniency, but that does not mean it was made in response to a promise of leniency."[67]

This brings us to minimization. Police use minimization tactics to make suspects more willing to confess. Police use minimization by framing a story for the suspect about the crime that minimizes his or her culpability. *Miller v. Fenton* is a great example; the detective minimized Miller's culpability by saying that the person who committed the murder was mentally ill and not responsible.

The problem is that each minimization story is, at the very least, an implied promise. In the words of the researchers who have studied this phenomenon, minimizations "can communicate promises of leniency indirectly through pragmatic implication."[68] In other words, the interrogator offers up the story, which seems to exculpate the suspect; all the suspect has to do to receive the benefit implied in the story ("you're not guilty if it's self-defense") is to utter a confession that agrees with the story offered. It is, in every sense, an exchange offered by the interrogator, if a more subtle one than the promise in *Miller v. Fenton*.

For these reasons, one could surely argue that promises (or anything that sounds like a promise) and minimization have no place in the interrogator's arsenal; the danger of pushing the innocent toward confession is simply too great. But, as a starting point, we need not go that far. Instead, we could simply say that anything that sounds like or functions as a promise will be considered one—any statement that might be understood by a reasonable person as an offer of leniency ("If you talk to me about this, it will go easier for you" or "If you tell me what happened, I'll put in a good word for you with the prosecutor") or help ("If I help you with the psychiatrist and your mental illness, will you talk to me about it?") is prohibited and would make a statement unusable in court. As for minimization, an implied promise, such as the one in *Miller v. Fenton*, ought to be beyond the pale, because it promises a get-out-of-jail-free card in exchange for a confession that matches the story.

Recommendation 10: Vulnerable individuals should never be questioned without an attorney present. There is disagreement about the problem of false confessions; certainly there is disagreement about its scope. But even those who minimize the problem agree on one thing: those most at risk for making a false confession share particular vulnerabilities. They are often young, inexperienced, and naïve in the extreme concerning police and the criminal justice system. Others suffer from mental disabilities or cognitive impairments or psychological disorders of different types and degrees, rendering them highly susceptible to suggestion, intimidation, and confusion, especially under the great stress of an interrogation by a police officer attempting to establish guilt. It is no wonder that Professor (and former judge) Paul Cassell of the University of Utah, who does not agree with most of the scholarship and science on exonerated individuals, does conclude that to the extent that there is a problem of false confessions, young people and the mentally impaired are uniquely vulnerable.[69]

The solution to this problem will not be popular with all law enforcement officials, many of whom have always opposed the *Miranda* decision's insistence on introducing legal representation into the interrogation process. But the solution is nevertheless both simple and obvious: no interrogation of persons in these vulnerable groups should take place without the presence of an attorney. This rule should apply any time a reasonable person would believe, given the facts of the case and the appearance and conduct of the suspect, that the suspect is a minor or is mentally impaired. This will, no doubt, keep some of these individuals from confessing. But that is a price worth paying to avoid false confessions and convictions of the innocent, which leaves the real perpetrators free.

Forensic Science: A Modest Set of Proposals for Better Tools to Pursue the Truth

Any fair reading of the landmark 2009 National Academy of Sciences report *Strengthening Forensic Science*[70] reveals the need for a substantial overhaul of the forensic science system, but attaining a comprehensive set of reforms will probably take years. Some of the proposals in the report may never fly; others are incredibly important, but even if enacted would not have an immediate impact on the day-to-day use of forensic evidence in ongoing cases. Yet the need for substantial improvement is both immediate and stark. Thus the reforms proposed here consist of a subset of those recommended in *Strengthening Forensic Science*. Those that are included here form the answer to the following question: What must be done *now* (1) to address the worst problems in forensic science and (2) to bring about immediate more positive changes that will move forensic science quickly toward producing accurate results? These changes will give us some immediate progress on forensic science issues, even if the need for other improvements remains.

Recommendation 11: The least accurate, least well-established forensic techniques should be banned until researchers produce work that demonstrates a solid scientific basis for these disciplines. I am not referring here to well-used methods such as the analysis of fingerprints and firearms identification (a discussion of those issues follows). Rather, I refer to other methods of forensic analysis that have consistently shown up in cases involving grievous miscarriages of justice. The mistakes stemming from them have been not isolated but common, and the lack of scientific underpinning and even outright fraud involving these techniques have called them into question repeatedly. These disciplines do not show up in the literature having caused an occasional mistake; rather, they produce consistently flawed outcomes. For these methods, only one approach will do: they should not be accepted in court at all until a significant body of research, accepted by the full scientific community, can prove their reliability.

This approach—excluding certain kinds of evidence from admissibility in court—has a long history. When the polygraph emerged in the early part of the twentieth century, its boosters claimed it could do nothing less than make perfect judgments about whether a person told the truth. The future looked promising for this new machine until judges began to face requests in court that the results of these lie detection tests be admitted as evidence. A consensus emerged in the judicial system that the technology had not become "sufficiently established" to have reached "general acceptance" in the scientific community,[71] and the polygraph was essentially banned from courtrooms across the country. The idea of general acceptance in the scientific community became known as the *Frye* rule, after one of the first and best-known cases to keep the early polygraphs out of court. The *Frye* case remains the governing law in some jurisdictions, though in others it has been replaced.[72] Nevertheless, it makes a good starting point for discussing when a method of testing simply has not demonstrated its reliability; it gives us a way to ask whether the method in question has a grounding in science such that we should rely on it. Under that standard, courts should not admit results that purport to identify a particular defendant from at least three forensic disciplines in any criminal case: bite mark analysis; analysis of patterns and impressions such as shoeprints and tire tracks; and hair analysis. All of these disciplines lack an adequate foundation upon which to base conclusions, and until that changes, they should not become part of the evidence used to convict defendants.

Forensic odontology, the application of principles of dentistry to law, plays several different roles in legal disputes. As explained in chapter 2, forensic odontology can help courts make determinations concerning allegations of dental malpractice or the origin or extent of oral injuries. It also has become a standard and reliable way to help identify unknown human remains. These uses of forensic odontology are not at all controversial, but another one is. The analysis of bite marks, which prosecutors sometimes use in criminal cases, engenders strong disagreement among scientific professionals; in the words of the National Academy of Sciences, "there is continuing dispute over the value and scientific validity of comparing and identifying bite marks."[73]

Bite mark evidence emerges most often in homicides, sexual assaults, and child abuse cases. Practitioners may use a variety of methods to obtain bite mark evidence from human skin, including taking photographs, making casts or clear overlays, using electron microscopes or computer imaging, or swabbing for DNA, all of which are considered scientifically acceptable.[74] Unfortunately, the problem is more basic than the way impressions are taken: bite marks "change over time and can be distorted by the elasticity of the skin, unevenness of the surface bite, and swelling and healing," all of which "severely limit the validity of forensic odontology."[75] The discipline's governing body, the American Board of Forensic Odontology, has established guidelines for its members, but the guidelines do not specify the criteria for deciding whether the bite mark in question can be connected to the suspect's teeth, and with what degree of certainty. No scientific work in the field tells us how well different methods might lead to conclusions of a match between a bite mark and a suspect; experts using the guidelines "provide widely differing results and a high percentage of false positive matches of bite marks" in rigorous comparison studies.[76] Moreover, there has been no systematic study of large populations to determine how unique the bite marks of individuals actually are.[77]

Bite mark analysis also suffers from the problems of bias that occur when police agencies supply the suspect marks for comparison, but only a very limited number of samples against which to compare the suspect marks. Add to this the fact that bite marks often emerge as evidence in cases that feature grisly, lurid, or depraved details, and the potential for pressure to make the match that police want becomes great. Further, there is "still no general agreement among practicing forensic odontologists about national or international standards for comparison."[78] According to the National Academy of Sciences researchers who wrote the *Strengthening Forensic Science* report, they "received no evidence of an existing scientific basis for identifying an individual to the exclusion of all others"[79]—the very kind of identification that much of forensic science seeks. Other scientists have confirmed this; in one study, the authors found "a lack of valid evidence to support many of the assumptions made by forensic dentists during bite mark comparisons."[80] All in all, bite mark analysis has so little scientific support that it should simply not be used, unless and until real data and analysis actually support the claims of those who practice it.

Analysis of hair includes the examination of hairs shed by people onto a crime scene. The analyst examines the hairs with a microscope for various physical characteristics that vary from person to person: color, form (straight, wavy, etc.), categories of shaft thickness, and length. Other, more particular characteristics may be noted as well. This sort of examination, across broad classes or categories of hair characteristics, can include or exclude a person as a suspect, but nothing more. Thus hair examination can create a class association, but not an identification of the person who committed the crime to the exclusion of all others.

Hair analysis that goes beyond these class exclusions or inclusions lacks any accepted statistical basis. In *Strengthening Forensic Science*, the authors surveyed all of the literature purporting to establish a statistical basis for identification of individual people using hair, and found all of the methods wanting.[81] None of the work done on this discipline so far has established a sufficient statistical foundation for judging the frequency with which any particular physical characteristics of hair appear in the general population, and no uniform standards exist on the number of physical features that two hair samples must share in order for an analyst to declare a match.

Hair analysis finds its way into fewer cases today than in the past, because laboratories can now extract small amounts of mitochondrial DNA from hair samples. Comparisons of mitochondrial DNA yield far more useful and accurate results than microscopic hair analysis can, and these DNA tests have begun to supplant the physical comparisons of hair.[82] In one FBI study comparing the two methods, DNA results showed that microscopic hair analysis was wrong more than 12 percent of the time.[83] Despite all of this, some courts continue to regard microscopic hair analysis as a generally accepted scientific technique and therefore usable in court.[84] All in all, the best one can say for hair analysis is that it could effectively exclude a suspect from the pool of potential perpetrators. But it cannot supply anything approaching an identification of a unique individual, and using hair to make such identifications should stop.

Impression evidence should receive the same treatment as bite marks and hair. While patent (visible) or latent (invisible) impressions can come from a variety of things—lips, ears, and blood, for example—most of the impression evidence that ends up in court comes from tires and shoes. As mass-manufactured objects, both tires and shoes will have characteristics common to every product in the group, according to product design and manufacture. These characteristics result from the repetition of the mass production process, with every tire or shoe having most of the same details. This allows an analyst to identify the class or group characteristics of a tire track or shoeprint. This information may help police, but it only narrows the field, just like a microscopic hair analysis would do. According to the authors of *Strengthening Forensic Science*, this means that the analysis at this level has only limited power: "class characteristics are not sufficient to conclude that any one particular shoe or tire made the impression."[85]

A second level of analysis of tires and shoes attempts to search for individual identifying characteristics in the impressions, and attempts to match them with those found on the suspect's tires or shoes. These characteristics come from everyday use, because the ground can make cuts, gouges, or cracks in the object's surface. Sometimes the individual characteristics result from objects sticking to the tires or shoes: pebbles, sticks, gum, or pieces of plastic. While these individual characteristics might serve to distinguish one tire track or shoeprint from another, the problem (as with other forensic disciplines) is that no one has collected and analyzed any data about these individualizing characteristics, and "there is no defined threshold that must be surpassed, nor are there any studies that associate the number of matching characteristics with the probability that the impressions were made by a common source."[86] Since these characteristics continue to change as the tires or shoes are used, any lapse of time undermines the confidence one might have in an impression match.

Without consensus regarding the number of characteristics necessary to declare a match, and without any data establishing the variability of these characteristics in the whole population of shoes and tires, impression evidence has only limited value. No scientist would take a chance on making a probabilistic assessment of a match between an impression and an individual tire or shoe without a statistical foundation for such an evaluation; it would be little more than a guess.

Recommendation 12: For the rest of the forensic disciplines, proficiency testing should be mandated. For the other, more established forensic disciplines, such as fingerprint analysis, tool mark identification, and the matching of firearms to markings on bullets and shell casings, we should be more willing to accept their results on an ongoing basis, on two conditions. First, research leading to real, statistically valid results must begin immediately in fields where it has not. But even more importantly, we must have real assurance that those producing this evidence conduct their work in a capable and competent fashion. Therefore these disciplines must immediately institute real proficiency testing for both individual practitioners and laboratories.

Proficiency testing is common in many disciplines. Those practicing a sensitive, important task undergo periodic testing of their skills under realistic conditions to assure that they have the degree of expertise necessary to produce reliable results. The utility of proficiency testing would assure consumers (for forensic science, that would include the police, the courts, and juries) that the results of forensic tests have credibility and can be relied upon when making momentous decisions about whom to charge and which defendants may or may not be guilty.

Proficiency testing for forensic disciplines must be constructed so that it resembles the actual situations faced by practitioners in the field. In other words, the testing should "[emulate] a realistic, representative cross-section of casework,"[87] so that it constitutes a real test of what people in the field actually do. The *Llera Plaza* case,[88] decided in 2002 in the U.S. District Court in Philadelphia, contains a valuable lesson about what proficiency testing should, and should not, look like. *Llera Plaza* is well known for the fact that Judge Louis Pollak granted a defendant's motion to exclude expert testimony concluding that a fingerprint was, in fact, the print of the defendant, because of deficiencies in the ACE-V procedure (see chapter 2). Judge Pollak found that no scientific or technical basis existed for the examiner's evaluations,[89] exactly as pointed out in the *Strengthening Forensic Sciences* report. When a huge outcry from law enforcement followed, Judge Pollak held hearings to reconsider his decision at the behest of the FBI, and changed his mind.[90] For our purposes, the most instructive part of this series of events came when the FBI presented evidence to Judge Pollack that some of its examiners had undergone proficiency testing.[91] Besides the government's witnesses, Judge Pollack heard testimony from an expert in fingerprint identification from New Scotland Yard in Britain. This expert testified that, in the U.K., fingerprint examiners undergo routine proficiency testing. Asked about the proficiency testing the FBI had given its own agents, the man from Scotland Yard scoffed. In his opinion, the testing used by the FBI was far too easy, so much so that it would have given his own agents a good laugh.[92] In the United States, it seems we have a long way to go: we rarely use proficiency testing, and even when our foremost police agency has used it, the testing done apparently would not meet any rigorous standard. Real periodic proficiency testing must become mandatory for any forensic scientist or technician, and the test should generate an overall proficiency score for each laboratory, too.

Recommendation 13: Terminology should be taken seriously. It is tempting to think that, in dealing with the results of forensic testing, it is only the science and the rigor of the methods used that matter. If the methods used do not reflect solid scientific principles and rigorous adherence to protocol, we should not give the results any credibility. This is true, but it represents only part of the story.

The ways in which forensic experts communicate the results of their work to judges, juries, and other decision makers also matter a great deal. Forensic scientists have used a variety of terms to characterize their work. Often, this terminology has lacked consistency or even well-understood definitions. And at no point is this more important, and more potentially damaging, than when these experts attempt to describe the association between materials that constitute evidence (such as fibers or fingerprints) and particular suspects or objects. A quick survey of the *Strengthening Forensic Science* report reveals a multitude of imprecise terminology: "consistent with," "similar in all respects," "cannot be excluded as a source of," "positive identification," "nonidentification," "nonconclusive," "could have come from the same individual," "probably made," "could have made," "inconclusive," "probably did not make," "elimination," "unsuitable," and "associated with," just to name a few.[93] Most dangerous of all, perhaps, are the terms "match" and "identical," when used in any context except perhaps DNA and chemical analysis. The danger lies in the implication that the method under discussion, whatever it is, can make an identification of the source of the evidence with one individual to the exclusion of all others. To be blunt, forensic disciplines other than DNA and chemical analysis simply have not established a statistical basis sufficient to make such claims.

Until the forensic disciplines other than DNA and chemical analysis complete studies that allow a valid claim that a particular piece of evidence is associated with a particular individual to the exclusion of all others, with an appropriate, statistically based degree of probability, the use of terms such as "match," "identical," "identification," and "conclusive" should be prohibited. The only acceptable terms should be ones that are limited and self-defining: "excludes," "includes," "inconclusive," or "sharing group characteristics with." Any other terminology threatens to portray these nonstatistical, interpretation-based disciplines as more precise than they can possibly be, given the current state of the science.

Recommendation 14: Procedures should be put in place for quality assurance and control, accreditation, and certification. In any field that requires precision, and in which practitioners desire to improve themselves continuously and learn from mistakes, one finds procedures in place for quality assurance and control. In medicine, quality assurance programs abound. Most hospitals have quality assurance programs to make certain that patients get the best possible care and that doctors and nurses continuously improve the delivery of the medical services. Medical quality-assurance officers can usually follow a patient's case all the way through the system to see whether the original diagnosis given was correct and whether the hospital and medical care providers actually helped the patient. This type of "systematic and routine feedback" plays a key role in helping practitioners in any field strive for improvement.[94] This must become the standard in each forensic discipline if it is to become "a self-correcting enterprise" that discovers, and works to avoid, past mistakes.[95] These quality assurance and control procedures should routinely "identify mistakes, fraud, and bias; confirm the continued validity and reliability of standard operating procedures and protocols; ensure that best practices are being followed; and correct procedures and protocols that need improvement."[96] All of this falls well within routine practice in industry.

Beyond quality assurance procedures, all laboratories and those who work in them should undergo accreditation and certification. Accreditation and certification remain spotty in the forensic disciplines, and not all states require it. This means that courts in some jurisdictions regularly receive forensic work from persons without any training and from laboratories that do not adhere to any regularized set of standards. Of course, this does not mean that the results produced are always, or even sometimes, wrong. But it does mean that courts have no assurance that these laboratories or individuals use accepted methods and adhere to them regularly. Some will argue that, because many laboratories are small "mom and pop" operations, a mandatory requirement for accreditation and certification would put them out of business. That may be, but if the forensic sciences wish to be accepted as scientific disciplines, accreditation and certification cannot wait. No one would accept anything less in a laboratory performing a crucial medical test on a loved one; we should not accept less regarding tests that have a direct impact on truth finding in our courts.

Recommendation 15: Begin to work toward eliminating human biases in laboratory testing. Researchers in all scientific fields know that human biases can creep into almost any kind of experimental work. The discussion of the experimenter-expectancy bias earlier in this book makes a good example. Without any intention of doing so and without realizing it, the person conducting an experiment with a human subject may communicate the "right" answer in a measurable percentage of instances. Unless researchers use well-developed and accepted protocols that safeguard against it, the effect is pronounced enough to throw off the results of experiments, so researchers routinely have a person who does not know the "correct" answer conduct the face-to-face interaction with the subject of the experiment, and they tell the subject that the administrator of the experiments does not know. This helps keep human bias out of the results. The problem is not that researchers are corrupt or bad people in any way. Rather, the issue is that they are human, and therefore subject to the same biases that all other people are subject to.

In general, forensic laboratories and forensic testing have evolved as parts of, and tools for, police departments and prosecutors' offices. Sometimes, these laboratories are even physically connected with these law enforcement operations; the labs are often funded by them and under their administrative control. In other words, the people who run the forensic laboratories and those who work in them performing the analyses know that, in some significant ways, they all work for and answer to the police. The natural human tendency in such situations is obvious: please the boss.

I do not mean to imply that forensic scientists and technicians would go so far as to consciously skew results to come up with the results they think detectives want. A few have done this, creating terrible miscarriages of justice on large scales,[97] but thankfully the numbers of such fraudulent actors seem to be low. The real danger is more subtle. As explained in chapter 2, with the exception of DNA analysis and chemical testing, most forensic disciplines retain some element of human judgment. An examiner decides whether or not one fingerprint "matches" another, and that judgment is not scientifically clear-cut; witness Brandon Mayfield's misidentification as one of the Madrid bombing terrorists, based on a fingerprint examined by some of the FBI's best.

In at least two specific ways, bias can creep into forensic judgments. First, those working in forensic labs may have contact with detectives working on individual cases, in the course of which they may learn what answers the detectives would like to see from the testing. Second, a routine part of finger-print examinations is to seek confirmation of the individual examiner's work by another examiner. This, of course, is a good thing—except that the routine fingerprint analysis procedures allow the confirming examiner to know of the first examiner's result prior to the confirmation examination. This introduces an obvious bias. It should be mandatory that the police officers, prosecutors, or other persons involved in or having knowledge of a case not have any contact with the persons in forensic laboratories performing any tests on evidence for the case, similar to the "blind lineup" procedure recommended earlier in this chapter. Second, confirmation of fingerprint examinations should never include any information concerning results of the initial examination. Unless the confirming examiner is blinded, such confirmations have little value.

Recommendation 16: There should be a post-conviction unit in every prosecutor's office. At least one other change must happen in order for us to move into the future. This one does not involve a particular area or type of police investigation, but rather the structure of prosecutors' offices: every prosecutor's office must create an internal unit dedicated to investigating post-conviction claims of innocence..

This innovation came to public notice with the election of Craig Watkins as district attorney in Dallas, Texas, in 2006. The criminal justice system in Dallas was under a cloud because of numerous reversals of convictions through DNA evidence, and a scandal involving both the police department and the Dallas forensic laboratory in which innocent men were framed for drug crimes. Watkins was elected with a mandate to clean up the system, and one of the first things he did was to set up a unit in his office—just like the units most prosecutors' offices have for major crimes, or sex crimes, or narcotics trials—with the specific task of examining cases in which previously convicted defendants made claims of innocence. Houston prosecutor Patricia Lykos, elected in 2008, established a similar unit within her office. In

Dallas, the conviction integrity unit confers a kind of legitimacy and public confidence on the district attorney's office that it had begun to lose through the many past errors that had come to light. It forms a kind of quality assurance mechanism that allows the prosecutor's operation to go forward with an established way of dealing with possible miscarriages of justice, instead of having to react on an ad hoc basis.

This kind of unit is something any prosecutor's office of any size simply must have. For offices too small to have the resources to dedicate personnel to it, a consortium could be formed between the elected prosecutors in several counties, and it could serve all of them.

How to Make It Happen

If the reforms recommended in this chapter represent a workable and effective package of possible changes, the question becomes how to make these proposals happen. Making changes, even modest ones, in a complex social system while it operates never comes easily. And given the resistance from so many police departments, prosecutors' offices, and their allies, the difficulty multiplies. Even so, we can increase the odds of progress by using a few critical strategies.

Focus on the Future, Not the Past (with One Important Caveat)

The first step in bringing about the reforms discussed in this chapter may seem counterintuitive: we must focus on the future. The main portion of our effort must target prospective reform, not retrospective correction. To many, this will seem the opposite of what we should do, because many of the problems with traditional methods of interrogation, eyewitness identification, and forensic science only came to light because of the exposure of the injustices of the past, usually through DNA testing. Indeed, we would probably not have had any extended public discussion about, or engagement with, the issue of wrongful convictions and what causes them except for the uncovering of miscarriages of justice of the past. Thus focusing forward, and not backward, will raise eyebrows, and it should. Nevertheless, with one essential caveat, concentrating on the future is the correct step to take *now*, for tactical and persuasive reasons.

At this point in the debate over what to do about police investigative techniques and forensic methods, the main question is no longer what the science indicates, because the science itself is largely unassailable. Rather, the issue now is how to persuade those resisting the science to open up to it, to see that they gain little and stand to lose much by insisting that no problems exist. Insisting that the ways of the past work just fine may play well inside police departments and prosecutors' offices and some law enforcement professional organizations, but taking a hard line against change has slowly become less and less tenable. In addition, the number of convictions subject to reversal with DNA has peaked, has been falling, and will continue only at a lower level than was true ten years ago. Thus a recalibration of overall strategy seems correct.

Recall the various cognitive barriers that motivate the resistance to reform (chapter 4). Cognitive dissonance looms as one of the most powerful. Police and prosecutors think of themselves as the good guys who spend their careers putting the bad guys in jail. They have much invested in this view of themselves, in which they stand up—at real personal risk, in the case of the police—to the worst elements of our society, and take those people off the street. The context in which the issues in this book have arisen—cases in which people have gone to prison, some for many years, for crimes they turned out not to have committed—constitutes an immediate and direct challenge to this self-image: good guys don't incarcerate innocent people. Accepting that mistakes occurred, and that they had a hand in those incidents—even though they may have acted at all times honestly, in good faith, and according to the best procedures available—causes great dissonance, so the drive to ignore or deny the existence of the mistakes of the past will remain strong. Only a rare and brave type of person can admit to making a mistake that resulted in someone else's wrongful imprisonment.

This shows why we must focus, in our public debates, on fixing the system prospectively, so that mistakes no longer happen. Except for the most doctrinaire members of the law enforcement establishment, almost everyone can support the idea of reforms that will improve things going forward, especially when (as with blind lineups, for example) doing so entails relatively small costs. Pushing for prospective change, while allowing for the continued use of improved, proficiency-tested versions of the better-developed forensic techniques (e.g., fingerprint analysis and tool mark identification), creates an opportunity to overcome this incredibly strong cognitive barrier. Allowing the continued use of the better forensic techniques (e.g., fingerprint analysis) while the improvement of them commences, along with the well-established methods of DNA testing and chemical analyses, will not put most current cases in jeopardy, thus shielding police and prosecutors from an attack on their ability to make arrests and get convictions.

The reason why focusing on the future can help overcome cognitive dissonance, or at least minimize opposition based on it, is that looking to future improvement does not center on affixing blame or finding culpability for past mistakes. Instead, it allows all parties to the discussion to ask, "How do we improve things going forward? How do we ensure that, in our current and future cases, justice is done?" For law enforcement, this will allow them to participate while maintaining their unshakeable "good guys" perception of themselves. By taking a role in the reforming of the system so that it convicts the guilty and minimizes the chances of harming the innocent, they do real and permanent good, and they are not focused on the mistakes law enforcement may have made in the past. Cognitive dissonance and the resistance to reform it engenders will be likely to decrease.

This is not to say, however, that nothing should be done about mistakes made in the past. On the contrary, justice absolutely requires that the errors of prior years be identified and rectified. But those efforts should now become institutionalized—something that happens as a matter of course, within a regularized framework. That is why the idea of focusing on the future comes with one essential caveat: every prosecutor's office must create a post-conviction review unit, as discussed in Recommendation 16. It must become absolutely routine for prosecutors to review closed cases in which new evidence has come to light, or a new form of testing has become available, or in which the lies of an informant or a witness have become known years after the fact. These units have begun to sprout in some of the larger prosecutors' offices around the country that, in the past, have had significant numbers of wrongful convictions, such as Dallas and Houston (see the earlier section of this chapter on this subject, and also chapter 7). Alternatively, instead of each prosecutor's office having its own conviction review unit, a state might enact legislation establishing an innocence commission. Several states have used this model (see chapter 7 for an in-depth discussion of innocence commissions, particularly the one in North Carolina). While the operational details of these commissions vary, reviewing claims of innocence from past cases constitutes the key function. In other words, the commission must serve the same purpose as a conviction review unit: providing an institutional place and a process for the routine review of innocence claims. Conviction review units would do this for individual prosecutor's offices; innocence commissions would do it statewide.

To make sure that cases of apparent wrongful conviction come to notice, and that the conviction review units and innocence commissions do their jobs thoroughly, organizations like the Innocence Project and its affiliates in states across the country must remain engaged, adequately funded, and supported in the work they do. They have, to this point, served as *the* key mechanisms for forcing law enforcement and courts to acknowledge mistakes and to take corrective action. Even in a world in which every prosecutor's office has a post-conviction unit, there will always be personal and bureaucratic forces at work that will attempt to slow this review work down or stop it. Thus a vital and vigorous network of innocence projects across the nation will keep the conviction review units or innocence commissions focused and honest, and will help to call the right cases to their attention.

Police and Prosecutors Must Lead the Effort

To fundamentally change policing and prosecution work so that the reforms highlighted here can succeed, we will need leadership. And if we want to reform the way police interrogate suspects, conduct eyewitness iden-tifications, and conduct forensic testing, and the way prosecutors use the results of these methods, leaders of the effort must come from the ranks of police and prosecutors themselves.

The job for reformers, at this juncture, is to persuade the people *inside* law enforcement's own institutions, and those members of the legislatures and courts who, for whatever reason, remain skeptical. The only advocates who might persuade those still resisting science are those who are, themselves, part of the law enforcement establishment: police chiefs and detectives and officers and prosecutors who have come around to the need for the types of changes advocated here. Law enforcement leaders who have altered their investigative methods out of hard-won experience, who have put changes into practice without their professional reputations and outcomes suffer-ing, may be able to persuade their colleagues who are not prone to listen to outsiders.

A related example shows how this can work. Five years ago, the Vera Institute of Justice, a nonpartisan think tank in New York City focused on justice and public safety issues, launched the Prosecution and Racial Justice (P&RJ) Project.[98] The P&RJ Project aimed to construct analytical tools for prosecutors to use that would enable them to see whether or not actions of their personnel might result in racial disparities in charging decisions, plea bargaining, sentencing, or other criminal justice outcomes. Racial bias in prosecutorial decisions had been the subject of discussions for years in minority communities, where some thought that prosecuto-rial operations suffered from the same kinds of racial bias seen in some police forces. The idea behind the P&RJ Project was to give prosecutors data and rigorous analysis to find out if this was true, and methods to cor-rect the situation if racial disparity problems had taken root.[99] The leader of the project, Wayne McKenzie, was himself a long-time prosecutor in the Brooklyn District Attorney's Office. McKenzie knew that to get the initiative started and give it credibility, he had to bring in nationally prominent veteran prosecutors who would make their offices the guinea pigs for the project. And McKenzie accomplished this: he recruited E. Michael McCann of Milwaukee County, Wisconsin, Peter Gilchrist of Mecklenberg County (Charlotte), North Carolina, and Bonnie Dumanis of San Diego County, California, all of whom had both national and local reputations as strong, no-nonsense district attorneys. McKenzie said, "I definitely believe that they saw themselves as test subjects" who understood "the importance of the work locally for them in their jurisdictions" as well as nationally.[100] Only by engaging such prosecutors could he hope to take the results of the P&RJ Project to other prosecutors across the country. McKenzie's approach worked. The credibility that these three established, well-respected prosecutors brought to the project helped interest other prosecutors, who will take up these tools as time goes on. After Michael McCann retired, his successor in Milwaukee, John Chisholm, became an enthusiastic supporter of the project, testifying about it in Congress and using it as a way to reach out to segments of his community who have harbored skepticism and suspicion about his office in the past. McKenzie and Chisholm have presented the project's work together to audiences of prosecutors around the country, and Chisholm's example in particular has inspired other prosecutors in the country to consider moving toward the project's model. "I do believe John's influence was key," McKenzie says, to bringing other prosecutors along. He calls the leadership of Gilchrist, McCann, Dumanis, and especially Chisholm "completely invaluable."[101]

Fortunately, there is now a small but growing pool of police officials and prosecutors who might serve well in this role when we think about reforming traditional police methods for interrogation, eyewitness identification, and forensics. Craig Watkins and Patricia Lykos, prosecutors in Dallas and Houston, respectively, would make the right kind of spokespersons. Thomas Sullivan, an esteemed Chicago lawyer and former United States attorney for the Northern District of Illinois, knows as much about the recording of suspect statements by police as anyone anywhere, and his writing shows his willingness to take a public stand on the issue. Police and prosecutors in Minnesota, such as former Hennepin County prosecutor and now U.S. senator Amy Klobuchar, have spoken about their experiences with recording interrogations. These people are only the most prominent examples; many others who have experience with these reforms might join the cause.

Reformers: Find Allies on the Right, Not Only on the Left

When we look at some of the successful efforts to reform traditional police methods and the use of forensic tools (see chapter 7), an important implication of the idea of putting police and prosecutors in the lead of the effort becomes clear. Reformers who wish to bring about change in the criminal justice system often seek out allies and kindred spirits on the Left. These people are likely to share with reform advocates the horror at wrongful convictions, and may already support many of the changes that reformers want. This is all well and good, but inadequate. Reformers must try to create alliances with police, prosecutors, and political actors on the Right. These people also share the abhorrence of injustice and can often be persuaded to join efforts to fix the system. Their motives may be different; for example, they may be more concerned about the integrity of the criminal justice system from the viewpoint of preserving the power to convict, rather than the damage done to the wrongfully convicted. No matter. They can still be strong allies, whatever their underlying motivations. More importantly, they are often less afraid than those on the Left of having foes label them "soft on crime." Since they have been part of or supported law enforcement and tough anticrime measures in the past, they have the political room and security to move toward reform. Thinking of the Cold War era, people often observe that perhaps only a staunch anti-Communist, such as Richard Nixon, could have begun the process of normalizing relations with the People's Republic of China. A Democratic, liberal president would have been too afraid of having opponents call him soft on communism. In the same way, allies on the Right can more easily move toward criminal justice reform than those on the Left.

An excellent example of this comes from Ohio. In 2010, Ohio passed legislation designed to address some of the shortcomings in police investigation and other issues uncovered by DNA exonerations.[102] The primary moving force behind the legislative effort that resulted in the new law was the University of Cincinnati College of Law's Ohio Innocence Project, led by Professor Mark Godsey. Godsey and his colleagues worked hard over a period of six years to bring the effort to change the law to a successful conclusion, but they could not have done this alone. They had a number of allies, both inside and outside the state legislature, but the most important was state senator Bill Seitz, a conservative Republican from the Cincinnati area. Godsey and his staff worked with Senator Seitz from the beginning of their efforts, and labored hard to demonstrate to him that their mission, if viewed objectively, was not a "liberal" cause but one that any fair-minded person could support.

This approach was consistent with the way the Ohio Innocence Project portrayed itself across the state. The project was careful to stick to its core mission—getting innocent people out of prison—something that Democrats and Republicans alike could support. The Ohio Innocence Project steered clear of advocacy on the death penalty and other issues that might antagonize people on the Right. Through time, with this strategy, the project gathered many important supporters on the Right, including Seitz and Attorney General Jim Petro, who also became very important to the passage of the bill. Godsey says that Seitz was the one person most responsible for assuring that the votes were there among the Republicans who joined with Democrats to pass the law. Godsey is emphatic: he says that to get significant criminal justice changes enacted into law, reformers must work with conservatives, who must take the leading roles in getting this done. The issue is, at bottom, the integrity of the system.

Money: Attaching Strings to Department of Justice Grants to Police Departments

Whatever else we wish to do to persuade people in police departments and prosecutors' offices of the importance and the necessity of the types of reform described here, reformers cannot afford to ignore one powerful tool: money. Every year, the federal government provides considerable resources to state and local police departments for a variety of purposes. Making this aid contingent on the acceptance of science-based improvements in the way that police investigate cases would give new leverage to reform efforts.

Unlike other countries, the United States has a completely decentralized law enforcement system. The U.S. Department of Justice runs the entire federal law enforcement system: the ninety-three U.S. attorneys offices around the nation that prosecute federal criminal cases; the FBI; the Drug Enforcement Administration; the Bureau of Alcohol, Tobacco, Firearms, and Explosives; and a host of other agencies. All of this federal bureaucracy gets its funding from the federal budget. But the Department of Justice has no supervisory role over nonfederal criminal justice agencies in the states, counties, towns, and cities. Every state and local police force, every county sheriff's office, and every township constable's office exists independently of the federal government and its authority. State and local law governs these agencies. The federal government cannot dictate policy or practice to these agencies, except to insist when necessary that they follow federal constitutional and civil rights laws. When the federal government does anything more, it oversteps its bounds.[103]

All of this is a customary part of our federal system, in which the federal, state, and local governments play different roles. But this does not mean that the federal government has no way to influence what goes on in the states. On the contrary, its ability to make itself heard and its will felt lies with another aspect of federal clout: the power of the purse. The federal government has, for years, given state and local governments funds for various purposes: everything from building and maintaining highways and transportation systems to performing law enforcement duties. And over the years, federal agencies have used this money to accomplish a variety of policy objectives in the states: everything from imposing a 55-mile-per-hour maximum speed limit[104] to forcing states to enact the minimum age of twenty-one for alcohol consumption.[105]

The federal government could help attain many of the reforms discussed here by conditioning receipt of federal aid to state and local law enforcement on the accomplishment of the goals outlined in this chapter. The formula need not differ from that used in past years to get states to change: if you want federal funds, you must comply with federal standards, or at least make demonstrated progress toward them. No state or town or city need comply, but if they do not, they would lose the opportunity to receive federal funding. And in times of ever leaner state and municipal budgets, any agency will think hard before throwing away the opportunity to get money.

Just how much money, and therefore how much leverage, would this involve? One of the main sources of federal money for state and local police departments involves COPS grants, which originate in the Department of Justice's Office of Community Oriented Policing Services. COPS grants support the addition of new officers to police departments, help pay for technology, and support other vital resources. According to Justice Department figures, a huge amount of money has reached state and local police departments in the form of COPS grants. In 2005, more than $315 million went to over eight hundred different grantees in every state; the vast majority of these agencies were police departments (a small number were other kinds of agencies with missions related to law enforcement), and these included a considerable number of the largest police departments in the country. These departments serve millions of Americans, both in big cities such as Dallas, Phoenix, Houston, Cincinnati, Atlanta, Boston, Memphis, and St. Paul, and in innumerable small towns. Subsequent years show a similar pattern. In 2006, more than $207 million in COPS grants went to 830 agencies: in 2007, $245 million went to 545 agencies. In 2009 and 2010, COPS funding reached a high point, with grants going to 2,000 (2009) and 1,300 (2010) agencies;

$1.263 billion was distributed in 2009, and $576 million in 2010. All in all, from the 2005 through the 2010 fiscal years, COPS awarded over six thousand grants worth a total of almost $3 billion.[106] Thus conditioning receipt of these funds on compliance with the reforms advocated here would give efforts aimed at change substantial leverage, and a much greater chance at success in departments that might otherwise ignore or resist calls for better practices.

Preserve Evidence

Over the past twenty years, DNA has accounted for over 250 exonerations. Whatever other facts these cases share, one commonality stands out: the presence of testable evidence. Without this evidence, no DNA testing can take place. Thus, when we hear that DNA testing has upended a case decided long ago, we know that the authorities preserved the evidence in the case for many years after the verdict, even though there may have been no reason to do so at the time; DNA testing may not have even existed when the courts heard the original case.

The preservation of evidence in these cases has followed no set pattern. Some jurisdictions preserved evidence, while others did not. Some even routinely destroyed or discarded evidence at some point after the legal proceedings in cases that had reached their final stages. Some states now have laws that require the evidence preservation; other states do not. In 1988, the Supreme Court ruled that the Constitution does not require the states to have laws mandating the preservation of evidence.[107] States may choose to do so, because they view it as fair or just or good practice. But the Constitution does not require that they do it.

The DNA revolution in criminal justice shows us that systematic failure or refusal to preserve evidence, even if constitutional, violates every rule of common sense. Nevertheless, the Supreme Court has not taken any opportunity to change this rule. If a technology like DNA can appear on the scene and absolutely transform what we can do with even the most minute amounts of evidence, we must surely see that even better technology could emerge sometime in the future. Evidence we might have no way to test now could turn out to hold the key to the truth in a few years. Thus failure to preserve evidence may not offend the Bill of Rights in the eyes of the Supreme Court, but it cannot stand in a system of criminal law concerned with finding the truth and doing justice. Every state must have an evidence preservation law; it is nothing less than a moral imperative.

The Courts and the Defense Bar: Make Daubert
Meaningful in Criminal Cases

One of the most important influences on forensic testing and scientific evidence is the legal standard courts use to decide whether to admit such evidence. This subject has grown increasingly important and visible over the last decade and a half. As explained earlier in this chapter, since the 1920s, courts assessing scientific or technical evidence decided whether or not to admit it using the *Frye* rule,[108] named for the case in which the court refused to allow the admission of the then-new lie detector machine. Under the *Frye* rule, courts would admit "testimony deduced from a well-recognized scientific principle or discovery," but only if the principle was "sufficiently established to have gained general acceptance in the particular field in which it belongs."[109] The lie detector, a forerunner of the polygraph, had not reached this point of general acceptance, and therefore could not be admitted.

The *Frye* rule remained the governing standard for admission of all scientific evidence for decades. In 1975, the Congress created the Federal Rules of Evidence,[110] a codification of evidence law that would govern the use of all evidence in federal courts. Among the new rules, Rule 702 governed the admission of expert testimony on scientific matters.[111] Despite the fact that Rule 702 said nothing about *Frye*, the *Frye* rule continued to govern the admissibility of scientific and technical evidence.

This changed dramatically in 1993, with the Supreme Court's decision in *Daubert v. Merrell Dow Pharmaceuticals, Inc.*[112] The *Daubert* case marked a sea change in the way federal courts would handle evidence involving expert testimony to explain scientific or technical matters. Nothing in Rule 702, the Court said, had anything to do with the old *Frye* "general acceptability" standard. Rather, Rule 702 emphasized evidentiary reliability. Writing for the Court, Justice Harry Blackmun said that the scientific methodology an expert witness uses must rest on "inference[s] or assertion[s] . . . derived by the scientific method." The methodology must come from a "body of known facts or [from] any body of ideas inferred from such facts or accepted as truth on good grounds." Thus, he said, "the requirement [in Rule 702] that an expert's testimony pertain to 'scientific knowledge' establishes a standard of evidentiary reliability."[113] Thus the *Daubert* case spelled out a reasonably detailed way in which courts should henceforth evaluate scientific and other evidence proffered to them by experts. No longer would courts allow juries to consider scientific evidence just because it had come from a method that experts in the field accepted. Rather, the evidence had to possess scientific reliability. From *Daubert* forward, it seemed, trial court judges would have a crucial role in passing judgment on scientific evidence. Judges would not just take the word of experts about their own expertise. Judges would, instead, serve as gatekeepers, charged with keeping unsubstantiated scientific evidence out of court.

The Supreme Court sharpened these points in two cases just a few years later. In *Khumo Tire Company v. Carmichael*,[114] the Court fleshed out its intentions for the role of trial judges vis-à-vis scientific evidence under *Daubert*. Reemphasizing the gatekeeper idea, the justices said that trial judges serve as sentinels, guarding the court and the jury from "junk science." Moreover, the gatekeeper role extended to all expert testimony, not only the testimony of scientists—for example, technicians skilled in the mechanics of failed machine parts, or persons with years of experience in reading street gang graffiti.[115] And in *General Electric Company v. Joiner*,[116] the Supreme Court made clear that trial judges would have wide discretion to make decisions about the admissibility of scientific evidence that litigants brought before them. Appeals courts should only overturn trial courts' decisions on the admissibility of scientific evidence, the justices said, when the trial court had abused its discretion[117]—making these gatekeeper decisions by judges very tough to reverse.

Daubert, *Khumo Tire*, and *Joiner* seemed to promise nothing less than a revolution in the use of scientific evidence in court. And although Rule 702, *Daubert*, and the cases that followed it came from the federal system, the Federal Rules of Evidence have always proven enormously influential in the states, inspiring almost all jurisdictions to adopt them whole or copy them closely, including these new expert evidence rules. Just as important, Rule 702 and *Daubert* applied equally to civil and criminal matters. Though *Daubert*, *Khumo Tire*, and *Joiner* all arose from civil disputes, nothing about those opinions or Rule 702 limited the application of the new standards to civil cases. Given all of this, one might have predicted that within a decade of the *Daubert* decision, the admission of evidence based on sloppy, groundless, and unsubstantiated pseudoscience would have ceased, or at least become much less common. Disciplines like fingerprint analysis and identification of firearms, which at least had some loose protocols, would need to develop data-based foundations for the judgments of examiners, and put into effect standard procedures to guard against human bias. Forensic disciplines with no real foundations, such as bite mark analysis, would be likely to fall into disuse entirely. All in all, forensic practices would have to come into compliance with scientific standards, as *Daubert* seemed to command.

Unfortunately, none of this has happened. Instead, courts have applied the *Daubert* rule in some curious ways. Courts in civil cases have become more skeptical of scientific evidence, and willing to exclude it, at least when offered by plaintiffs. But courts seem to "employ Daubert more lackadaisically in criminal trials—especially in regard to prosecution evidence"—than they do in civil cases.[118] In criminal cases, most of the expert evidence is offered by the government, in its effort to prove guilt; defendants rarely offer this kind of evidence.[119] According to Professor Michael Risinger, Daubert-type challenges by defendants in criminal cases rarely succeed—only 10 percent of the time. But prosecution challenges to expert evidence offered by the defense succeed two-thirds of the time.[120] Risinger says, correctly, that "none of this goes to the validity of any given decision," but these results "are still fairly striking in their own right."[121] Other researchers have come to similar conclusions, noting that "even a casual glance at many courts' treatment of prosecution experts, from police officers to bitemark identification, suggests a leniency applied to the state"[122] in criminal matters, which would systematically disadvantage defendants. Peter Neufeld, who with Barry Scheck established the Innocence Project and conducted many DNA-based challenges, says that "whereas civil defendants prevail in their Daubert challenges, most of the time criminal defendants almost always lost their challenges to [prosecution evidence]. But when the prosecutor challenges a criminal defendant's expert evidence, the evidence is almost always kept out of the trial."[123]

Two things must happen. First, judges must take Daubert seriously in criminal cases. Nothing in Rule 702 or Daubert or the cases that followed it made any distinction between civil and criminal cases; it must apply with the same vigor to both types of matters. It is impossible to conceive of a reasonable rationale for energetically applying Rule 702 and Daubert to civil matters, usually to the benefit of defendants seeking to protect themselves against damage awards, but not to criminal matters, where the scientific evidence offered by the prosecution may play the major role in sending a defendant to prison. Judges in criminal cases may feel they cannot apply a rigorous standard to common forensic practices such as fingerprinting, if this might cause them to have to exclude that evidence or limit its applicability. A few lonely judges have done this, following Daubert properly to its logical and legal conclusion. For example, in State v. Rose, a Maryland judge ruled that, given the existing science, the ACE-V method for evaluation of latent fingerprints (see chapter 2) did not rest on a reliable factual foundation. Therefore, the fingerprint examiner in the case could not testify that the latent fingerprint found at the scene of the crime matched the defendant.[124] But few judges, it seems, will do anything like this. Instead, most simply quote the opinion of the expert that the method used is valid—hardly a surprise—and then ground their decisions upon cases in which other judges have decided the same way on the same circular basis.[125] Proponents of shaky forensic methods such as bite mark analysis insist that the fact that judges, in previous cases, have accepted these techniques somehow validates them; through vigorous cross-examination, they argue, the science underlying these methods undergoes the toughest kind of close scrutiny, something akin to the peer review process. But this assertion has no basis. In fact, expert testimony about scientific evidence rarely encounters any rigorous challenge. Examining the most well-known cases of forensic science fraud, incompetence, and misfeasance going back to the mid-1980s, Peter Neufeld shows that not a single one came to light because of aggressive adversarial legal investigation and cross-examination at trial. The idea that the courtroom can serve as a kind of "crucible" in which the truth will out on questions of forensic science simply does not square with the evidence.[126] Judges, therefore, must shoulder the burden by confronting scientific evidence in criminal cases at least as vigorously as they do scientific evidence in civil cases.

The second thing that must happen involves other actors in the system: criminal defense lawyers. If judges have failed to act as the gatekeepers that *Daubert* demands they be, defense counsel have done little to hold judges' feet to the fire. While judges now have the authority to exclude evidence as unreliable, this will only happen in our adversary system when defense lawyers put motions to exclude before the courts. And criminal defense lawyers have not done the job of bringing these challenges forward. Neufeld points out that in the first seven years following *Daubert*, defense counsel challenged prosecution experts in only 211 reported cases.[127] From August of 1999 through August of 2000, Neufeld says that only fifty reported challenges to admissibility under *Daubert* took place in state criminal cases; to get a sense of comparison, in 2000, the states accounted for fifteen million criminal cases.[128] The lack of challenges by the defense may not come from pure laziness, though that is surely sometimes true; it may also be simple habit ("these things never work, so no one does them, so I'm not going to bother"), lack of resources, or lack of understanding of the basic principles of science and the methods forensic practitioners use. Whatever the reason, this must change.

The Big Picture

As we began this chapter, we had a clear idea of the problem of law enforcement's resistance to science (chapter 2) and law enforcement's explanations for this (chapter 3). We also knew the real reasons for this resistance. They included cognitive barriers, such as cognitive dissonance, threats to status, and endowment and wealth effects (chapter 4), as well as institutional and political barriers, such as the imperatives of arrest and conviction and the desire for political advancement (chapter 5).

This chapter brought us to solutions. What must be done to right the system? And how can we make these things happen? On the question of what should be done, the approach was modest: not how to fix every problem, but rather what must be done now, to move forward toward a better system. Sixteen recommendations covered eyewitness identification (e.g., use blind lineups, take confidence statements before giving feedback), interrogation (e.g., conduct electronic recording, limit interrogations time, limit deception), and forensic science (e.g., require proficiency testing, eliminate human biases). We then took an equally pragmatic view of how to accomplish these goals: making law enforcement the leaders of reform, focusing on the future, establishing post-conviction units, and working with leaders on the political Right, for example.

All of this describes an agenda that, while pragmatic and modest, still makes one wonder: Can this be done? The answer is yes. Chapter 7 will tell the stories of how these changes have been accomplished in some places, and the men and women who have led these efforts.

7

Reasons for Hope

Examples of Real Change

Having come this far, we know the problem is real, and solutions are within reach. Not every law enforcement agency and prosecutor's office has resisted better methods. While still relatively few, a growing number have decided to make changes to their basic procedures to bring them into line with the best current science. Most of these agencies have adopted reforms governing a single category of problems: eyewitness identifications or suspect interrogations, for example. Others have been more ambitious. In some cases, these agencies have initiated changes themselves; at other times, another government authority—a state legislature or a court—has forced these changes on them. The origins of these changes matter; sometimes a disaster brings change in its wake, but in other instances it may come from another source. Most important, we need to see that some of the leaders in policing and prosecution have made choices and taken positions different from the majority of their colleagues, and have gained by doing so. Their stories have great value, and can serve as examples with which to lead others in their professions. When others see that they can move toward best practices without the sky falling, and without arrests and convictions disappearing, law enforcement as a whole may begin to take a different view toward science.

Over the last five to six years, the examples discussed in this chapter have begun to seem less like one-off anomalies and more like the beginnings of a sustainable trend. Among them: the creation of conviction review units in prosecutors' offices in Dallas and Houston; the adoption of eyewitness reforms in New Jersey and elsewhere; the creation of a permanent innocence commission in North Carolina to handle claims of innocence; and the spread of requirements to record interrogations to a growing number of jurisdictions. Together, these developments tell us that moving police work and prosecution in the direction that science points can happen. And when it does, this will benefit not only innocent persons saved from illegitimate convictions but also those police and prosecutors who now continue to resist.

Innocence Commissions
Types, Necessity, and Efforts

As the controversies over DNA-based exonerations began to bubble up in state after state over the last two decades, demands for action sometimes resulted in the appointment of committees to address and sort out the issues. Some of these bodies, though perhaps appointed as a way to stave off a crisis, did impressive work and produced worthwhile guidance for governors, state legislatures, and others to follow. In Illinois, Governor George Ryan appointed the Governor's Commission on Capital Punishment in 2000.[1] Ryan appointed the commission in the aftermath of thirteen exonerations of men from death row; all of these exonerations occurred during the same period in which the state executed twelve men. The commission worked on systemic problems in the Illinois criminal justice system for two years. In 2002, it issued a report containing eighty-five recommendations for reform of eyewitness identification practices, recording of interrogations, the use of jailhouse snitches, and evidence produced through forensic science.[2] Some of the reforms recommended by the governor's commission have found their way into Illinois law. The state legislature has enacted requirements for recording police interrogation in some homicide cases,[3] required a pilot study of changes in eyewitness identification procedures,[4] prescribed rules for disclosure to the defense of investigatory materials and exculpatory evidence,[5] and created rules for the use of informant testimony.[6] The state senate in California created the California Commission on the Fair Administration of Justice in 2004, with the same purpose as the governor's commission in Illinois: examining the system as a whole in order to make recommendations for reforms needed to assure justice and prevent wrongful convictions.[7] The California commission issued reports and made recommendations, and some of these recommendations—requirements for electronic recording of interrogations of suspects in homicides and other serious felony cases, guidelines for the use of photo lineups, and corroboration requirements for jailhouse informants—were enacted by the legislature.[8] Governor Schwarzenegger vetoed all of them when law enforcement opposition arose.[9] In Virginia, a group of "lawyers, academicians, and activists" formed a commission of their own to study wrongful convictions in the state and to make recommendations to avoid them in the future. The group, called the Innocence Commission of Virginia, had no state support; rather, it subsisted on pro bono contributions from law firms and work contributed by three law schools. Nevertheless, it produced a comprehensive report that summarized known wrongful convictions and discussed their causes, and it suggested reforms that would address issues such as eyewitness identification, interrogation tactics, and forensics, among others.[10] These commissions represent one type of innocence commission: a body created to examine a state's criminal justice apparatus or police procedure as a whole, with the aim of making recommendations to policy makers for changes designed to avoid miscarriages of justice and conviction of the innocent. Their beginnings have differed, and their tasks have varied in scope and complexity. All have in common the idea of spotting the flaws in the entirety of the criminal justice system and proposing solutions, rather than examining individual cases.

These types of innocence commissions serve an essential purpose. Examining the big picture in order to see where major criminal justice errors may originate, and making recommendations that will correct the system going forward, could not be more important. Two decades and more into the DNA revolution, because of the hundreds of wrongful convictions uncovered, we see a set of recurring, systemic difficulties. Such problems demand wide-ranging investigation and general solutions.

The North Carolina Innocence Inquiry Commission

But another type of innocence commission has emerged from the DNA era as well. This type of commission focuses not on systemic improvements generally but on hearing claims of actual innocence by individuals who have no legal avenue to be heard in courts. At this writing, one such commission exists: the North Carolina Innocence Inquiry Commission (NCIIC). It is a model worth examining, and imitating. And the story of how the NCIIC came into existence teaches us a number of important lessons: about the types of innocence commissions (big-picture systemic-problems commissions versus those that hear claims of innocence in individual cases), about what motivates change, and about the importance of the right leadership on the issues if we hope to see real reform.

Like other states, North Carolina has had a number of high-profile miscarriages of justice in which innocent men went to jail for considerable lengths of time for crimes they did not commit.[11] Ronald Cotton of Burlington, North Carolina, served eleven years for two rapes; DNA testing resulted in his release in 1995.[12] Lesly Jean of Jacksonville, North Carolina, went to prison for nine years for rape and sexual assault; DNA evidence also cleared him.[13] Terence Garner served four years for an armed robbery and shooting in Johnston County, North Carolina; the emergence of three alibi witnesses and the confession of another man upended his case, and the district attorney dismissed all charges against him.[14] Leo Waters served twenty-one years in prison for rape and sexual assault; DNA cleared him.[15] Alan Gell served nine years for murder, but a jury acquitted him in a retrial based on new evidence.[16] There were others exonerated, too. Other states have had as many or more problem cases as North Carolina has, but the reaction to the accumulation of these injustices in North Carolina differed in one crucial respect. During the time when these cases became known in the state, I. Beverly Lake served on the North Carolina Supreme Court.[17] Lake was already a well-known figure in the state's legal and political world when he became chief justice in 2001; he had served seven years as an associate justice on the Supreme Court and had been a superior court judge, a two-term state senator, and the governor's legislative liaison. He recalls that the release of wrongfully convicted men in North Carolina after they had served long prison terms made a strong impression on him for two reasons beyond the sheer injustice of innocent men spending time in prison. First, Lake had always had a strong interest in preserving the public's trust in the integrity of the judicial system, and as chief justice he made it a priority. Any time a person is exonerated after a long prison term, Lake says, "that certainly damages the public's trust and confidence in the reliability and integrity" of the process.[18] Second, it happened that, during this same period of time, Chief Justice Lake had a law clerk named Christine Mumma. Mumma had taken a keen interest in wrongful conviction cases; in fact, she represented Dwayne Dale, one of the exonerated men.[19] Mumma therefore knew the issues, and had become well versed in the causes of these miscarriages of justice. The mutual interest of Chief Justice Lake and Christine Mumma in the reasons for wrongful convictions, and in ways to fix the criminal justice system, created a powerful partnership. Mumma says that Chief Justice Lake felt able to act on the issue "because he trusted me" to make sure that he had all the right information and understood the issues.[20] And Chief Justice Lake was the kind of leader who could bring all the people that counted to the table to make things happen. Mumma calls their teaming up on the issue "a unique combination."[21] Mumma worked on her own time on individual cases of innocence, but Chief Justice Lake came at the issue of wrongful convictions from a different perspective. He describes himself as a "staunch conservative" and a law-and-order judge; no less a conservative icon than Senator Jesse Helms had talked him into leaving the Democratic Party and joining the Republicans.[22] Lake remains a strong supporter of the death penalty;[23] Christine Mumma recalls that, as a state senator, Lake "brought the death penalty back to North Carolina" in new legislation after the U.S. Supreme Court found the old law unconstitutional in the 1970s.[24] Chief Justice Lake might have seemed an unlikely reformer. But his background as a tough-on-crime conservative, combined with his strong political skills, enabled him to engage and convince the right people of the need for change. Mark Rabil, the codirector of the Innocence and Justice Clinic at Wake Forest University School of Law and the attorney for exonerated defendant Darryl Hunt, says that North Carolina now has the mechanisms to guard against wrongful convictions precisely because Chief Justice Lake brought people from all over the political spectrum together around the common idea of the integrity of the system.[25] Real, lasting reform, Rabil says, only happens "when you bring both sides of the aisle together" with "leadership from the conservatives," not just from reformers on the Left. The changes in North Carolina would not have happened without Chief Justice Lake's "direct involvement," along with his work with Christine Mumma.[26]

Chief Justice Lake's first action was the creation a study commission called the North Carolina Actual Innocence Commission (NCAIC) in 2002.[27] The chief justice anticipated considerable resistance to the commission "from the establishment" in his state. He knew that creating the commission would represent a real political risk for him if he ever wished to run for another office, but given his concerns about damage to the integrity of the system and the public's confidence in it, his own political future "seemed to be a relatively small matter."[28] Lake's prediction proved correct: resistance to his efforts quickly materialized. Former supporters questioned his law-and-order bona fides, and many wondered whether he had changed his conservative philosophy. Some of his former supporters felt that digging into the question of wrongful convictions would actually undercut the public's faith in the system.[29] Lake asked more than two dozen prominent actors in the state's criminal justice system—prosecutors, defense attorneys, judges, professors, and many others—to join the commission. In his letter to prospective members, Lake recalls that he said that "in my very strong opinion, we have the very best criminal justice system in the world, but it [is] not perfect and [is] subject to mistakes like any other endeavor created by man." Since the system was not perfect, it was "incumbent on us to try to improve it in any way that we could, to strengthen it."[30] With the NCAIC, Chief Justice Lake did not attempt to examine the facts of individual cases but instead looked at the big picture: what systemic factors caused these miscarriages of justice, and how could the flaws in the system be addressed? In that respect, the NCAIC resembled the Illinois governor's commission. The NCAIC's recommendations, he hoped, would make the conviction of the innocent less likely, strengthen the state's criminal justice system, and restore the public's faith in the system.[31] He appointed Christine Mumma, still serving as his law clerk, executive director of the commission, and the work began. Mumma remembers that the group established two ground rules early on. First, the commission would not discuss or investigate individual cases with an eye to fixing blame; cases would serve only as examples for study, with an eye toward remedying overall problems. Second, there would be no discussion of the death penalty, because members of the commission held very strong and deeply divergent opinions on capital punishment. Attempting to address the death penalty would not only sidetrack the commission but perhaps derail it permanently.[32]

The NCAIC began by studying the problems with eyewitness identification; after two years of study, it made recommendations to reform those procedures,[33] and its recommendations eventually became law. These reforms on eyewitness testimony would constitute a huge achievement, standing alone, but the NCAIC then moved to another problem: the inability of convicted defendants now claiming that they were in fact innocent to have their claims heard in court. Both Chief Justice Lake and Christine Mumma understood the problem: the court system, as traditionally structured, provides no real avenue for the wrongfully convicted to argue their innocence. Once the trial, appeals, and other post-trial proceedings have run their course, Mumma says, "innocence was really off the table" and could not be considered in any existing legal forum.[34] After considerable study of the issue, the members of the NCAIC agreed "that neither the appellate nor adversarial process is conducive to post-conviction claims of innocence."[35] In other words, those already convicted of crimes but who now say they have evidence creating plausible claims of innocence had no opportunity to have these claims addressed. As in all other states, appeals of guilty verdicts in North Carolina consider only legal issues; facts are almost always considered settled after trial. Federal courts only rarely grant habeas corpus petitions for actual innocence, because they use a very high standard that usually proves impossible to meet.[36] In *Herrera v. Collins*,[37] the U.S. Supreme Court declared that actual innocence, in itself, does not constitute an adequate legal basis for federal courts to grant relief; in other words, the Constitution created no right to have a claim of actual innocence heard after a conviction.[38] Thus a person who obtains evidence of his innocence after conviction might have no venue in which to ask for relief, and the U.S. Constitution does not obligate any court to hear such a claim. Therefore, with all of the usual doors of the legal system shut tight, the NCAIC drafted a proposal that would create a permanent body under North Carolina law to review actual innocence claims.[39] The NCAIC modeled the proposal on a similar body in the United Kingdom, called the Criminal Cases Review Commission.[40] The NCAIC sent the proposal to the North Carolina General Assembly, and that body passed the law; the state's governor signed it in August 2006, creating the nation's first innocence commission designed to hear individual claims of actual innocence: the North Carolina Innocence Inquiry Commission (NCIIC).[41]

The NCIIC has one purpose: the review of individual claims of actual, fact-based innocence ("I did not commit the crime"); it does not review legal claims (e.g., an argument that the judge made a mistake when she ruled on a point of evidence).[42] The NCIIC's staff begins the process by doing a preliminary screening of all of the claims it receives, filtering out those based on alleged legal errors and any that lack credibility.[43] The defendant making the claim must assert his or her complete innocence; he cannot claim a reduced level of responsibility for the crime.[44] "I didn't commit murder, because it was only manslaughter" would not fly. The defendant must also present credible, verifiable evidence of innocence that no court has seen before in a previous hearing.[45] Further, the defendant must sign a waiver of all procedural safeguards and privileges, agree to cooperate with NCIIC, and agree to provide full disclosure to all inquiries by NCIIC.[46] If the NCIIC investigation uncovers any evidence of criminal activity by the defendant related to the offense for which the defendant claims innocence, NCIIC will send the evidence to the prosecution.[47] With the preliminary screening complete and these promises by the defendant in place, the NCIIC will undertake a full investigation. The statute that created NCIIC and the promises of the defendant to NCIIC entitle it to full disclosure from both the prosecution team and the defense lawyers involved in the defendant's original case, and the NCIIC can use subpoenas to compel attendance of witnesses and the presentation of evidence it wants.[48] Once the NCIIC completes the investigation, the members vote on whether "there is sufficient evidence of factual innocence to merit judicial review."[49] If five of the eight members vote yes, the NCIIC refers the case to a three-judge panel appointed by the state's chief justice; the panel cannot include any trial judge with substantial prior involvement in the case.[50] The panel holds a hearing on the evidence and then decides "whether the [defendant] has proved by clear and convincing evidence that the [defendant] is innocent of the charges."[51] A unanimous vote of yes means that the panel dismisses the charges against the defendant.[52]

Some might imagine that the NCIIC would open a floodgate through which hundreds of previously convicted felons could escape, but the data do not support this belief. As of May 2010, the NCIIC has reviewed over 650 cases.[53] It has rejected the vast majority. Five hundred and thirty-two cases have not made the cut because they concerned only legal issues, contained no new evidence or only partial evidence of innocence, or had no reliable evidence.[54] The NCIIC has sent only three cases to a formal hearing before a panel of judges, and only one of them resulted in an exoneration.[55]

Texas: Conviction Integrity Units in Dallas and Houston

Few states approach the number of miscarriages of justice seen in Texas. As of December 2010, Texas had had forty wrongful conviction cases;[56] Dallas alone produced more wrongful convictions than any *state* except New York, Illinois, and Texas itself.[57] For decades, the District Attorney's Office of Dallas County had a reputation as one of the toughest prosecution offices in the country, regularly churning out death sentences and unimaginably long prison terms. Thus it may seem surprising to find one of the most promising models of reform emerging from Dallas. But the reason this has happened in Dallas has everything to do with that hard-nosed, lock-'em-up history.

To understand the Dallas County DA's office and its culture, begin with one man: Henry Wade. Wade cut a legendary figure in Dallas, presiding over the DA's office from 1951 until his retirement in 1987. The Wade years virtually defined the idea of strict law and order prosecution.[58] Under Wade, each prosecutor's trial record defined his or her professional standing. "A major consideration for promotion was the trial stats: the number of trials you had, and your win-loss record," said Royce West, a former prosecutor under Wade who went on to serve in the state senate.[59] Some call this "the Henry Wade mentality: convictions at all costs."[60] Anne Wetherholt, who worked in Wade's office beginning in 1981, told the *Dallas Morning News* that winning cases played a huge role for prosecutors under Wade.[61] The DA's office also discriminated against minorities in jury selection during this time; its office manual told prosecutors, "Do not takes Jews, Negroes, Dagos, Mexicans, or a member of any minority race on a jury."[62]

Into this world in 2006 came an outsider: Craig Watkins, a South Dallas lawyer who was not part of the city's legal power structure. Watkins has upended much of the prevailing culture in the Dallas DA's office, and with it some convictions of innocent men. Watkins had an early passion to become a lawyer. Twice he applied for a job as a prosecutor with the Dallas DA's office; both times, he did not get the job. He worked at the public defender's office, and later, when he set up his private practice, he chose to do so not in the tony North Dallas office towers most establishment lawyers favored but in predominantly black South Dallas. Doing this made him stand out, and allowed him to build a political base in the community. In 2002, he mounted an upstart campaign for district attorney, and to widespread surprise came within ten thousand votes of winning against one of Henry Wade's protégées. In the next election, Watkins ran against another former Wade staffer, and won. He became the first African American ever to hold the office in any county in Texas.

Given Watkins's background as a legal outsider and an African American deeply enmeshed in Dallas's black community, Watkins seemed likely to do some things differently than his predecessors. By the time Watkins took the oath of office, ten exonerations of wrongfully convicted defendants had already taken place, and confidence in the DA's office and the criminal justice system had suffered. Given DNA cases already in the pipeline for review at that point, more exonerations and further blows to public confidence were likely to follow. Watkins moved boldly to confront this set of problems, and to get ahead of them. At the suggestion of his chief of staff, Terri Moore (herself an experienced prosecutor from the Tarrant County, Texas, district attorney's office and the United States Attorney's Office), Watkins established a Conviction Integrity Unit, dedicated to the review of claims of wrongful convictions through DNA testing and other methods. This promised to create a very direct confrontation with the DA office's former convictions-at-any-cost culture, and to unsettle the status quo in a big way. It has done both—and at the same time, served as a national model for how prosecutors might tackle the problems highlighted in this book in an open, straightforward way.

The Conviction Integrity Unit (CIU) works just like any other unit within the Dallas DA's office; it has a leader and a small number of staff members. But instead of pursuing active charges against a particular type of crime, it looks at cases in which doubts have arisen about a conviction already obtained, and so the focus shifts from present cases to past convictions in light of new evidence. The CIU also works hand in hand with the Innocence

Project of Texas, a nonprofit organization with its own small staff, board of directors, and volunteers, which helps screen the cases of the many persons asserting their innocence in Texas. This partnership with the Innocence Project illustrates the magnitude of the change in attitude since the Wade era. Texas criminal defense attorney Gary Udashen, who has represented men convicted in Texas and later found innocent, says that in the past in Dallas, like the rest of Texas, if the DA obtained a conviction, the office defended it even when strong scientific evidence came to light that seemed to prove the defendant's innocence. Udashen says that Watkins and his partnership with the Innocence Project have taken "a completely different approach," cooperating with the Innocence Project and giving it any records, materials, or access needed for a thorough review. This kind of "active involvement in proving people innocent is something I've never seen a district attorney do before."[63]

Since 2001, some inmates in Texas have had the right to petition for DNA testing in their cases after their convictions,[64] but district attorneys, including those in Dallas, usually opposed these requests. With the new CIU in place, the Dallas DA's office under Watkins began to examine these requests more carefully, and even to reexamine some requests that Watkins's predecessor had opposed. Watkins's efforts to reexamine old cases then found traction in an unexpected way. For years, Dallas County had contracted with a private company to do its forensic testing. Contrary to the practice of most public forensic laboratories that handled the bulk of this scientific activity in Texas (and elsewhere), the private laboratory used by Dallas County preserved all of the biological samples it tested.[65] Thus unlike most jurisdictions in Texas, Dallas "has a treasure trove of potentially exonerating evidence" available for testing.[66] This has proven unimaginably lucky for some wrongfully convicted persons, who would no doubt still remain in prison if not for this strange twist of fate.

The results of the CIU reviews have upset some in Dallas's legal community, to say the least. Since Watkins became DA, thirteen people have had their innocence proven through DNA testing. In total, twenty wrongful convictions in Dallas County have been thrown out. At the beginning of 2011, hundreds of cases remained under review. The CIU reviews claims of innocence in cases with and without DNA; the latter are more difficult to sort out, but get the same treatment as the others.[67]

But the CIU's efforts have produced another effect, something too often unnoticed and 180 degrees different from the exonerations of the innocent. The CIU's work has *confirmed* the guilt of twenty-one defendants who have undergone DNA testing.[68] In four other cases, DNA tests have done even more: they have both exonerated the wrongfully convicted and identified the actual perpetrators.[69] Thus the CIU has contributed directly to a restoration of the credibility of the system. Watkins's efforts have not turned out to focus only on the mistakes of the past; they have also revealed that, much more often, the police and prosecutors got it right, and that those who escaped at first can sometimes still be found.

And it is this restoration of the criminal justice system's integrity that seems to supply the lion's share of Watkins's motives for establishing the CIU. As a result of his "life experience," Watkins says, he came to the post "with a different mindset of what it means to be a prosecutor" and what the law compelled him to do.[70] Growing up in Dallas in the black community, he often saw that law enforcement did not serve people the way it did else- where, and that people from his community sometimes found themselves on the wrong side of the law, blamed and even convicted for things they had not done. All of this, combined with revelations (which seemed surprising only to those outside the black community) that prosecutors kept blacks and other minorities off juries, meant that "people had a distrust of law enforce- ment."[71] Watkins says that when he came into office, "you talk to a lot of folks, they'll tell you that their faith in the criminal justice system is gone."[72] And he knows that that lack of faith has played a part in propelling him to the DA's office. "The reason I'm here is a result of what happened in the past."[73] Thus he knows that his top priority must be to restore the integrity and credibility of the office in the eyes of all of the people of Dallas, who had begun to see the parade of exonerations of the wrongfully convicted as evidence of rot in the system.

Watkins is not without critics. Those who served for years under his predecessors did not take kindly to the idea that the integrity of the DA's office needed restoring.[74] But others have been critical as well—especially some prominent prosecutors across the country. To them, Watkins is noth- ing more than another politician eager to smear his predecessors from the easy position of hindsight for the sake of some good publicity and political advantage for himself.[75] The comments of Joshua Marquis, himself an elected district attorney (of Clatsup County, Oregon), give a good sense of how some of his peers see Watkins. Marquis has served as an occasional spokesperson and board member of the National District Attorney's Association. "Where I think he's doing a grave disservice is trying to create this image that the criminal-justice system is fatally flawed, and only people like Craig Watkins can save it," Marquis says. Some members of the criminal defense bar echoed Marquis' criticisms, commenting that Watkins's actions had more to do with what would help him and his image in the national press than with assisting the wrongfully convicted. Jeff Blackburn, a long-time Texas criminal defense attorney who has had the lead role in representing many wrongfully convicted people in Texas, serves as one of the leaders of the Innocence Project of Texas, headquartered at Texas Tech School of Law in Lubbock. He worked with Watkins and his office in the beginning of his first term in office, helping Watkins to establish the CIU by staffing it with students from the Project. An early admirer of Watkins, Blackburn now says that Watkins's thirst for publicity seems to have gotten the better of him.[76] Watkins's judgment and his actions have become erratic, Blackburn says, turning Watkins into "a train wreck" who will eventually discredit all the good his office has done.[77]

Watkins, who has a reputation as almost legendarily thin skinned,[78] says none of his bothers him. "I encounter resistance every day," he says, but "[it] doesn't make any difference. Let [the critics] be on the wrong side of history."[79] Perhaps, for all his faults, Watkins has discovered something that other prosecutors have missed: the old saw that good policy is good politics applies even in the arena of criminal justice.

In 2008, Houston elected a new district attorney: Patricia Lykos.[80] Lykos, who served one term before losing her re-election bid in 2012, was almost the opposite of everything that Craig Watkins was when he became DA in Dallas. She is white; she is also a Republican who defeated a black Democrat. If Watkins came to office as an outsider, Lykos took the oath in Houston with a consummate insider's pedigree. She'd long played a part in the criminal justice system in Houston, serving as a criminal court judge for fourteen years, hearing over twenty thousand criminal cases.[81] She had also worked for other judges in the county courts, and spearheaded numerous criminal justice, judicial, and civic projects.[82] She was in every way the establishment candidate, in contrast to the insurgent Watkins. Yet one of the first things Lykos did after taking office was to establish a post-conviction review unit in her office, modeled on the CIU in Watkins's office. As Lykos said in testimony given to the U.S. Senate's Judiciary Committee in November of 2009, "one of my first initiatives was to create a post-conviction review section that was separate and apart from our excellent appellate division." The goal, she told the senators, was independent, objective, and timely review of cases "where evidence suggests that the defendant may be innocent."[83]

The efforts of Lykos's post-conviction unit paid off. Within one week during the summer of 2010, the post-conviction unit's work resulted in the freeing of two innocent men who had languished in prison for a combined forty-six years. First, DNA showed that Allen Wayne Porter had not had any involvement in a 1990 home invasion and rape. Then, after extraordinary efforts by Lykos's post-conviction section staff, DNA testing proved that

Michael Anthony Green had served twenty-seven years in prison for a brutal 1983 gang rape he had not committed.[84] Sandra Guerra Thompson, a professor of law at the University of Houston and a long-time observer of the city's criminal justice system, says she has no doubt about how Lykos's predecessors in the Houston DA's office would have responded to the DNA results. In the past, when DNA showed that a convicted defendant had not taken part in the crime, Thompson says, the typical response from the DA's office in Houston was to defend the conviction anyway: the defendant was "probably there and took part and we stand by the conviction. . . . [The defendant is] just as guilty" regardless of the DNA results.[85] The attitude of the DA's office under Lykos changed; Lykos and her prosecutors took the duty to seek justice as seriously as the job of pursuing convictions. The proof, for Thompson, came when Michael Anthony Green, upon his release from prison, went out of his way to thank the prosecutors in Houston for working to free him.[86] All of this, Thompson says, signal that "a new era in criminal justice may be dawning" in Houston.[87] Lykos has summed up her willingness to pursue cases of possible wrongful convictions in the same way that she explained it in her Senate testimony: "When innocent people are convicted, it is a triple tragedy: injustice for those individuals; denial of justice for the victims; and the lack of justice for society, as the actual criminals are free to continue their depredations."[88]

Lykos surprised people: despite her insider background and her impeccable law enforcement credentials, she became a strong advocate for reform, both in Texas and nationally. Jeff Blackburn, the criminal defense attorney and leader of the Innocence Project of Texas, say that while Houston's district attorney's office had formerly occupied the darkest corners of the justice system, "now it's light-years ahead of everyone else. . . . I think [Pat Lykos] has brought about a sea change in attitude and perspective for that office. I wish every DA in the state would do what she has proven herself capable of doing in these cases. It's something that requires a lot of moral authority and a lot of courage."[89]

New Jersey: An Unusual Way to Create Change

When it comes to making change happen in police departments and prosecutors' offices, several possibilities exist. Sometimes, change can come from internal agency leadership, as in the Dallas and Houston DA's offices. Sometimes, change must come from outside. For example, in two states, courts forced police to change interrogation methods by requiring them to record interrogations: Alaska[90] in 1985 and Minnesota[91] in 1994. In some other states,

legislatures have acted, passing laws that have required new police procedures. In Illinois, in the wake of the freeing of more than a dozen wrongfully
convicted defendants, the legislature passed a new law mandating recording
of interrogations in some cases; any *unrecorded* statement made during an
interrogation in a homicide case will be presumed inadmissible.[92] In 2008,
the legislature in North Carolina enacted a broad package of eyewitness
identification reforms, based on the recommendations of Chief Justice Lake's
Actual Innocence Commission.[93] In 2010, Ohio's state legislature mandated
significant changes to the methods police must use for eyewitness identification.[94] Ohio also created an incentive for police to electronically record interrogations by declaring that all recorded statements would be presumed to
be voluntary in court.[95] Wisconsin has also enacted laws to require police
departments to adopt policies for eyewitness identification procedures that
"reduce the potential for erroneous identifications" by utilizing recognized
best practices,[96] and mandated recording of interrogations in felony cases.[97]

New Jersey makes a very interesting example, because of the way it has
made major changes in eyewitness identification methods. And what makes
this intriguing is that the impetus came not from the legislature or the
courts but from the executive branch. Recall that in 1999, the U.S. Department of Justice issued a document called *Eyewitness Evidence: A Guide for
Law Enforcement* (discussed in chapter 6).[98] Developed by the National
Institute of Justice's Technical Working Group on Eyewitness Evidence, the
NIJ's *Guide* was the first comprehensive, research-based source on how law
enforcement should handle eyewitnesses to crimes, from the point of first
contact in the field through photographic and live lineup procedures. Using
the *Guide*, any law enforcement agency could follow the best practices in the
field in order to avoid errors and the wrongful convictions that sometimes
followed. The *Guide* was, in every sense, a landmark document, except for
one fact: it did not bind any police department or agency; no one had to follow its recommended practices. On the federal level, where the Department
of Justice could have mandated federal police practices, the statements made
in the *Guide* only had the status of recommendations that agencies such as
the FBI might follow if they wished. As for state and local police agencies,
the federal government had no authority to order them to follow its lead
on eyewitnesses. In fact, the *Guide* went out of its way to make clear that
no agency, anywhere, had to do what it said. Police and prosecutors should
view the document only "as a guide to recommended practices for the collection and preservation of eyewitness evidence. Jurisdictional, logistical, or
legal conditions may preclude the use" of the recommended practices.[99] It
was not a "legal mandate" and was "not intended to state legal criteria for the

admissibility of evidence."[100] So, despite its status as a document issued by the U.S. Department of Justice based on the best scientific evidence available, almost all of the states did exactly what one would expect: they ignored it.

But New Jersey did not. And the story of why that happened and how it made New Jersey a national leader in the reforming of eyewitness identification practices makes a powerful lesson. As in the stories from North Carolina and Texas, this one also centers on a leader who recognized and grasped an opportunity for change: Attorney General John Farmer Jr.

In New Jersey, the attorney general does not run for office; the governor nominates a candidate for attorney general, and the state senate must confirm the nominee.[101] In 1999, Governor Christine Todd Whitman nominated Farmer to be attorney general, and the Senate confirmed him. When Whitman later resigned as governor to take a cabinet post in the administration of President George W. Bush, Farmer remained attorney general, serving until 2002. Nothing in Farmer's background or record suggested he might become a reformer. Few would have expected to find in him anything other than the kind of mainstream Republican values that Governor Whitman represented. He had practiced law privately, and had then worked as a prosecutor in the U.S. Attorney's Office in New Jersey for four years. He then joined Governor Whitman's legal team, and eventually became her chief counsel.[102] When Whitman appointed Farmer attorney general in 1999, he became one of the most powerful officials in the state; under New Jersey's constitution and statutes, the attorney general has extensive power over all levels of state law enforcement, with direct supervisory authority over all twenty-one county prosecutor's offices and all six hundred police departments in the state. As Farmer sees it, having this power means "you can really set policy for law enforcement" in a way that few other officials in any state can.[103]

In April of 2001, Farmer took an extraordinary step. Using his broad powers as attorney general, he issued rules for eyewitness identification procedures for the state: *The Attorney General Guidelines for Preparing and Conducting Photo and Live Identification Lineups*.[104] In one bold stroke, Farmer made New Jersey "the first state in the Nation to officially adopt the recommendations issued by the U.S. Department of Justice" on the subject.[105] In his memorandum to all of the police chiefs and law enforcement executives in the state, Farmer explained that he knew that neither the law as it then stood nor the federal and state constitutions compelled any change; in other words, practices then in use in police departments in New Jersey complied with the law. But he had determined that police and prosecutors must do more. Eyewitness identification often played a crucial role in identifying criminals, but then-recent cases in which DNA testing led to the exoneration of individuals convicted on the basis of eyewitness identifications had proven "that [eye-witness] evidence is not fool-proof."[106] The adoption of the new guidelines, Farmer said, would "enhance the accuracy and reliability of eyewitness identifications and will strengthen prosecutions in cases that rely heavily, or solely, on eyewitness evidence."[107] The New Jersey *Attorney General Guidelines* did a thorough job of revamping law enforcement procedures in this area. They put in place everything recommended by the Justice Department's *Guide*, from required instructions to be given to witnesses to the minimum numbers of fillers in lineups to the proper method for recording the witness's identification and level of certainty. But Farmer went further: his *Guidelines* mandated the use of blind lineups whenever practical, and required the use of sequential lineups when possible. Farmer understood that taking these two additional steps represented the biggest changes yet for New Jersey's law enforcement agencies on the subject of eyewitness identification, and would probably require the biggest adjustment.[108] But he mandated them anyway, even featuring them at length in his memorandum announcing the changes to the state's law enforcement apparatus.[109]

So far, this tells us what John Farmer did, and how he did it: as the New Jersey attorney general, he had extraordinary powers over law enforcement. But the more intriguing question is *why* Farmer did this. Surely, no one in law enforcement clamored for such changes; on the contrary, almost all hated the idea. Debra L. Stone, a senior member of Farmer's staff who helped develop and implement the *Attorney General Guidelines*, told the *New York Times* that the plan "elicited howls of protest" from prosecutors and police departments.[110] In one of the milder reactions, one New Jersey police chief said that "[e]very time you see something coming along that makes your job a little harder, you kind of cringe a little."[111] To his credit, Farmer knew that he had to do more than simply order prosecutors and police to follow the *Guidelines* he had issued. If he wanted anything more than mere lip service, he needed to get law enforcement on board. So Farmer and his staff held meeting after meeting with groups of skeptical police and prosecutors, understanding that buy-in mattered; for the police especially, Farmer knew he'd need to get support at least at the commander level.[112] So, given the tough, almost thankless job of making this happen, what motivated him?

Farmer had absorbed some powerful lessons on his way to the attorney general's office. During his years as an assistant U.S. attorney, the office had handled a rape case. (Most rapes are prosecuted as state crimes, but this one occurred at Fort Dix, making it a federal matter.) The defendant had a record as a habitual offender but no record of violence. Nevertheless, the victim identified the defendant, saying she felt absolutely certain that the defendant had committed the crime. Three years later, the authorities apprehended a serial killer at another army base, and it turned out that he had committed the rape at Fort Dix. Farmer still recalls the impact this had on him: "through no prosecutorial excesses and no misconduct on anybody's part, we convicted the wrong guy"—something he found "scarier" than a conviction that resulted from some kind of wrongdoing. "[I]t just shows that if you do everything right . . . the system is a human system and mistakes can be made and prosecutors sometimes lose sight of that human dimension of the system."[113] This occurred, Farmer remembers, at about the same time that DNA exonerations, especially those resulting from incorrect eyewitness identifications, began to emerge regularly in the news.

A second formative experience for Farmer resulted from the biggest case he faced as he took up the attorney general's post. Since the early 1990s, New Jersey had fought lawsuits that alleged that members of the state police engaged in racial profiling of African American drivers on the New Jersey Turnpike. The state police had fought the accusations vigorously, insisting that no profiling had occurred, despite persuasive statistical and other evidence that it had.[114] In 1999, the state was finally forced to admit the truth: racial profiling on the Turnpike was "real— not imagined."[115] As the new attorney general, coming to this crisis just after it peaked and then shepherding the state police through the process of federally mandated reforms, Farmer was struck by the waste of time and resources the state had put into "defending things that were indefensible" after the fact; he saw the damage inflicted by this sort of rear-guard action. For his part, Farmer remembers thinking, "I'd like to get ahead of some of these issues."[116]

The third factor impelling Farmer concerned his personal legal philosophy. He'd practiced law privately and for the government, as a prosecutor and as a public official, and he understood that one thing mattered above all else in the law: the integrity of the legal system. Without it, law was just words on paper, and police officers' authority was little more than state power. He and his staff, especially Deputy Attorney General Debra Stone, worked tirelessly to persuade prosecutors and police that the eyewitness guidelines were "the right way to go in order to preserve and defend 'the integrity of the entire system'" from the damage and erosion it would experience in the event of false convictions.[117]

For all these reasons, Farmer forged ahead. He understood what happened when eyewitness identifications, which "can be more or less accurate," go wrong. He wanted to "give law enforcement a way in which we think we can at least narrow the risk that a mistake will be made."[118] His vision on this issue instantly made New Jersey the leader on the reform of eyewitness identification.

To get a sense of how far in front of the rest of criminal justice officialdom Farmer and New Jersey put themselves, note that not until 2005, four years later, did any other public official or body anywhere make such a move, when the attorney general of Wisconsin did not mandate but instead recommended the use of blind and sequential lineup procedures.[119] And not until 2008 did another state (North Carolina) require improved lineup procedures.[120]

One thing to note about the New Jersey *Attorney General Guidelines* is that they contained no mandatory enforcement mechanism. In other words, if a police department chose in a particular case to ignore the *Guidelines*, what effect would this have on the case? Should a court suppress the identification evidence? The New Jersey *Attorney General's Guidelines* did not give a definitive answer. In a case stemming from the arrest of a man named Larry Henderson in a fatal shooting in 2003, failure to follow the *Guidelines* eventually led to clarification on that point. In the course of the investigation of Henderson, officers used a photo lineup procedure that did not comply with the *Guidelines*.[121] The jury convicted Henderson, but he appealed, arguing that police had failed to abide by the *Guidelines* when they conducted the photo lineup, leading to a mistaken identification.[122] The appeals court agreed with Henderson and ordered that a hearing be held on the admissibility of the photo lineup identification, but the state appealed before that hearing could be held. The New Jersey Supreme Court then took up the Henderson case and decided that it wanted a full-blown inquiry into witness identification procedures not just in the Henderson case, but throughout all of New Jersey law enforcement.[123] The Supreme Court appointed a special master, a retired judge, to hold plenary hearings and gather evidence on eyewitness identification. The special master's report went to the New Jersey Supreme Court in June of 2010,[124] and in August 2011 the court affirmed the special master's conclusions and effectively made the *Guidelines* mandatory for police in New Jersey. All of the changes in eyewitness identification in New Jersey stem from the foresight, courage, and leadership of John Farmer and his staff. The fact that the whole state stepped forward, led the way, and proved to everyone in other jurisdictions that the sky would not fall if police procedures for eyewitness identification came into line with the best science on the subject all comes down to them, and to the many police officers and prosecutors they persuaded to go along with these reforms, instead of resisting.

The New DNA

When it first appeared in courts in the late 1980s and early 1990s, DNA quickly demonstrated that it had the power to convict defendants like nothing seen before. It could determine the likelihood that the defendant had left a tiny bit of tissue or fluid at a crime scene, with a highly precise, data-based estimate of the probability. Experts testified, for the first time, that the odds that anyone other than the defendant had perpetrated the crime were millions— even tens or hundreds of millions—to one. But this powerful tool could also exonerate those already convicted, with equal strength and precision. A long procession of exonerations began in 1989 with Gary Dotson, and it continues even now. With each exoneration, we began to see the pattern explored in chapter 2: DNA proved that the basic tools of forensic science, as well as the routine methods of eyewitness identification and suspect interrogation, had fundamental flaws. Sometimes, they produced grave miscarriages of justice. No matter what we had long believed, DNA made it obvious that these standard tools of police investigation did not work nearly as well as we had assumed; compared to DNA analysis, they had little or no scientific basis. DNA thus undermined our long-held beliefs in these methods, and set the stage for much of what we have learned in this book. DNA ultimately forced the reexamination of all of the basics of police investigation.

Thus, we cannot end the discussion of the resistance of law enforcement to science without noting a potentially huge development in DNA analysis itself. Scientists have begun to reexamine the methods used to make identifications with DNA for the last two decades. It seems that DNA analysis, which damaged confidence in all of the other investigative methods examined here, is having its own "DNA moment." Scientific advances have come along that can vastly improve the identifications we can make with tiny bits of biological material.

The coming challenge to DNA does not question the results of testing under current methods of DNA analysis; the status of convictions and exonerations with DNA over the last two decades will not change at all. Rather, researchers have begun to use improved science to challenge the protocols of DNA identification as practiced during those years. This new way of using DNA will make the methods we have used obsolete, and in the bargain will make DNA more accurate and powerful—a scenario that should look quite familiar to readers of this book.

Cybergenetics, a company based in Pittsburgh, Pennsylvania, has created a better method for using DNA for forensic purposes. Dr. Mark Perlin, the founder of Cybergenetics, holds doctorates in mathematics and computer science as well as a medical degree. He was a senior research faculty member in the School of Computer Science at Carnegie Mellon University in Pittsburgh for ten years before leaving to start Cybergenetics, and he serves as the company's chief executive and chief scientific officer.[125] While on the faculty at Carnegie Mellon, Perlin began to study diagnostic tests that examined DNA, and the way that the testing process and the interpretation of results produced artifacts: phantom data created by the testing and interpreting process itself. Perlin came up with a solution: he created mathematical models to effectively neutralize the artifacts, and these models could be built into computer software. The software filtered out the phantom data efficiently and very quickly.[126] In 1998, British forensic scientists noticed his work, and asked if he could apply it in a different context.[127] Britain's criminal justice system had built up a backlog of more than 350,000 DNA samples; even with a department of about one hundred people at work processing the samples around the clock, the backlog only grew larger. Could Perlin's model be adapted to processing forensic DNA samples? Perlin accomplished the task, virtually eliminating the backlog with two people and two powerful computers.[128]

The British forensic DNA work brought Perlin fully into the world of forensic DNA analysis, and he ended up challenging the way law enforcement in the United States and the world over have always used and interpreted DNA. Among the problems he discovered was that the protocols set by the FBI in the early 1990s for interpreting and explaining DNA testing relied on rules and procedures set up to allow relatively easy processing by lab personnel, and simplified testimony in court. The protocols set a threshold for testing samples; a measurement of the sample above the threshold made it usable, and below the threshold, it was not. Using a threshold made some sense in the context of the early testing of reference samples of DNA; the reference samples were typically large, clear, and uncomplicated, and the work of interpretation had to be done by people.[129] But the use of the threshold had negative consequences. DNA samples that came from actual cases were often not as large or as simple as the reference samples. In fact, they were often quite small, and sometimes contained complex mixtures of the DNA of several people. This meant that many samples would not meet the threshold, and could not be used. Thus use of the threshold effectively left most data from the DNA samples unused. If a sample was above the threshold, all DNA samples looked the same, no matter how strongly they actually registered; no measurement quantified how far above the threshold the sample scored, and data that would have indicated the strength of the sample went unexploited. Below the threshold, the samples simply did not register; for all practical purposes, that data disappeared altogether. So everything above the threshold looked the same, and everything below it didn't exist. This would generate false negatives: perpetrators whose DNA was present but whose DNA fell below the threshold would be excluded and not matched, allowing them to escape justice and victimize others. In other cases, the threshold would effectively depress the strength of possible DNA matches—that is, the likelihood that the defendant had left the DNA at the crime scene would still be reported, but perhaps at a much *lower* number than was possible.[130]

Using his mathematical models, Perlin constructed software, called TrueAllele, to meet these problems. The software, running on very fast and powerful computers, works without any threshold. It can process DNA samples much too small for any other technique, and it does this much faster, more efficiently, and more accurately than prior methods had. And, most importantly, the software allowed the computers to use all the data present in the DNA sample, including all that would have been discarded as above or below the threshold.[131] The upshot is that with TrueAllele, law enforcement will get many more "hits" from DNA samples that would have been considered far too small in the past (since they were below the threshold), resulting in convictions of perpetrators who would have walked free. Also, since data above the threshold can now be quantified, TrueAllele will produce results in some cases that are many times stronger than what would have been possible before. There will also be exonerations in cases with small samples or DNA mixtures that would not have been possible before. In late 2011, the *Journal of Forensic Sciences* will publish Perlin's validation study of the use of TrueAlelle for the interpretation of DNA mixtures—the first such peer-reviewed validation of any DNA technique.[132]

Since Perlin founded Cybergenetics in 1994, he has spoken countless times to law enforcement organizations about his new and better approach to DNA analysis. Unfortunately, progress has been slow. The general reaction to TrueAllele in law enforcement will not surprise readers of this book: there has been resistance to the new method in most of law enforcement, especially among those lab personnel whose primary role has been the processing of samples according to the current protocols. Most state police crime laboratories have been unwilling to even consider TrueAllele technology, frustrating Perlin's efforts,[133] even though it promises to make their DNA-based investigations considerably faster, more efficient, and accurate, greatly increasing the odds of catching perpetrators. Much of the forensic science community, Perlin says, is "embedded" in the prevailing practices.[134] He finds most forensic scientists strongly attached to the status quo[135]—a concept familiar to us from our examination of cognitive barriers in chapter 4. As of 2011, Perlin had achieved some breakthroughs with a few important law enforcement organizations. After about ten years of working to convince crime lab specialists and others in the organization,[136] the New York State Police has recently accepted TrueAllele for use in case work.[137] Perlin has also put in considerable time attempting to persuade the FBI to consider TrueAllele, and there are indications that the agency has begun to consider how it might use the technology.[138] In 2011, Virginia's Department of Forensic Sciences decided to reevaluate the DNA testing in 375 cases,[139] this time using TrueAllele.[140] The Allegheny County, Pennsylvania, Medical Examiner's Office (covering Pittsburgh and the surrounding area), under the leadership of Dr. Karl Williams, has moved relatively quickly to evaluate the technology with an eye toward adopting it.[141] But these agencies are the exception. Despite the fact that TrueAllele has been accepted for some years in Great Britain, and despite the promise of improved, more accurate police work and more convictions of predators of all kinds, law enforcement resists. Perlin wants to see his work succeed, but he has broader concerns. Perlin is a scientist, and in his mind good science leading to the truth is just better than any other alternative.[142] He has a hard time understanding why others might cling to methods that do not do as well at reaching the truth. Moreover, current DNA methods allow some very dangerous people to walk the streets. His goal is to have his product used because of "the impact it will have on public safety."[143]

The Common Threads

The examples in this chapter—the innocence commissions in North Carolina and other states, the conviction integrity units in Dallas and Houston, and the reform of eyewitness identification procedures in New Jersey—share some important connections. In all three, a determined figure within the state's power structure took ownership of the issue and exercised the leadership necessary to bring it forward. Except in the case of Craig Watkins, all of these leaders came from the political Right, ranging from the moderate Republican Farmer to the Jesse Helms conservative Lake. All took some degree of political risk by moving toward reform, but they all did so willingly, seeing it as worth the gamble. In the cases of DAs Watkins and Lykos, the risks taken have resulted in political benefits for them. And all of them saw the task of fixing the system as more than just compelled by the overwhelming weight of scientific work in these fields. Rather, they went ahead on these initiatives because they genuinely valued the criminal justice system and saw the importance of preserving its integrity. Preserving that integrity was worth the political risks taken and the work done.

8

Conclusion: From the Task to the Solutions

When most people think about modern law enforcement and prosecution, they believe that science propels police work and proof in court in the twenty-first century. Popular entertainment portrays police work as 90 percent test tubes and lab coats and 10 percent old-fashioned hustle; news reports feature DNA implicating the bad guys in both new crimes and cold cases. Science has become the handmaiden of police work.

This view rests on a skewed and incomplete version of the facts. The science-driven police investigation that seals a case in the courtroom makes great television and movies, but the real world of law enforcement usually does not resemble this picture. We are, instead, stuck in the past. Most of those who work in law enforcement and prosecution—not all, but most—do not use the knowledge that science offers about a host of traditional police investigative methods. And, more to the point, they do not wish to change things—the way that they perform eyewitness identifications, or interrogate suspects, or conduct forensic testing—even though solid scientific research tells them that doing what they have done for years can lead to incorrect results.

Let me be clear: our police officers and prosecutors do not want to convict the wrong people. They have no desire to put people in jail only to see them emerge years or even decades later, exonerated. They only wish to convict the guilty. There is no evidence, anywhere, that any but the tiniest number of police or prosecutors would ever even consider intentionally putting innocent people behind bars. Unfortunately, however, plenty of evidence exists that many members of these honorable professions continue to use methods that increase the likelihood of unintentional miscarriages of justice. The evidence shows that many police and prosecutors actively resist changes in investigative methods in the face of science that shows that the usual ways of gathering and testing evidence sometimes lead to wrongful convictions. And many voices from within policing and prosecution have spoken, loudly and clearly, against even acknowledging the existence of a problem, and against any contribution that science can make to greater certainty of guilt. All of this comes against a backdrop of more than 250 DNA-based exonerations, with every indication that this number represents only the tip of the proverbial iceberg. One need only think of the aftermath of the Brandon Mayfield fingerprint identification debacle—a "100 percent match" by the FBI's best analysts, for which the FBI later apologized and paid damages—which other fingerprint experts followed by continuing to call fingerprint analysis infallible on national television. And we must keep in mind that when outmoded methods implicate the wrong person, the injustice goes beyond a wrongful conviction. As Houston district attorney Pat Lykos says, a wrongful conviction constitutes a triple tragedy: the victim does not get justice, the convicted person suffers the nightmare of unjust imprisonment, and the real predator remains at large, free to kill or rape or rob again. Obviously, this benefits no one. Yet, much of the law enforcement establishment remains at best curiously uninterested, and at worst actively resistant, and even hostile, to aligning their efforts with the best of what science has to offer.

No one should look for perfection in the American criminal justice system. It is naïve to imagine that, if we can get our investigative and prosecutorial procedures just right, we will always get the right answer and a just outcome in every case. After all, we cannot know what constitutes the truth in many cases; the prosecution and the defendant dispute what happened, and why. More than that, humans have constructed the laws, procedures, and institutions of our justice system, and humans run every aspect of it. Expecting perfection from human institutions run by human beings could stand as the very definition of folly. But we should—indeed, we must—aspire to another goal: we must strive to do all that we as human beings can to increase the likelihood that we will get important decisions in the justice system right, and to decrease the chances that we will get these things wrong. We cannot be perfect, but we can do the best that our knowledge and reasoning allow us to do. We owe that to our fellow men and women who find themselves at the defendant's table in court. And, because our society values justice and fairness, we also owe this to ourselves. Ignoring science, when doing so increases the risk of wrongful convictions, simply does not square with justice or fairness.

And the scientific work in these areas comes to us well grounded, rigorously conducted, and replicated by others in the field. It doesn't just ferret out the mistakes of the past and present; it also gives us detailed blueprints for how to do better in the future. For example, scientific research on eyewitness identification tells us that using traditional simultaneous lineups—in which the witness sees the suspect and some number of fillers at the same time—leads to a built-in level of inaccuracy because of relative judgment, in which witnesses look for the person in the lineup who looks most like the perpetrator they remember instead of looking for the perpetrator. The research also shows that instead of using the simultaneous lineup of suspect and fillers, witnesses should see each person in the lineup sequentially: one at a time. This removes the relative judgment problem and forces a direct comparison of the witness's memory of the perpetrator to the person in the lineup, instead of a relative comparison of the persons in the lineup to each other to determine who looks most like the suspect. When solid research tells us that what we are doing that makes us less accurate than we can be, and also how to be more accurate, no good excuse exists for failing to pay heed.

If that is true, then why the resistance? The rejection of science by much of law enforcement has little to do with the stated reasons we often hear, such as costs, or the difficulty of the changes proposed, or that these adjustments would make it impossible to catch and convict criminals. Instead, police and prosecutors have resisted change for reasons that have remained hidden to most people. Some of these barriers to change come from cognitive factors. Cognitive dissonance makes it almost impossible for some in law enforcement to admit the need for change, because acknowledging past mistakes creates a strong dissonance between their self-image and what the facts show. They fear the reduction in status that might come with admitting that their bedrock knowledge and beliefs concerning what they consider their core areas of expertise actually have deep flaws, and that scientific testing has shown that their conceptions of how things work do not stand up. This would diminish their status as experts, and with it their value. They fear wealth effects: the natural sense that movement from the status quo is a loss and the reality that people experience losses more painfully than they do possible gains denied to them. And group polarization sets in when any relatively close group interacts and communicates only with those who share their own points of view. This tends to move the members of the group, especially strongly cohesive and insular ones (like police), toward more extreme versions of their original positions.

Other barriers come from institutional and professional factors. Among them, the imperative of arrests (for police) and convictions (for prosecutors) ranks high. As things stand, police advance in their careers by making arrests, and prosecutors by accumulating convictions. Any new arrangements that might threaten the ability of police to arrest or of prosecutors to convict will generate resistance. Second, law enforcement generally takes an us-versus-them view of the world, with the views of outsiders distrusted and not easily accepted. Third, for prosecutors, political ambition may enter into the picture. Being a tough prosecutor remains one of the best ways to carve out a political identity with the public; those who wish to attain elected office or become judges will want to preserve their ability to convict, and will not wish to see changes to the law or police procedure that might make that harder. Fourth, the power of police unions, and the voices of police and prosecutorial professional groups in legislatures, tends to make it difficult to bring about change that law enforcement sees as potentially threatening to their power in, and control of, the criminal justice system. Fifth, the portrayals of crime and violence in the media generally make it difficult to build public support for anything but very traditional kinds of tough enforcement; any push for reform, by contrast, looks like "soft" measures aimed at "helping criminals," even if the objective is helping the justice system to attain fairness.

Fortunately, there are concrete ideas regarding what changes we need, and how to make these things happen (chapter 6). Again using eyewitness identification as our example, we must change police procedures to require proper pre-identification instructions, the use of blind procedures, the use of sequential lineups, and the immediate taking of confidence statements from witnesses without any feedback. To make this happen takes a combination of focusing on the future (while creating dedicated conviction review units), putting law enforcement members—prosecutors and police chiefs experienced with these reforms—in the lead of reform efforts, attaching conditions to federal funding, requiring the preservation of evidence, and making *Daubert* standards meaningful in criminal cases.

There has been so much science produced on these questions, and so many wrongful convictions overturned by DNA, and yet resistance remains. Given this, can sweeping change really occur? The answer is a qualified, cautious yes. Ten years ago, much of what science tells us about eyewitness identification was known, yet only New Jersey had even a set of guidelines based on the best available knowledge. Now, a small number of other states, and many individual jurisdictions, have made at least some changes to their eyewitness identification procedures. Ten years ago, only Minnesota and Alaska had court-mandated requirements for the recording of police interrogations; now, some states have taken steps in that direction, and a small but growing number of local jurisdictions have become enthusiastic supporters of recording interrogations. Ten years ago, forensic evidence still carried the luster of science, with few questioning its findings; now, after DNA has exposed many serious forensic mistakes, and after the highly critical 2009 National Academy of Sciences report, the need for real science in forensic disciplines is widely acknowledged. Thus we see some small first steps in the long journey we must take to bring police investigation and prosecution in tune with the best that science has to offer, and we can see progress, even if most would agree that it has come too slowly and in too few places. But at least we have begun to move in the right direction. We see this through the actions of leaders like Chief Justice I. Beverly Lake and attorney Christine Mumma in North Carolina in their work establishing the state commission to examine wrongful convictions; through the establishment of conviction review units by district attorneys Craig Watkins and Pat Lykos in Texas; and through the actions of former New Jersey attorney general John Farmer, issuing guidelines for eyewitness identification for every police department in his state before any executive official, anywhere, had done anything like this.

The resistance remains, but perhaps now, with a better understanding of the reasons for that resistance, change will begin more widely, and its pace will quicken. Justice demands no less.

Notes

CHAPTER 1

1. *CSI: Crime Scene Investigation*, official website, accessed March 12, 2010, at http://www.cbs.com/primetime/csi/about/.

2. For example, the video introduction to the original *CSI* for its tenth season shows almost all video of lab work, test simulations, and the like; a policeman with a gun shows up only at the end. *See CSI 10: Season Introduction Video*, YouTube, http://www.youtube.com/watch?v=tRZZlnKBrVk, accessed March 12, 2010.

3. Paul Rincon, *CSI Shows Give "Unrealistic View,"* BBC News, Feb. 21, 2005, accessed March 12, 2010, at http://news.bbc.co.uk/2/hi/science/nature/4284335.stm (*CSI* portrays forensic science as infallible, forensic testing as impossibly fast, and every mystery as susceptible to solution through forensic science.); Richard Willing, *"CSI Effect" Has Juries Wanting More Evidence*, USA Today, Aug. 5, 2004 ("[T[he programs also foster what analysts say is the mistaken notion that criminal science is fast and infallible and always gets its man."). For a scholarly treatment of this point, see N. J. Schweitzer and Michael J. Saks, *The CSI Effect: Popular Fiction about Forensic Science Affects Public Expectations about Real Forensic Science*, 47 Jurimetrics 357 (2007) ("Compared to non-*CSI* viewers, *CSI* viewers were more critical of the forensic evidence presented at the trial, finding it less believable.").

4. Justin Fenton, *State, City Police Laud Increase in Arrests Using DNA*, Baltimore Sun, Jan. 22, 2010.

5. Mehan Mattteucci, *Georgia DNA Solves 1,500 Cases*, Atlanta Journal-Constitution, July 30, 2009.

6. Chris Conley, *DNA Databanks Allow Police to Solve at Least Four Murders*, Memphis Commercial Appeal, July 19, 2009.

7. Ryan Haggerty, *With Added Lab Staff, DNA Tests Resolve String of Old Killings*, Milwaukee Journal Sentinel, Aug. 29, 2009.

8. Application for Material Witness Order and Warrant Regarding Witness: Brandon Bieri Mayfield, In re Federal Grand Jury Proceedings, 03-01, 337 F. Supp. 2d 1218 (D. Or. 2004) (No. 04-MC-9071).

9. Simon A. Cole, *More Than Zero: Accounting for Error in Latent Fingerprint Identification*, 95 J. Crim. L. & Criminology 985, 986 (2005).

10. *Id.* at 985.

11. Sarah Kershaw, *Spain and U.S. at Odds on Mistaken Terror Arrest*, N.Y. Times, June 5, 2004.

12. Press Release, Federal Bureau of Investigation, *Statement on Brandon Mayfield Case*, May 24, 2004. The press release of May 24 is mostly devoted to explaining its error in the most favorable terms it can manage, and ends with the following sentence: "The FBI apologizes to Mr. Mayfield and his family for the hardships that this matter has caused." The real apology in the case came more than two years later, well after the case had faded from the headlines, and begins with "The United States of America apologizes to Mr. Brandon Mayfield and his family for the suffering cause by the FBI's misidentification of Mr. Mayfield's fingerprint," and includes an acknowledgment that the events were "deeply unsettling" to Mr. Mayfield and his family. It states that Mayfield's identification and arrest were a result of FBI mistakes, and does not repeat the excuses that appeared in the May 24 statement. *Apology Note,* Washington Post, Nov. 29, 2006.

13. Eric Lichtblau, *U.S. Will Pay $2 Million to Lawyer Wrongly Held*, N.Y. Times, Nov. 30, 2006.

14. Flynn McRoberts, Steve Mills, and Maurice Possley, *Unproven Techniques Sway Courts, Erode Justice,* Chicago Tribune, Oct. 17, 2004 (admission by one of the verifying examiners that he knew "another examiner had already declared a match").

15. *Id.*

16. Steve Scarborough, *They Keep Putting Fingerprints in Print*, Weekly Detail, Dec. 13, 2004, http://www.clplex.com/Articles/TheDetail/100-199/TheDetail174.htm, quoted in Simon A. Cole, *More Than Zero: Accounting for Error in Latent Fingerprint Identification*, 95 J. Crim. L. & Criminology 985, 987 (2005).

17. *60 Minutes: Fingerprints*, CBS Television, Jan. 5, 2003.

18. National Research Council, STRENGTHENING FORENSIC SCIENCE IN THE UNITED STATES: A PATH FORWARD 40-41 (2009) ("Thus, DNA analysis—originally developed in research laboratories in the context of life sciences research—has received heightened scrutiny," including tests, evaluations, development of guidelines for analysis and proficiency testing and requirements for blind trials.).

19. For a description of these advances, see Barry Scheck, Peter Neufeld, and Jim Dwyer, ACTUAL INNOCENCE: WHEN JUSTICE GOES WRONG AND HOW

TO MAKE IT RIGHT (2003, updated edition), chapter 2, "The Invention," describing the advent of DNA testing on very small samples due to the use of polymerase chain reaction, or PCR, which made it possible to replicate tiny amounts of DNA many times for testing purposes.

20. The Innocence Project, *Know the Cases: Innocence Project Case Files* ("There have been 251 post-conviction DNA exonerations in United States history."), accessed March 17, 2010, at http://www.innocenceproject.org/know/.

21. The Innocence Project, *Understand the Causes: Eyewitness Identification* ("Eyewitness misidentification is the single greatest cause of wrongful convictions nationwide, playing a role in more than 75% of convictions overturned through DNA testing."), accessed March 17, 2010, at http://www.innocenceproject.org/understand/Eyewitness-Misidentification.php.

22. The Innocence Project, *Understand the Causes: Unvalidated or Improper Forensic Science* (Unvalidated or improper forensic science constitutes "the second-greatest contributor to wrongful convictions that have been overturned with DNA testing."), accessed March 17, 2010, at http://www.innocenceproject.org/understand/Unreliable-Limited-Science.php.

23. The Innocence Project, *Understand the Cause: False Confession* ("In about 25% of DNA exoneration cases, innocent defendants made incriminating statements, delivered outright confessions or pled guilty."), accessed March 17, 2010, at http://www.innocenceproject.org/understand/False-Confessions.php.

24. National Research Council, *supra* note 18, at 41.

25. National Research Council, *supra* note 18.

26. *Id.* at 42–43 ("The fact is that many forensic tests . . . have never been exposed to scientific scrutiny. . . . [C]omparisons of their results with DNA testing in some cases has revealed that some of these analyses, as currently performed, produce erroneous results. . . . Some non-DNA forensic tests do not meet the fundamental requirements of science, in terms of reproducibility, validity, and falsifiability.").

27. Saul M. Kassin et al., *Police-Induced Confessions: Risk Factors and Recommendations,* Law & Human Behavior (2009).

28. E.g., Jennifer Mnookin, *The Validity of Latent Fingerprint Identification: Confessions of a Fingerprinting Moderate,* 7 Law, Probability & Risk 127 (2008) (advocating that "the fingerprint identification community" move strongly toward implementing "carefully-designed, appropriately challenging proficiency tests. There are not insurmountable technical obstacles to proficiency tests that accurately mirror the degrees of difficulty encountered in actual casework.").

CHAPTER 2

1. National Research Council, National Academy of Sciences, STRENGTHENING FORENSIC SCIENCE IN THE UNITED STATES: A PATH FORWARD 42 (2009).

2. *Id.* at 112-13.

3. Interview with Professor Andrew Taslitz, Dec. 2, 2010 (copy on file with the author).

4. National Academy of Sciences, *supra* note 1.

5. U.S. Congress, Office of Technology Assessment, GENETIC WITNESS: FORENSIC USES OF DNA TESTS, OTA-BA-438 (1990).

6. National Research Council, DNA TECHNOLOGY IN FORENSIC SCIENCE 55 (1992).

7. National Research Council, THE EVALUATION OF FORENSIC DNA EVIDENCE: AN UPDATE (1996).

8. For example, the FBI set up guidelines for DNA analysis and proficiency testing in the early 1990s, and just four years later set up a national system designed to allow federal, state, and local crime labs to exchange and compare DNA results. National Academy of Sciences, *supra* note 1, at 40.

9. The Innocence Project, *Know the Cases: Gary Dotson*, accessed April 30, 2010, at http://innocenceproject.org/Content/89.php.

10. *Id.*

11. The Innocence Project, *Know the Cases: David Vasquez*, accessed April 30, 2010, at http://innocenceproject.org/Content/276.php.

12. *Id.*

13. The Innocence Project, *Know the Cases: Innocence Project Case Profiles* (graph showing year-by-year totals of exoneration from 1989 through the present), accessed April 30, 2010, at http://innocenceproject.org/know/.

14. *Id.*

15. A large number of sources, to which I will return, substantiate this claim. Among them are Samuel R. Gross, Kristen Jacoby, Daniel J. Matheson, Nicholas Montgomery, and Sujata Patel, *Exonerations in the United States, 1989 through 2003*, J. Crim. L. & Criminology 523 (2004); Gary L. Wells and Eric P. Seelau, *Eyewitness Identification: Psychological Research and Legal Policy on Lineups*, 1 Psychology, Pub. Pol'y & L. 765 (1995) ("[M]istaken eyewitness identification is the single largest source of wrongful convictions.").

16. The Innocence Project, *Understand the Causes: Unvalidated or Improper Forensic Science*, accessed April 30, 2010, at http://www.innocenceproject.org/understand/Unreliable-Limited-Science.php.

17. S. Rep. No. 109-88, at 46 (2005).

18. National Academy of Sciences, *supra* note 1.

19. *Id.* at 22.

20. *Id.* at 23.
21. *Id.*
22. *Id.* at 24.
23. *Id.* at 24-25.
24. Simon A. Cole, *More Than Zero: Accounting for Error in Latent Finger-print Identification*, 95 J. Crim. L. & Criminology 985, 987 ("Latent print examiners have long claimed that fingerprint identification is 'infallible.' The claim is widely believed by the general public" and "even appears to survive exposed cases of error, which would seem to puncture the claim of infallibility.").
25. Federal Bureau of Investigation, THE SCIENCE OF FINGERPRINTS: CLASSIFI-CATION AND USES iv (1985).
26. According to Robert Epstein, the litigator who first challenged fingerprint validity in the post-*Daubert* era, the first American case in which latent fingerprint evidence was introduced was People v. Jennings, 96 N.E. 1077 (Ill. 1911). Robert Epstein, *Fingerprints Meet Daubert: The Myth of Fingerprint "Science" Is Revealed*, 75 S.Cal. L. Rev. 605, n. 1 (2002).
27. See, e.g., Simon A. Cole, *supra* note 24, at 990 n. 27 (2005) (quoting the federal government's Combined Report to the Court and Motions in Limine concerning Fingerprint Evidence in U.S. v. Mitchell, 199 F.Supp. 2d 262 (E.D. Pa. 2002), as stating that "[b]y following the scientific method of analysis, comparison, evaluation and verification, the error rate remains zero."). Other examples abound, including those quoted in chapter 1's telling of the aftermath of Brandon Mayfield's mistaken identification.
28. Jonathan Saltzman and Mac Daniel, *Man Freed in 1997 Shooting of Officer: Judge Gives Ruling after Fingerprint Revelation*, Boston Globe, Jan. 24, 2004.
29. David Weber and Kevin Rothstein, *Man Freed after 6 Years: Evidence Was Flawed*, Boston Herald, Jan. 24, 2004.
30. Professor Simon Cole of the University of California at Irvine has amassed evidence of twenty-two cases (including Mayfield and Cowans) of fingerprint misidentification, using conservative criteria that probably underestimate the total number. Simon A. Cole, *supra* note 24. Robert Epstein, an attorney who brought one of the first challenges to the scientific validity of fingerprint identification in the modern era, calls the idea "that there is a 'science of fingerprints'" nothing but "an unfounded creation of law enforcement fingerprint examiners." Robert Epstein, *supra* note 26, at 607.
31. Keith Inman and Norah Rudin, PRINCIPLES AND PRACTICE OF CRIMINAL-ISTICS: THE PROFESSION OF FORENSIC SCIENCE 123 (2001).
32. Scientific Working Group for Friction Ridge Analysis, Study, and Technology [hereinafter, SWGFAST], *Friction Ridge Examination Methodology for*

Latent Print Examiners, at §3.3.1, accessed Jan. 26, 2012, at http://swgfast.org/Friction_Ridge_Examination_Methodology_for_Latent_Print_Examiners_1.01.pdf.

33. National Academy of Sciences, *supra* note 1, at 137-38.
34. *Id.*
35. *Id.* at 138.
36. *Id.*
37. *Id.*; see also Simon A. Cole, *supra* note 24, at 992-93.
38. National Academy of Sciences, *supra* note 1, at 138.
39. David R. Ashbaugh, QUANTITATIVE-QUALITATIVE FRICTION RIDGE ANALYSIS: AN INTRODUCTION TO BASIC AND ADVANCED QUANTITATIVE-QUALITATIVE FRICTION RIDGE ANALYSIS 22 (1999).
40. SWGFAST, *supra* note 32.
41. David Ashbaugh, *supra* note 39, at 98.
42. Christophe Champod, *Numerical Standards and "Probable" Identifications*, 45 J. Forensic Identifciation 136, 138 (1995).
43. Federal Bureau of Investigation, U.S. Dep't of Justice, LAW ENFORCEMENT BULLETIN: AN ANALYSIS OF STANDARDS IN FINGERPRINT IDENTIFICATION 6 (June 1972).
44. International Association for Identification, IAI STANDARDIZATION COMMITTEE REPORT 1 (1973).
45. National Academy of Sciences, *supra* note 1, at 139 (emphasis supplied).
46. *Id.*
47. National Academy of Sciences, *supra* note 1, at 141-42.
48. International Association for Identification, *Resolution VII*, 29 Identification News 1 (Aug. 1979) ("[A]ny member, officer, or certified latent print examiner who provides oral or written reports, or gives testimony of possible, probable, or likely [print] identification shall be deemed to be engaged in conduct unbecoming a member, officer, or certified latent print examiner."); International Association for Identification, *Resolution V*, 30 Identification News 3 (Aug. 1980) (allowing probabilistic testimony when there is threat of a court sanction for failing to do otherwise).
49. National Academy of Sciences, *supra* note 1, at 122.
50. *Id.*
51. Itiel E. Dror, David Charlton, and Ailsa E. Peron, *Contextual Information Renders Experts Vulnerable to Making Erroneous Identifications*, 156 Forensic Science International 74-78 (2006).
52. *Id.* at 75.
53. *Id.* at 75-76.
54. *Id.* at 76.

55. *Id.*

56. *Id.* at 77.

57. In a related follow-up study, Dror and Charlton gave six other experienced fingerprint examiners eight pairs of fingerprints. Itiel E. Dror and David Charlton, *Why Experts Make Errors*, 56 Journal of Forensic Identification 600 (2006). Unbeknownst to the examiners, they had examined each pair before, making matches in four and exclusions in the other four. Again, these prior determinations were verified by independent examiners. *Id.* at 607. For each examiner, four of the pairs served as controls, and the examiners received them without any extraneous context information. For two of the remaining pairs, for which the examiners had found a match in prior examinations, the examiners were given routine, nonextreme contextual information that seemed to imply that the suspect could not have committed the crime (e.g., a statement such as "suspect was in police custody at the time of the crime"). For the other two remaining pairs, which the examiners had excluded (i.e., found a nonmatch) in prior examinations, examiners received routine, nonextreme contextual information that implied guilt (e.g., "suspect confessed to the crime.") *Id.* at 608. The results both replicated and enlarged upon the results in the prior study: fully two-thirds of the examiners came to decisions inconsistent with those they had already come to in the past on the same pairs of prints. *Id.* at 610-12.

58. *Theory of Identification, Range of Striae Comparison Reports, and Modified Glossary Definitions: An AFTE Criteria for Identification Committee Report,* 24 Journal of the Association of Firearm and Toolmark Examiners 336-40 (1992).

59. *Id.* at 336.

60. National Academy of Sciences, *supra* note 1, at 155.

61. *Id.* at 153.

62. *Id.* at 153-54.

63. W. J. Bodziak, Footwear Impression Evidence: Detection, Recovery, and Examination 329 (1999, 2nd ed.).

64. National Academy of Sciences, *supra* note 1, at 147.

65. *Id.*

66. M. J. Cassidy, Footwear Identification (1980).

67. National Academy of Sciences, *supra* note 1, at 147-49.

68. *Id.* at 149.

69. *Id.*

70. M. Houck and B. Budowle, *Correlation of Microscopic and Mitochondrial DNA Hair Comparisons,* 47 J. Forensic Sciences 974 (2002).

71. National Academy of Sciences, *supra* note 1, at 160-61.

72. *Id.* at 161.
73. *Id.* at 161.
74. *Id.* at 161.
75. *Id.* at 163.
76. J. A. Kieser, *Weighing Bitemark Evidence: A Postmodern Perspective*, 1 Journal of Forensic Science, Medicine, and Pathology 75-80 (2005).
77. American Board of Forensic Odontology, accessed July 1, 2011, at www.abfo. org.
78. National Academy of Sciences, *supra* note 1, at 173-74.
79. American Board of Forensic Odontology, *supra* note 77.
80. National Academy of Sciences, *supra* note 1, at 174, quoting C. M. Bowers, *Problem-Based Analysis of Bite Mark Misidentifications: The Role of DNA*, 159 Supp. 1 Forensic Science International s104-s109 (2006).
81. I. A. Pretty and D. Sweet, *The Scientific Basis for Human Bitemark Analyses: A Critical Review*, 41 Science and Justice 85-92 (2001).
82. National Academy of Science, *supra* note 1, at 176.
83. *Id.* at 178.
84. *Id.*
85. Contrary to what most people seem to believe, most people interrogated by the police talk to them voluntarily, even after receiving *Miranda* warnings, which tell suspects that they need not talk, and that if they do, the state will try to use their statements against them. More than 70 percent of those with previous felony records, and 90 percent of those with no previous record, speak to the police despite these warnings. See Richard A. Leo, *The Impact of Miranda Revisited*, 86 J. Crim. L. & Criminology 621 (1996).
86. In place of the idea that innocent people would never confess to a crime they did not commit, we must acknowledge the myth of psychological interrogation. Richard A. Leo, *False Confessions: Causes, Consequences, and Solutions*, in WRONGLY CONVICTED: PERSPECTIVES ON FAILED JUSTICE (S. D. Westervelt and J. A. Humphreys, ed.) (2001), 36-37. While we have always thought that psychological pressure during interrogation could not produce false confessions, this is an illusion; "police-induced false confessions occur with troubling frequency in the American criminal justice system." Richard A. Leo, POLICE INTERROGATION AND AMERICAN JUSTICE 38 (2008).
87. Tom Wells and Richard A. Leo, THE WRONG GUYS: MURDER, CONFESSIONS, AND THE NORFOLK FOUR (2008).
88. *Id.*
89. *Id.*
90. *Id.*

91. *Id.*
92. *Id.*
93. Richard A. Leo and Deborah Davis, "From False Confession to Wrongful Conviction: Seven Psychological Processes," 38 Journal of Psyoliatry and Law 9 (2010).
94. Tom Wells and Richard A. Leo, *supra* note 87.
95. *Id.*
96. *Id.*
97. *Id.* at 255 (quoting Peter Neufeld of the Innocence Project, saying that it would be very rare for a prosecutor to go ahead with a case in which DNA excluded even one suspect, let alone more than one. "[I]n 99 percent of those instances, those charges will be dismissed.").
98. *Id.* at 55.
99. *Id.* at 120, 163.
100. Id. at 184.
101. *Id.*
102. John E. Reid & Associates, Inc., Company Information, accessed May 9, 2010, at http://www.reid.com/r_about.html.
103. *Id.* at 212.
104. For a history of the Reid Technique and its various incarnations and appearances, see Brian R. Gallini, *Police "Science" in the Interrogation Room: The Use of Pseudo-Psychological Interrogation Methods to Obtain Seventy Years of Inadmissible Confessions*, 61 Hastings Law J. 529 (2010).
105. *Id.* at 531, 533.
106. Fred E. Inbau, John E. Reid, Joseph P. Buckley, and Brian C. Jayne, CRIMINAL INTERROGATION AND CONFESSIONS (2001, 4th ed.).
107. *Id.* at chapter 13, "The Reid Nine Steps of Interrogation," 209-397.
108. See, e.g., Carol Tavris and Elliot Aronson, MISTAKES WERE MADE (BUT NOT BY ME): WHY WE JUSTIFY FOOLISH BELIEFS, BAD DECISIONS, AND HURTFUL ACTS 141 (2007) (characterizing the Reid and Inbau text as "[the] Bible of interrogation methods"); Welsh S. White, MIRANDA'S WANING PROTECTIONS 25 (2001) ("Of all the interrogation manuals, the Inbau Manual, as it is commonly known, has been the most influential."); Miriam S. Gohara, *A Lie for a Lie: False Confessions and the Case for Reconsidering the Legality of Deceptive Interrogation Techniques*, 33 Fordham Urb. L.J. 791, 808 (2006) ("The interrogation method most widely publicized and probably most widely used is known as the Reid Technique."); Max Minzner, *Detecting Lies Using Demeanor, Bias, and Context*, 29 Cardozo L. Rev. 2557, 2560 (2008) (describing the Reid technique as "[t]he most influential current training method for law enforcement [for interrogation]"); Charles

Weisselberg, *Mourning Miranda*, 96 Cal. L. Rev. 1519, 1532 (2008) (citing John E. Reid & Associates as "[t]he largest national provider of training in interrogation techniques"); Marvin Zalman and Brad Smith, *The Attitudes of Police Executives toward Miranda and Interrogation Policies*, 97 J. Crim. L. & Criminology 873, 919 (2007) (Reid & Associates training "is the largest and best-known training program for police interrogations."); see also Richard J. Ofshe and Richard A. Leo, *The Social Psychology of Police Interrogation: The Theory and Classification of True and False Confessions*, 16 Stud. L. Pol. & Soc'y 189, 190 (1997) (calling the Inbau and Reid manual "the most popular police training manual"). In fact, the company itself says the Inbau, Reid, et al. book "is considered by the courts and practitioners to be the 'Bible' for interviewing and interrogation techniques." John E. Reid & Associates, Company Information, supra note 102.

109. Fred E. Inbau, John E. Reid, Joseph P. Buckley, and Brian C. Jayne, et al., *supra* note 106, at 5.

110. *Id.* at 5-6.

111. *Id.* at 6-7.

112. *Id.* at 7-8.

113. *Id.* at 8.

114. *Id.* at 173.

115. *Id.*

116. Richard A. Leo, *The Third Degree and the Origins of Psychological Interrogation in the United States*, in INTERROGATIONS, CONFESSIONS, AND ENTRAPMENT 66 (G. Daniel Lassiter, ed.) (2004).

117. Fred E. Inbau, John E. Reid, Joseph P. Buckley, and Brian C. Jayne, et al., *supra* note 106, at 8.

118. *Id.*

119. *Id.*

120. *Id.* at 57-64.

121. *Id.* at 218-19.

122. *Id.* at 219.

123. Richard A. Leo, *supra* note 116, at 67.

124. *Id.* at 67. See also Saul M. Kassin, *The Psychology of Confessions*, 4 Annual Rev. Law Soc. Sci. 193, 197 (2008) ("[T]here is no evidence to support the diagnostic value of the verbal and nonverbal cues that investigators [using the Reid technique] are trained to observe.").

125. Richard A. Leo, *supra* note 116, at 67.

126. Saul M. Kassin and Christina T. Fong, *I'm Innocent! Effects of Training on Judgments of Truth and Deception in the Interrogation Room*, 23 Law & Hum. Behav. 499 (1999).

127. S. M. Kassin, C. A. Meissner, and R. J. Norwick, *"I'd Know a False Confession If I Saw One": A Comparative Study of College Students and Police Investigators*, 29 Law and Human Behavior 211-27 (2005).

128. E.g., Aldert Vrij, Detectng Lies and Deceit: Pitfalls and Opportunities (2008, 2nd ed.); Aldert Virj, Samantha Mann, and Ronald P. Fisher, *An Empirical Test of the Behaviour Analysis Interview*, 30 Law & Human Behavior 329 (2006) (demonstrating that the evocation of different verbal and nonverbal responses from truth tellers and deceivers, as predicted by the Reid Technique, did not work and therefore the Reid Technique would have little or no value in ferreting out lies); Charles F. Bond and Bella M. DePaulo, *Accuracy of Deception Judgments*, 10 Personal Soc. Psychol. Rev. 214, 230 (2006) (meta-analysis noting that "the average person discriminates lies from truths at a level slightly better than he or she could achieve by flipping a coin"); Saul M. Kassin and Gisli H. Gudjonsson, *The Psychology of Confessions: A Review of the Literature and Issues*, 5 Psych. Sci. in the Pub. Int. 33, 37 (2004) ("Despite popular conceptions, psychological research conducted throughout the Western world has failed to support the claim that groups of individuals can attain high average levels of accuracy in judging truth and deception. Most experiments have shown that people [including police investigators] perform at no better than chance levels," citing numerous contemporary studies.); B. M. DePaulo, J. J. Lindsay, B. E. Malone, L. Muhlenbruck, K. Charlton, and H. Cooper, *Cues to Deception*, 129 Psychological Bulletin 74-112 (2003).

129. Steven A. Drizin and Richard A. Leo, *The Problem of False Confessions in the Post-DNA World*, 82 N.C. L. Rev. 891 (2004).

130. *Id.* at 891.

131. *Id.* 915.

132. *Id.*

133. *Frazier v. Cupp*, 394 U.S. 731 (1969).

134. Steven A. Drizin and Richard A. Leo, *supra* note 129, at 914.

135. *Id.* at 892.

136. *Id.* at 907, tbl. 1.

137. *Id.* at 921.

138. *Id.* at 922.

139. Saul Kassin and K. Neumann, *On the Power of Confession Evidence: An Experimental Test of the "Fundamental Difference" Hypothesis*, 21 Law & Human Behavior 469-84 (1997).

140. Richard Leo and Richard Ofshe, *The Consequences of False Confessions: Deprivations of Liberty and Miscarriages of Justice in the Age of Psychological Interrogation*, 88 J. Crim. L. & Criminology 429 (1998).

141. Steven Drizin and Richard Leo, *supra* note 129.
142. Saul Kassin and Gisli Gudjonsson, *supra* note 128, at 56.
143. E. E. Jones, INTERPERSONAL PERCEPTIONS (1990); L. Ross, *The Intuitive Psychologist and His Shortcomings: Distortions in the Attribution Process*, 10 Advances in Experimental Social Psychology 174-221 (1977).
144. S. M. Kassin, C. A. Meissner, and R. J. Norwick, *supra* note 127.
145. *Id.*
146. Saul M. Kassin, *A Critical Appraisal of Modern Police Interrogations*, in INVESTIGATIVE INTERVIEWING: RIGHTS, RESEARCH, REGULATION (T. Williamson, ed.) (2006), 207-28.
147. Gary L. Wells, Amina Memon, and Steven D. Penrod, *Eyewitness Evidence: Improving Its Probative Value*, 7 Psych. Sci. in the Public Interest 45, 60 (2006) (citing numerous sources demonstrating the unique persuasive power of eyewitness testimony).
148. The Innocence Project, *Understand the Causes: Eyewitness Identifications*, accessed May 24, 2010, at http://www.innocenceproject.org/understand/ Eyewitness-Misidentification.php (Mistaken eyewitness identifications play "a role in more than 75 percent of convictions overturned through DNA testing.").
149. *Id.*
150. The Innocence Project, *Know the Causes: Unvalidated or Improper Forensic Science*, accessed May 24, 2010, at http://www.innocenceproject.org/understand/Unreliable-Limited-Science.php.
151. The Innocence Project, *Know the Causes: False Confessions/Admissions*, accessed May 24, 2010, at http://www.innocenceproject.org/understand/ False-Confessions.php.
152. These percentages add up to more than 100 percent because in some cases, more than one error becomes the source of the wrongful conviction.
153. Gary L. Wells, Amina Memon, and Steven D. Penrod, *supra* note 147, at 49-50.
154. The facts of the Kirk Bloodsworth case come from *State of Maryland v. Kirk N. Bloodsworth*, 84-CR-3138 (Baltimore Co., MD, 1984); Gary L. Wells, Amina Memon, and Steven D. Penrod, *supra* note 147, at 46; the Innocence Project, *Know the Cases: Kirk Bloodsworth*, accessed May 24, 2010, at http:// www.innocenceproject.org/Content/54.php.
155. Hugo Munsterberg, ON THE WITNESS STAND (1908).
156. See, e.g., Gary L. Wells, Amina Memon, and Steven D. Penrod, *supra* note 147, at 47, for works cited there by many early-twentieth-century psychologists.
157. *Id.*

158. *Id.*

159. One can get a sense of Wells's prominence among his colleagues from Atul Gawande, *Under Suspicion, Science on Trial*, New Yorker, Jan. 8, 2001, discussing Wells as the leading researcher in the field. For a large, yet not quite complete, accounting of Wells's work and its wide influence in the world, see his website at Iowa State University, archiving a considerable amount of his work and articles about it generated elsewhere. Gary L. Wells, website, Iowa State University, accessed May 24, 2010, at http://www.psychology.iastate.edu/~glwells/.

160. Gary L. Wells and E. Luus, *Police Lineups as Experiments: Social Methodology as a Framework for Properly-Conducted Lineups*, 16 Personality and Social Psychology Bulletin 106-17 (1990).

161. Gary L. Wells, Mark Small, Steven Penrod, Roy S. Malpass, Solomon M. Fulero, and C. A. E. Brimacombe, *Eyewitness Identification Procedures: Recommendations for Lineups and Photospreads*, 22 Law & Human Behavior 1, 13 (1998).

162. *Id.* at 13-14.

163. Gary L. Wells, *The Psychology of Lineup Identifications*, 14 Journal of Applied Social Psychology 89-103 (1984).

164. See Gary L. Wells, Amina Memon, and Steven D. Penrod, *supra* note 147, at 61.

165. *Id.*

166. Roy Malpass and Patricia Devine, *Eyewitness Identification: Lineup Instructions and the Absence of the Offender*, 66 Journal of Applied Psychology 482-89 (1981).

167. *Id.*

168. It is worth noting that one recent meta-analysis indicated that rate of correct identifications might be slightly depressed by the instruction. Steven Clark, *A Re-Examination of the Effects of Biased Lineup Instructions in Eyewitness Identification*, 29 Law and Human Behavior 395-424 (2005). But "the decline in accurate identifications when the target is present is much smaller than the decline in mistaken identifications when the target is absent," Gary L. Wells, Amina Memon, and Steven D. Penrod, *supra* note 147, at 62, thus obtaining a significant reduction in mistaken identifications for the cost of a much smaller reduction in correct identifications. Still, assuming that Clark's analysis is correct, it is important to recognize the tradeoff as real, and to say that the question of whether the cost is worthwhile is ultimately one for policy makers.

169. C. A. E. Luus and Gary L. Wells, *Eyewitness Identification and the Selection of Distracters for Lineups*, 15 Law and Human Behavior 43-57 (1991).

170. Gary L. Wells, S. Rydell, and E. Seelau, *On the Selection of Distracters for Eyewitness Lineups,* 78 Journal of Applied Psychology 835-44 (1993).

171. *Id.*

172. This also shows up in the AP/LS white paper, if in a slightly different form. See Gary L. Wells, Mark Small, Steven Penrod, Roy S. Malpass, Solomon M. Fulero, and C. A. E. Brimacombe, *supra* note 161, at 23-27.

173. Gary L. Wells, Amina Memon, and Steven D. Penrod, *supra* note 147, at 63.

174. R. Haw and R. Fisher, *Effects of Administrator-Witness Contact on Eyewitness Accuracy,* 89 Journal of Applied Psychology 1106-12 (2004).

175. L. Garrioch and C. A. E. Brimacombe, *Lineup Administrators' Expectations: Their Impact on Eyewitness Confidence,* 25 Law and Human Behavior 299-314 (2001).

176. *Id.*; see also Gary L. Wells, Mark Small, Steven Penrod, Roy S. Malpass, Solomon M. Fulero, and C. A. E. Brimacombe, *supra* note 161, at 21-22.

177. O. MacLin, L. Zimmerman, and R. Malpass, *PC Eyewitness and the Sequential Superiority Effect: Computer-Based Lineup Administration,* 29 Law and Human Behavior 303-21 (2005) (describing how such a computer program would work).

178. R. C. L. Lindsay and Gary L. Wells, *Improving Eyewitness Identification from Lineups: Simultaneous versus Sequential Lineup Presentations,* 70 Journal of Applied Psychology 556-64 (1985).

179. Gary L. Wells, Amina Memon, and Steven D. Penrod, *supra* note 147, at 63.

180. *Id.*

181. N. Steblay, J. Dysart, S. Fulero, and R. C. L. Lindsay, *Eyewitness Accuracy Rates in Sequential and Simultaneous Lineup Presentations: A Meta-Analytic Comparison,* 25 Law and Human Behavior 459-74 (2001).

182. Gary L. Wells, Amina Memon, and Steven D. Penrod, *supra* note 147, at 63.

183. C. Meissner, C. Tredoux, J. Parker, and O. MacLin, *Eyewitness Decisions in Simultaneous and Sequential Lineups,* 33 Memory and Cognition 783-92 (2005).

184. Gary L. Wells, Amina Memon, and Steven D. Penrod, *supra* note 147, at 64.

185. Recently, the state of Illinois conducted a field test comparing the simultaneous and sequential lineup identification methods. Illinois Pilot Program on Double-Blind Sequential Procedures (2006), accessed at May 26, 2010, at http://www.chicagopolice.org/IL%20Pilot%20on%20Eyewitness%20ID.pdf. It was the first such study by a major American jurisdiction, and many felt it presented the opportunity to demonstrate the superiority of the new and improved sequential approach. The results of the study sent shock waves through the community of scientists who study eyewitness

identification and lineups: the report on the experiment stated that the traditional approach of simultaneous lineups produced fewer identifications of fillers, and more correct identifications, than the sequential lineups did. *Id.* at iii-v. But analysis of the methods used uncovered a fundamental mistake in the structure of the test. The sequential lineups in the study always utilized the double-blind method discussed above, in which the experimenter—in this instance, the person conducting the lineup—does not know which member of the lineup police have selected as the target for their suspicions. *Id.* at 32 ("[T]he Illinois Pilot Program protocol required that every sequential lineup be conducted by a blind administrator—no exceptions."). Recall that this constitutes standard operating procedure for credible science, because of the experimenter-expectancy effect: the subtle cues given to the subject by the person conducting any face-to-face experiment who knows the correct answer. The simultaneous lineups, on the other hand, "were always conducted by the case detectives" —they were not blind tests, because detectives conducting them knew the "right" answer. Gary L. Wells, Amina Memon, and Steven D. Penrod, *supra* note 147, at 64. Thus the simultaneous lineups produced more correct and fewer incorrect identifications: the witnesses in those lineups received subtle hints of which selection the detective preferred. This result is exactly what the many studies of the experimenter-expectancy effect would have predicted.

186. A. Bradfield and Gary L. Wells, *The Perceived Validity of Eyewitness Identification Testimony: A Test of the Five Biggers Criteria*, 24 Law and Human Behavior 581-94 (2000).

187. *Manson v. Brathwaite*, 423 U.S. 98, 115 (1977) (Court stated that "[t]he witness's level of certainty" is one of the five prime factors in deciding how reliable an identification is.).

188. Gary L. Wells, Amina Memon, and Steven D. Penrod, *supra* note 147, at 65.

189. S. Sporer, Steven Penrod, D. Read, B. Cutler, *Choosing, Confidence, and Accuracy: A Meta-Analysis of the Confidence-Accuracy Relation in Eyewitness Identification Studies*, 118 Psychological Bulletin 315-27 (1995).

190. Gary L. Wells, E. Olsen, and S. Charman, *Eyewitness Identification Confidence*, 11 Current Directions in Psychological Science 151-54 (2002).

191. Gary L. Wells, Amina Memon, and Steven D. Penrod, *supra* note 147, at 65.

192. Gary L. Wells and A. Bradfield, *"Good, You Identified the Suspect": Feedback to Eyewitnesses Distorts Their Reports of the Witnessing Experience*, 83 Journal of Applied Psychology 360-76 (1998).

193. Gary L. Wells, Amina Memon, and Steven D. Penrod, *supra* note 147, at 66.

194. A. Bradfield, Gary L. Wells, E. Olsen, *The Damaging Effect of Confirming Feedback on the Relation between Eyewitness Certainty and Identification Accuracy*, 87 Journal of Applied Psychology 112-20 (2002).

195. Gary L. Wells, Amina Memon, and Steven D. Penrod, *supra* note 147, at 67, citing Gary L. Wells and A. Bradfield, *Distortions in Eyewitnesses' Recollections: Can the Post-Identification Feedback Effect Be Moderated?* 10 Psychological Science 138-44 (1999).

CHAPTER 3

1. Curtis Steven, *Record Time*, City Limits, Oct. 15, 2003, accessed June 8, 2010, at http://www.citylimits.org/news/articles/2993/record-time.

2. *Id.*

3. Cornelia Grumman, Editorial, *When Believing Isn't Seeing*, Chicago Tribune, Sept. 30, 2002.

4. Bill Moushey and Nathan Crabbe, *Questionable Identifications Sent 2 to Jail*, Pittsburgh Post-Gazette, May 9, 2005, accessed June 14, 2011, at http://www.post-gazette.com/pg/05129/501377-85.stm.

5. *Id.*

6. Susan Saulny, *National Law Group Endorses Videotaping of Interrogations*, N.Y. Times, Feb. 10, 2004, accessed June 9, 2010, at http://www.nytimes.com/2004/02/10/nyregion/national-law-group-endorses-videotaping-of-interrogations.html.

7. Barry Scheck, Peter Neufeld, and Jim Dwyer, ACTUAL INNOCENCE: WHEN JUSTICE GOES WRONG AND HOW TO MAKE IT RIGHT (2003, updated edition).

8. *Id.*

9. Maurice Possley, Steve Mills, and Flynn McRoberts, *Scandal Touches Even Elite Labs*, Chicago Tribune, Oct. 21, 2004.

10. *Id.*

11. *Id.*

12. The work of Tom Tyler of New York University helps to explain the importance of citizens' belief in the integrity of the system. If people do not believe that the criminal justice system will treat them fairly, Tyler says, they become less willing and less likely to obey the law. See, e.g., Tom R. Tyler, WHY PEOPLE OBEY THE LAW (2006) (suggesting that citizens obey the law because they see it and legal institutions like the police as legitimate). Thus the failure of the system to bear the costs necessary to avoid incorrect outcomes strikes at the heart of what the law does for society.

13. *Witness to the Prosecution*, Texas Lawyer, June 9, 2008.

14. *Id.*

15. *Id.*

16. Video, NDAA Message to Prosecutors Regarding the National Academy of Sciences Forensic Science Report, National District Attorneys Association, accessed June 7, 2010, at http://www.wininteractive.com/NDAA/NAS.html.

17. *Id.*

18. Solomon Moore, *Exoneration Using DNA Brings Change in Legal System*, N.Y. Times, Oct. 1, 2007 (quoting letter from California State Sheriffs Association to the California Commission on the Fair Administration of Justice).

19. Testimony of Barry D. Matson, Committee on Judiciary, United States Senate, Sept. 9, 2009.

20. *Id.* at 2.

21. *Id.* at 4.

22. Patrik Jonsson, *The Police Lineup Is Becoming Suspect Practice*, Christian Science Monitor, Feb. 6, 2007, accessed July 1, 2010, at http://www.csmonitor.com/2004/1208/p11s01-usju.html (noting that "a handful of police departments" had changed lineup practices, but "resistance to top-down reform from the majority of American police chiefs and prosecutors is pushing the debate into the legislative chamber.").

23. Bruce Gerstman, *Governor to Take Up Lineup Bill*, Contra Costa Times, Oct. 13, 2007.

24. IACP Capitol Report Update, November 2009, accessed June 8, 2010, at http://theiacp.org/LegislativeAction/CapitolReportUpdate/tabid/626/Default.aspx.

25. *Id.*

26. E.g., *Brown v. Mississippi*, 297 U.S. 278 (1936) (Confession cannot be used in court when police use force to make defendant speak.).

27. *Arizona v. Fulminante*, 499 U.S. 279 (1991) (Police informant offered to protect inmate from physical violence inside prison, but only if inmate would confess to him.).

28. Randy Dotinga, *Criminal Lineups Get a Makeover*, Christian Science Monitor, Dec. 8, 2004, accessed June 11, 2010, at http://www.csmonitor.com/2004/1208/p11s01-usju.html.

29. Cornelia Grumman, *supra* note 3.

30. *Id.*

31. Patrik Jonsson, *supra* note 22.

32. *Id.*

33. See chapter 2, *supra*.

34. *Id.*

35. Gabrielle Banks, *Pennsylvania Panel to Study Wrongful Convictions,* Pittsburgh Post-Gazette, May 31, 2007, accessed Dec. 23, 2010, at http://www.post-gazette.com/pg/07090/774016-85.stm.

36. Bobby Kerlik, *Pittsburgh-Area Police May Test Interrogation Changes,* Pittsburgh Tribune-Review, July 27, 2009, accessed June 14, 2009, at http://www.pittsburghlive.com/x/pittsburghtrib/news/pittsburgh/s_635409.html.

37. *Id.*

38. Bill Moushey and Nathan Crabbe, *supra* note 4.

39. Richard Willing, *Police Lineups Encourage Wrong Picks, Experts Say,* USA Today, accessed June 14, 2002, at http://www.usatoday.com/news/nation/2002-11-25-police-lineups-cover-usat_x.htm.

40. Written Testimony of Matthew F. Redle, County and Prosecuting Attorney, Sheridan County, Wyoming, Senate Committee on the Judiciary, Hearing, Strengthening Forensic Science in the United States, Sept. 9, 2009.

41. *Id.*

42. Curtis Stephen, *supra* note 1.

43. *Id.*

44. Testimony of Barry D. Matson, *supra* note 19.

45. American Bar Association Criminal Justice Section, The Prosecution Function, Standard 3-1.2(b) ("The prosecutor is an administrator of justice, an advocate, and an officer of the court; the prosecutor must exercise sound discretion in the exercise of his or her functions.") and (c) ("The duty of the prosecutor is to seek justice, not merely to convict.").

46. American Bar Association Criminal Justice Section, The Defense Function Standard 4-1.2(b) ("The basic duty defense counsel owes to the administration of justice and as an officer of the court is to serve as the accused's counselor and advocate with courage and devotion and to render effective, quality representation.").

47. Rick Hepp, *DNA Tests Topple Murder Conviction,* Newark Star-Ledger, July 30, 2005.

48. *Id.*

49. See discussion in chapter 2 of Tom Wells and Richard A. Leo, THE WRONG GUYS: MURDER, FALSE CONFESSIONS, AND THE NORFOLK FOUR (2008).

50. *Id.*

51. Steve Mills, *Prosecutor, DNA at Odds,* Chicago Tribune, Dec. 15, 2008.

52. *Id.*

53. *Id.*

54. *Id.*

55. *Id.*

56. *Id.*

57. *Id.*

58. *Id.*

59. *DNA, Exoneration, and Compensation: A Discussion*, National Public Radio, June 13, 2007, accessed June 10, 2010, at http://www.npr.org/templates/ story/story.php?storyId=11012152.

60. *Id.*

61. Peter A. Modafferi, *Eyewitness Identification: A View from the Trenches*, The Police Chief, October 2009, accessed April 29, 2010, at http://policechiefmagazine.org/magazine/index. cfm?fuseaction=display&article_id=1926&issue_id=102009.

62. Written Testimony of Matthew F. Redle, *supra* note 40.

63. Testimony of Honorable Paul A. Logli, State's Attorney, Winnebago County, Illinois, and Chair, National District Attorneys Association Capital Litigation Subcommittee before a Hearing of the Committee of the Judiciary on the Innocence Protection Act, June 18, 2002.

64. Mark Hansen, *Untrue Confessions*, ABA Journal, July 1999.

65. Ken Armstrong, Steve Mills, and Maurice Possley, *Coercive and Illegal Tactics Torpedo Scores of Cook County Murder Cases*, Chicago Tribune, Dec. 16, 2001, accessed June 7, 2010, at http://www.chicagotribune.com/news/ watchdog/chi-011216confession,0,1748927.story.

66. April Witt, *Allegations of Abuse Mar Murder Cases*, Washington Post, June 23, 2001, accessed June 15, 2001, at http://www.washingtonpost.com/wp-dyn/content/article/2008/02/15/AR2008021501521.html.

67. *Id.*

68. *Id.*

69. Susan Saulny, *supra* note 6.

70. The Innocence Project, *Understanding the Causes: False Confessions*, accessed June 15, 2010, at http://www.innocenceproject.org/understand/ False-Confessions.php.

71. The Innocence Project, *Understanding the Causes: Unvalidated or Improper Forensic Science*, accessed June 15, 2010, at http://www.innocenceproject. org/understand/Unreliable-Limited-Science.php.

CHAPTER 4

1. Stanley Z. Fisher, *In Search of the Virtuous Prosecutor: A Conceptual Framework*, 15 Am. J. Crim. L. 197, 204-13 (explaining influences that result in prosecutors pursuing guilty verdicts and sentences "overzealously"); Bennett L. Gershman, *The New Prosecutors*, 53 U. Pitt. L. Rev. 393, 458 (1992) (describing as "ingrained" the "ethos of overzealous prosecutorial advocacy"); Judith L. Maute, *"In Pursuit of Justice" in High-Profile Criminal*

Matters, 70 Fordham L. Rev. 1745, 1747 (2002) (concerning "overzealous prosecutors" inclined to "become too closely aligned" with witnesses willing to trim their testimony to get a conviction).

2. Bennett L. Gershman, *The Prosecutor's Duty to the Truth*, 14 Geo J. Legal Ethics 309, 350 (2001); see also Anthony V. Alfieri, *Prosecuting Race*, 48 Duke L.J. 1157, 1242-45 (1999) (ways in which "moral norms" guide prosecutorial discretion).

3. Rule 3.8, comment 1, of the American Bar Association's Model Rules of Professional Conduct (2001) obligates prosecutors not only to act as the advocate for the state but also to ensure that justice is done ("A prosecutor has the responsibility of a minister of justice and not simply that of an advocate.").

4. See Tracey L. Meares, *Rewards for Good Behavior: Influencing Prosecutorial Discretion and Conduct with Financial Incentives*, 64 Fordham L. Rev. 851, 890 (1995) ("Prosecutorial misconduct is readily apparent to any lawyer who keeps abreast of appellate review of criminal convictions.").

5. Alafair Burke, *Improving Prosecutorial Decision Making: Some Lessons of Cognitive Science*, 47 Wm. & Mary L. Rev. 1587, 1590 (2006).

6. *Id.* at 1593.

7. Leon Festinger, A Theory of Cognitive Dissonance (1957).

8. Andrew M. Colman, A Dictionary of Psychology 144 (2009) (definition of cognitive dissonance, explaining "cognitions" as "items of knowledge or belief").

9. Elliot Aronson, *Back to the Future: Retrospective Review of Leon Festinger's "A Theory of Cognitive Dissonance,"* 110 Am. J. Psychol. 127, 128 (1997).

10. Andrew J. McClurg, *Good Cop, Bad Cop: Using Cognitive Dissonance Theory to Reduce Police Lying*, 32 U.C. Davis L. J. 389, 393 (1999).

11. Leon Festinger, *supra* note 7, at 1-31.

12. Carol Tavris and Elliot Aronson, Mistakes Were Made (But Not by Me) 13 (2007).

13. Elliot Aronson, The Social Animal 176 (1995, 7th ed.).

14. This process, of course, repeated itself each time the DNA tests revealed that the second defendant, the third defendant, etc., had not been the source of the DNA. See chapter 2. Though I have described what happened in the case through the concept of cognitive dissonance, one could also view it as a case demonstrating confirmation bias: "a tendency to seek and interpret evidence in ways that support existing or favored beliefs." Barbara O'Brien, *A Recipe for Bias: An Empirical Look at the Interplay between Institutional Incentive and Bounded Rationality in Prosecutorial Decision Making*, 74 Missouri L. Rev. 999, 1011 (2009).

15. *Mapp v. Ohio*, 367 U.S. 643 (1961). Mapp applied this exclusionary rule to the states for the first time; the rule had applied in federal courts for decades. *U.S. v. Weeks*, 232 U.S. 383 (1914).

16. See, e.g., Remo Franceschini, A MATTER OF HONOR: ONE COP'S LIFELONG PURSUIT OF JOHN GOTTI AND THE MOB (1993), describing how the advent of *Mapp* caused police officers in New York to begin to lie about the seizure of narcotics in order to escape suppression of the evidence.

17. Irving Younger, *The Perjury Routine*, The Nation, May 8, 1967, at 596.

18. Alan M. Dershowitz, THE BEST DEFENSE xxi-xxii (1982).

19. Alan M. Dershowitz, REASONABLE DOUBTS 60 (1996).

20. *Id.* at 61.

21. Report, The City of New York Commission to Investigate Allegations of Police Corruption and the Anti-Corruption Procedures of the Police Department (1994) (hereinafter the Mollen Commission Report).

22. *Id.* at 36.

23. Andrew J. McClurg, *supra* note 10, at 391.

24. *Id.* at 391-92.

25. *Id.* at 392-93.

26. *Id.* at 411-15.

27. The Mollen Commission Report, *supra* note 21, at 41.

28. *Id.*

29. John K. Cochran and Max L. Bromley, *The Myth (?) of the Police Sub-culture*, 26 Policing: An International Journal of Police Strategies & Management 88, 90 (2003) ("[The police] come to see themselves as the 'thin blue line' that prevents society from slipping permanently into moral decay and unrest.").

30. Mark Baker, COPS: THEIR LIVES IN THEIR OWN WORDS 247-48 (1985) ("If we're going to catch these guys, fuck the Constitution, fuck the Bill of Rights, fuck them, fuck you, fuck everybody. The only ones I care about are my partners.").

31. Testimony of Barry D. Matson, Committee on Judiciary, United States Senate, Sept. 9, 2009, accessed at http://www.ndaa.org/pdf/matson_testimony.pdf.

32. Video recording, *NDAA's Message to Prosecutors Regarding the National Academy of Sciences Forensics Sciences Report, 2009*, accessed at http://www.wininteractive.com/NDAA/NAS.html.

33. Andrew J. McClurg, *supra* note 10, at 391-92.

34. Video recording, *NDAA's Message to Prosecutors Regarding the National Academy of Sciences Forensics Sciences Report, 2009*, *supra* note 32.

35. Testimony of Honorable Paul A. Logli, State's Attorney, Winnebago County, Illinois, before a Hearing of the Committee of the Judiciary on the Innocence Protection Act, June 18, 2002, at 2.

36. Testimony of Barry D. Matson, *supra* note 31, at 2.

37. William R. Levesque, *Police Can Be Dead Certain, and Wrong*, St. Petersburg Times, April 6, 2003, accessed July 1, 2010, at http://www.psychology.iastate.edu/~glwells/StPetersburgTImes.pdf.

38. According to the Innocence Project, as of December 9, 2007, the day that District Attorney Fleming's comments appeared in the press, five men had been exonerated in Georgia. Each case involved a faulty eyewitness identification. Between that time and the time this is written, three more exonerations have occurred, for a total of eight. The Innocence Project, *National View, Exonerations by State, Georgia*, accessed July 1, 2010, at http://www.innocenceproject.org/news/state.php?state=GA.

39. Jonathan Springston, *State House Committee Releases Draft of Eyewitness ID Bill*, Atlanta Progressive News, Dec. 9, 2007, accessed July 1, 2010, at http://www.atlantaprogressivenews.com/news/0264.html.

40. David A. Harris, GOOD COPS: THE CASE FOR PREVENTIVE POLICING (2005), chapter 7, "Bending Granite or Curving Wood: Changing the Culture of Police Departments."

41. Mark Baker, *supra* note 30, at 247-48.

42. Alafair S. Burke, *Prosecutorial Passion, Cognitive Bias, and Plea Bargaining*, 91 Marquette L. Rev 183, 187 (2007).

43. S. Moscovici and M. Zavalloni, *The Group as a Polarizer of Attitudes*, 12 J. Personality and Social Psychol. 125-35 (1969).

44. Daniel J. Isenberg, *Group Polarization: A Critical Review and Meta-Analysis*, 50 J. Personality and Social Psychology 1141 (1986) (emphasis supplied).

45. Cass R. Sunstein, *The Law of Group Polarization*, 10 Journal of Political Philosophy 175, 176 (2002).

46. *Id.*

47. Gary S. Becker, THE ECONOMIC APPROACH TO HUMAN BEHAVIOR 14 (1976).

48. Thomas Gilovich, *Amos Tversky*, MIT ENCYCLOPEDIA OF THE COGNITIVE SCIENCES (Robert A. Wilson and Frank C. Keil, eds.), online version accessed June 15, 2010, at https://sremote.pitt.edu/library/erefs/mitecs/,DanaInfo=cognet.mit.edu+gilovich.html.

49. William Samuelson and Richard Zeckhauser, *Status Quo Bias in Decision Making*, 1 Journal of Risk and Uncertainty 7-8 (1988).

50. Daniel Kahneman and Amos Tversky, *Prospect Theory: An Analysis of Decision under Risk*, 47 Econometrica 263 (1979).

51. Milton Friedman, *The Methodology of Positive Economics*, in A SURVEY OF CONTEMPORARY ECONOMICS, Vol. II (B.F. Haley, ed.) (1952), 455-57.

52. Daniel Kahneman and Amos Tversky, *supra* note 50.

53. *Id.* at 268-69.

54. *Id.* at 273.

55. *Id.*

56. *Id.* at 277.

57. *Id.*

58. *Id.* at 279.

59. Thomas Gilovich, *supra* note 48.

60. Richard Thaler, *Toward a Positive Theory of Consumer Choice*, 1 Journal of Economic Behavior and Organization 39-60 (1980).

61. *Id.*

62. *Id.*

63. William Samuelson and Richard Zeckhauser, *supra* note 49.

64. *Id.* at 36.

65. *Id.* at 8.

66. *Id.*

67. *Id.*

68. *Id.*

69. *Id.* at 9.

70. *Id.* at 9-10, 37-38.

71. For the full discussion of the information summarized in the two sentences preceding this note, see chapter 2.

72. William Samuelson and Richard Zeckhauser, *supra* note 49.

73. For a discussion of social status, see, e.g., *Social Status*, New World Encyclopedia, accessed July 13, 2010, at http://www.newworldencyclopedia.org/entry/Social_status.

74. Dae H. Chang and Charles H. Zastrow, *Police Evaluative Perceptions of Themselves, the General Public, and Selected Occupational Groups*, 4 Journal of Criminal Justice 17 (1976) (Contrary to police expectations, members of the public perceive them not negatively but with considerable esteem.).

75. Lori H. Colwell, Holly A. Miller, Rowland S. Miller, and Phillip M. Lyons Jr., *U.S. Police Officers' Knowledge Regarding Behaviors Indicative of Deception: Implications for Eradicating Erroneous Beliefs through Training*, 12 Psychology Crime & Law 489 (2006).

76. *Id.* at 491.

CHAPTER 5

1. Interview with Bob Stewart, Jan. 19, 2011 (copy on file with the author).

2. April Witt, *Allegations of Abuses Mar Murder Cases*, Wash. Post, June 3, 2001, accessed Aug. 13, 2010, at http://www.washingtonpost.com/wp-dyn/content/story/2008/10/03/ST2008100302485.html.

3. Peter K. Manning, *The Police: Mandate, Strategies, and Appearances*, in THE POLICE AND SOCIETY: TOUCHSTONE READINGS (Victor E. Kappler, ed.) (1999, 2nd ed.), reprinted from Peter K. Manning and John Van Maanen, eds., POLICING: A VIEW FROM THE STREET (1978).

4. William F. Walsh, *Patrol Officer Arrest Rates: A Study of the Social Organization of Police Work*, 2 Justice Quarterly 271, 272 (1986).

5. *Id.* at 275-76.

6. *Id.* at 282.

7. Harry G. Levine, Jon B. Gettman, Craig Reinarman, and Deborah Peterson Small, *Drug Arrests and DNA: Building Jim Crow's Database*, 21 GeneWatch 9, 10 (Nov.–Dec. 2008) (extract from the full paper).

8. Richard R. Johnson, *Explaining Patrol Officer Drug Arrest Activity through Expectancy Theory*, 32 Policing: An International Journal of Police Strategies & Management 6 (2009).

9. *Id.*

10. Todd S. Purdom, *Transit Scandal: Do Arrest Incentives Motivate the Police or Invite Abuse?* N.Y. Times, Dec. 16, 1987.

11. Judith A. Goldberg and David M. Seigel, *The Ethical Obligations of Prosecutors in Cases Involving Postconviction Claims of Innocence*, 38 Cal. W. L. Rev. 389, 409 (2002).

12. Daniel S. Medwed, *The Zeal Deal: Prosecutorial Resistance to Post-Conviction Claims of Innocence*, 84 B. U. L. Rev. 125, 134 (2004).

13. George T. Felkenes, *The Prosecutor: A Look at Reality*, 7 Sw. U. L. Rev. 98, 114 (1975).

14. Daniel S. Medwed, *supra* note 12, at 134-35.

15. Abbe Smith, *Can You Be a Good Person and a Good Prosecutor?* 14 Geo. J. Legal Ethics 355, 388 (2001) ("In view of the institutional culture of prosecutors' offices and the culture of the adversary system generally, it is perhaps inevitable that the overriding interest of prosecutors would be winning.").

16. Barbara O'Brien, *A Recipe for Bias: An Empirical Look at the Interplay between Institutional Incentives and Bounded Rationality in Prosecutorial Decision Making*, 74 Missouri L. Rev. 999 (2009).

17. George T. Felkenes, *supra* note 13, at 99, 109-10 (While prosecutors care about fairness, nearly one-third of those queried indicated that their job was to secure convictions, "what may be termed the 'conviction psychology.'"); Stanley Z. Fisher, *In Search of the Virtuous Prosecutor: A Conceptual Framework*, 15 Am J. Crim. L. 197, 207 (1988) ("The moral and political climate in an agency can foster a 'conviction psychology' more powerfully than can any specific policy basing promotions on an assistant's conviction rate.")

18. George T. Felkenes, *supra* note 13, at 110.

19. Barbara E. Armacost, *Organizational Culture and Police Misconduct*, 72 Geo. Wash. L. Rev. 453 (2004).

20. E. Reuss-Ianni and F. A. J. Ianni, *Street Cops and Management Cops: The Two Cultures of Policing*, in CONTROL IN THE POLICE ORGANIZATION (M. Punch, ed.) (1983), 251-74.

21. Eugene A. Paoline III, *Taking Stock: Toward a Richer Understanding of Police Culture*, 31 Journal of Criminal Justice 199-214 (2003).

22. *Id.* at 200-202.

23. It is important to point out that some scholars of policing have said that the idea of a monolithic, unvarying police culture is outdated, and that, due to demographic changes and changes in agency philosophy (e.g., greater emphasis on community support and interaction and the like), policing and police agencies have a greater diversity of people and attitudes within them. John K. Cochran and Max L. Bromley, *The Myth (?) of the Police Sub-Culture*, 26 Policing: An International Journal of Police Strategies & Management 88 (2003); David Alan Sklansky, *Seeing Blue: Police Reform, Occupational Culture, and Cognitive Burn-In*, in POLICE OCCUPATIONAL CULTURE: NEW DEBATES AND DIRECTIONS (Megan O'Neill and Monique Marks, eds.) (2007). This is certainly a fair point. But as even these commentators seem to concede, this does not by any means tell us that the fundamental aspects of police culture—the belief that only fellow officers understand, that they have only each other to rely on, and that the public and command staff are to be distrusted—have disappeared. As long as the basic precepts of the culture remain in place, "us versus them" will never go away.

24. Malcolm K. Sparrow, Mark H. Moore, and David M. Kennedy, BEYOND 911: A NEW ERA FOR POLICING 51 (1992).

25. Steve Herbert, *Morality in Law Enforcement: Chasing "Bad Guys" with the Los Angeles Police Department*, 30 Law & Society Review 799, 800 (1996).

26. Michael Tooley, Jeffrey Linkenbach, Brian J. Lande, and Gary M. Lande, *The Media, the Public, and the Law Enforcement Community: Correcting Misperceptions*, 76 Police Chief Magazine, June 2009, accessed June 23, 2010, at policechiefmagazine.org/index.cfm?fus.

27. Dae H. Chang and Charles H. Zastrow, *Police Evaluative Perceptions of Themselves, the General Public, and Selected Occupational Groups*, 4 Journal of Criminal Justice 17-27 (1976).

28. *Id.* at 22. This is quite literally true: of all the groups included in the survey, "prison inmates" ranked dead last in terms of police esteem.

29. H. L. Mencken and George Jean Nathan, THE AMERICAN CREDO: A CONTRIBUTION TO THE INTERPRETATION OF THE NATIONAL MIND 84 (1920).

30. The Economist, *American Politics: Democracy in America*, *"Prosecutor or Politician?"* accessed July 29, 2010, at http://www.economist.com/blogs/democracyinamerica/2010/01/prosecutor_or_politician.

31. *Id.*

32. Wendy McElroy, *Prosecutorial Indiscretion*, The Freeman: Ideas on Liberty, January/February 2008, p. 25, accessed July 30, 2010, at http://www.fee.org/pdf/the-freeman/0801McElroy.pdf.

33. Sheldon Goldman, Sara Schiavoni, and Elliot Slotnic, *W. Bush's Judicial Legacy: Mission Accomplished*, 92 Judicature 258 (May–June 2009).

34. *Id.* at 279 tbl. 3 (The actual percentages for prior judicial experience prior to appointment to the district courts were Carter 54 percent, Reagan 46.2 percent, G. H. W. Bush 46.6 percent, Clinton 52.1 percent, and G. W. Bush 52.1 percent.).

35. *Id.* at 284 tbl. 6 (The actual percentages for prior judicial experience prior to appointment to the appellate courts were Carter 53.6 percent, Reagan 60.3 percent, G. H. W. Bush 62.2 percent, Clinton 59 percent, and G. W. Bush 61 percent.).

36. *Id.* at 279 tbl. 3 (The actual percentages for prior prosecutorial experience prior to appointment to the district courts were Carter 38.1 percent, Reagan 44.1 percent, G. H. W. Bush 39.2 percent, Clinton 41.3 percent, and G. W. Bush 47.1 percent.).

37. *Id.* at 284 tbl. 6 (The actual percentages for prior prosecutorial experience prior to appointment to the appellate courts were Carter 30.4 percent, Reagan 28.2 percent, G. H. W. Bush 29.7 percent, Clinton 37.7 percent, and G. W. Bush 33.9 percent).

38. Theresa M. Beiner, *How the Contentious Nature of Federal Judicial Appointments Affects "Diversity" on the Bench*, 39 U. Richmond Law Rev. 849, 863-64 (2005).

39. Susan D. Rozelle, *Daubert, Schmaubert: Criminal Defendants and the Short End of the Science Stick*, 43 Tulsa L. Rev. 597, 604-5 (2008).

40. Chicago Appleseed Fund for Justice and the Criminal Justice Project, *A Report on Chicago's Felony Courts*, December 2007, 26–33.

41. Kan Ori, *The Politicized Nature of the County Prosecutor's Office, Fact or Fancy: The Case of Indiana*, 40 Notre Dame Lawyer 289, 303 (1965).

42. *Id.* at 293, tbls. 5 and 6.

43. *Id.* at 294, tbl. 7.

44. *Id.* at 297, tbl. 8.

45. *Id.* Ori did not find any pattern of former prosecutors holding the office of either governor or U.S. senator.

46. Data on file with the author. I thank Library Research Fellow Derek Candela, University of Pittsburgh School of Law Class of 2011, for painstakingly sifting through the online biographies of all 435 House members and 100 senators. The use of the word "approximately" is deliberate, because some House members listed positions that might or might not have been prosecutorial jobs.

47. Bob Papper, The Future of News, p. 7, the Radio and Television News Directors Foundation (2006).

48. *Key News Audiences Now Blend Online and Traditional Sources*, Pew Research Center for the People and the Press, Aug. 17, 2008, accessed Aug. 2, 2010, at http://people-press.org/report/444/news-media.

49. Matthew R. Kerbel, If It Bleeds, It Leads: An Anatomy of Television News (2000).

50. *Id.*

51. *Id.* at 52.

52. Pew Research Center, Project for Excellence in Journalism, *The State of the News Media, 2006: An Annual Report on American Journalism*, accessed August 3, 2010, at http://www.stateofthemedia.org/2006/narrative_localtv_contentanalysis.asp?cat=2&media=7.

53. Jeff Cohen and Norman Solomon, *On Local TV News, If It Bleeds It (Still) Leads*, Media Beat, accessed Aug. 3, 2010, at http://www.fair.org/media-beat/951213.html.

54. Martin Kaplan and Matthew Hale, *Local TV News in the Los Angeles Media Market: Are Stations Serving the Public Interest?* March 11, 2010, accessed Aug. 3, 2010, at http://www.learcenter.org/pdf/LANews2010.pdf.

55. *Id.* at 1. The researchers quote "a recent Pew poll" for this information.

56. *Id.* at 3.

57. *Id.* at 3, 4.

58. Federal Bureau of Investigation, *Crime in the United States: Preliminary Semiannual Uniform Crime Report*, January to June, released Dec. 21, 2009, accessed Aug. 4, 2010, at http://www.fbi.gov/ucr/2009prelimsem/index.html ("[L]aw enforcement agencies throughout the Nation reported a decrease of 4.4 percent in the number of violent crimes brought to their attention for the first six months of 2009 when compared with figures reported for the same time in 2008. . . . The number of property crimes in the United States from January to June of 2009 decreased 6.1 percent when compared with data from the same time period in 2008."); U.S. Census Bureau, *The 2010 Statistical Abstract: The National Data Book*, tbl. 295, accessed Aug. 4, 2010, at http://www.census.gov/compendia/statab/2010/tables/10s0295.

pdf (showing decreases in all categories of crime per 100,000 people, with violent crimes falling from 714 (1994) to 467 (2007) per 100,000, and property crimes falling from 4,660 (1994) to 3,264 (2007) per 100,000).

59. Federal Bureau of Investigation, *supra* note 58, at tbl. 3, accessed Aug. 4, 2010, at http://www.fbi.gov/ucr/2009prelimsem/table_3.html (showing 2006-2005 jump in violent crimes rate for that period, but drops in all subsequent years afterward).

60. David Von Drehle, *What's Behind America's Falling Crime Rate*, Time, Feb. 22, 2010, accessed Aug. 4, 2010, at http://www.time.com/time/magazine/article/0,9171,1963761,00.html (Crime, especially murder, began falling in the mid-1990s, and now is at levels not seen since the 1960s.); Basil Katz, *New York City Crime Rates at Record Low: Police*, Reuters, Dec. 28, 2009, accessed Aug. 4, 2010, at http://www.reuters.com/article/idUS-TRE5BR38320091228 (record low crime rates in New York City, including rates of murder that were the lowest since beginning of record keeping in 1963).

61. Lydia Saad, *Worry about Crime Rains at Last Year's Elevated Levels*, Gallup, accessed July 26, 2010, at http://www.gallup.com/poll/25078/Worry-About-Crime-Rains-at-Last-Year's-Elevated-Levels.aspx ("Currently 68% of Americans say there is more crime in the United States than there was a year ago.").

62. Lydia Saad, *Perceptions of Crime Problem Remain Curiously Negative*, Gallup, Oct. 22, 2007, accessed Aug. 4, 2010, at http://www.gallup.com/poll/102262/perceptions-crime-problem-curiously-negative.aspx (showing that in 2007, 71 percent of Americans believed there was more crime in the United States than the year before, and 57 percent of Americans rated the problem of crime as either extremely or very serious, with another 39 percent rating it at least moderately serious).

63. *Crime*, Gallup, accessed Aug. 5, 2010, at http://www.gallup.com/poll/1603/Crime.aspx (showing that in 2008, 67 percent of Americans believed there was more crime in the United States than the year before, and 51 percent of Americans rated the problem of crime as either extremely or very serious, with another 43 percent rating it at least moderately serious).

64. Jeffrey M. Jones, *Americans Perceive Increased Crime in the U.S.*, Gallup, Oct. 14, 2009, accessed July 26, 2010, at http://www.gallup.com/poll/123644/Americans-Perceive-Increased-Crime.aspx.

65. Joseph F. Sheley and Cindy D. Ashkins, *Crime, Crime News, and Crime Views*, 45 Public Opinion Quarterly 492-506 (1981).

66. Allen E. Liska and William Baccaglini, *Feeling Safe by Comparison: Crime in the Newspapers*, 37 Social Problems 360-74 (1990).

67. Garrett J. O'Keefe and Kathleen Reid-Nash, *Crime News and Real-World Blues: The Effects of the Media on Social Reality*, 14 Communications Research 147-63 (1987).

68. Bernard C. Cohen, THE PRESS AND FOREIGN POLICY 13 (1963) ("[T]he press may not be successful much of the time in telling people what to think, but it is stunningly successful in telling its readers what to think about.").

69. Dennis T. Lowry, Tarn Ching Josephine Nio, and Dennis W. Leitner, *Setting the Public Fear Agenda: A Longitudinal Analysis of Network TV Crime Reporting, Public Perceptions of Crime, and FBI Crime Statistics*, 53 Journal of Communication 61-73 (2003).

70. *Id.* at 70.

71. *Id.* at 72.

72. *Report of the National Advisory Commission on Civil Disorders, Summary of Report, Introduction*, p. 6, accessed Aug. 12, 2010, at http://www.eisenhowerfoundation.org/docs/kerner.pdf ("'Prior' incidents, which increased tensions and ultimately led to violence, were police actions in almost half the cases; police actions were 'final' incidents before the outbreak of violence in 12 of the 24 surveyed disorders.").

73. *Id.* at 1.

74. *Id.* at 14.

75. *Id.* at 310.

76. *Id.* at 311.

77. For an excellent summary of these developments in New York and Philadelphia, see Samuel Walker, POLICE ACCOUNTABILITY: THE ROLE OF CITIZEN OVERSIGHT 26-31 (2001).

78. *Id.* at 27-28.

79. *Id.* at 28.

80. *Id.* at 29-31.

81. *Id.* at 31.

82. *Id.* at 31, 35.

83. *Id.* at 32-40.

84. Walker notes that even as the 1990s ended and the new century was about to begin, "[p]olice unions continued to fight [civilian] oversight," even as they saw that both police leaders and public opinion were increasingly moving in the other direction. He gives the example of the police union in Seattle, which opposed proposals for civilian oversight but eventually realized "that some form of oversight would be created" and participated in negotiations that resulted in the creation of the independent auditor overseeing the police department. *Id.* at 43.

85. Office of the Governor, *Governor Ryan Declares Moratorium on Executions, Will Appoint Commission to Review Capital Punishment System*, Jan. 31, 2000, accessed Aug. 12, 2010, at http://www.illinois.gov/PressReleases/ShowPressRelease.cfm?SubjectID=3&RecNum=359.

86. *Id.* Ultimately, Ryan emptied Illinois' death row before he left office.

87. Office of the Governor, *Governor Ryan's Commission on Capital Punishment Completes Comprehensive Review of Illinois System Delivers Final Recommendations to Governor Ryan*, April 15, 2002, accessed Aug. 12, 2010, at http://www.illinois.gov/PressReleases/ShowPressRelease.cfm?SubjectID=3&RecNum=1742.

88. *Report of the Illinois Commission on Capital Punishment* 24 (April 15, 2002), accessed Aug. 12, 2010, at http://www.idoc.state.il.us/ccp/ccp/reports/commission_report/chapter_02.pdf.

89. Pam Belluck, *Murder Charges Dropped against 2 Boys in Chicago*, N.Y. Times, Sept. 5, 1998, accessed Aug. 12, 2010, at http://www.nytimes.com/1998/09/05/us/murder-charges-dropped-against-2-boys-in-Chicago.html?ref=ryan_harris.

90. Henry Weinstein, *Illinois Governor to Set Taped Interrogations Rule*, N.Y. Times, July 17, 2003, accessed Aug. 12, 2010, at http://articles.latimes.com/2003/jul/17/nation/na-confess17/2.

91. *Id.*

92. Monica Davey, *Illinois Will Require Taping of Homicide Interrogations*, N.Y. Times, July 17, 2003, accessed Aug. 12, 2010, at http://www.nytimes.com/2003/07/17/us/illinois-will-require-taping-of-homicide-interrogations.html.

93. Telephone conversation with Tim Richardson, national FOP legislative affairs staff, Aug. 19, 2010 (notes on file with the author).

94. *Id.*

95. *Id.* Mr. Richardson explained that this "locals do local legislative advocacy" approach is vital to the FOP, because different locals may come up with diametrically opposed positions on the same issue. As an example, he discussed concealed carry permit laws. Some FOP locals strongly favor these laws, in order to have more armed citizens on the street; other locals oppose them just as strongly, because they want fewer people with guns in their jurisdictions. Thus the national FOP must allow locals to come to their own conclusions. This sometimes makes formulating national policy for the organization difficult, according to Mr. Richardson.

96. *Id.*

97. California Senate Committee on Public Safety, Bill Analysis: S.B. 511 (Alquist), as amended April 9, 2007, 2007-2008 Regular Session, accessed

Aug. 13, 2010, at http://info.sen.ca.gov/pub/07-08/bill/sen/sb_0501-0550/ sb_511_cfa_20070416_151508_sen_comm.html.

98. Letter from Robert Baker, President, Board of Directors Los Angeles Police Protective League, to Gerald F. Uelman, Executive Director, California Commission on the Fair Administration of Justice, July 18, 2007, accessed Aug. 13, 2010, at http://www.ccfaj.org/documents/Legislation/2007/SB%20756/ Los%20Angeles%20Police%20Protective%20League%20Opposition.pdf.

99. *President's Message: Killing Bills, Paying Tribute, and Taking Care of Our Own*, Badge & Gun, July 2009, accessed Aug. 13, 2010, at http://www.hpou. org/badgeandgun/index.cfm?fuseaction=view_news&NewsID=569.

100. Bruce Lambert, *No Retrial in '88 Double Killing on Long Island*, N.Y. Times, July 1, 2008, accessed Aug. 13, 2010, at http://www.nytimes.com/2008/07/01/ nyregion/01tankleff.html?ref=martin_tankleff.

101. Michael Amon, *Release Puts Focus on Interrogations*, Newsday, Jan. 6, 2008.

102. Yale Kamisar, Wayne R. LaFave, Jerold H. Israel, Nancy J. King, and Orin S. Kerr, MODERN CRIMINAL PROCEDURE, CASES, COMMENTS, QUESTIONS 18 (2008, 12th ed.).

103. The only exceptions at the state level might be in situations where a state executive officer (such as in New Jersey) or a state commission might take the laboring oar on these issues. But even with changes proposed by a commission, legislative action would probably be necessary to implement reforms. For more on both possibilities, see chapter 7.

104. Along with the material on the legislative activities of police professional organizations, the author conducted a survey at the end of August and the beginning of September 2010. The author searched for websites for police chiefs' and sheriffs' professional organizations. Each website was then examined for any indication that the organization had an active lobbying presence in legislative matters in its state, either through active lobbying activities (usually performed by executives, leaders, and members of the organizations, or sometimes [though rarely] by paid lobbyists). This activity consisted of legislative monitoring, the giving of testimony, or the supplying of information to legislators and members of their organizations. Some organizations also endorse candidates for office who backed their efforts. A few organizations were found on the web that did not articulate any such activities, and they were not included in the list of organizations in the three following footnotes. Other states may have such organizations that may engage in similar political activities, but do not have a web presence; those do not appear, either.

105. E.g., Alabama Association of Chiefs of Police (AACOP) (provides "Legislative and State Committee Support"), accessed Sept. 1, 2010, at http://web.

memberclicks.com/mc/page.do?sitePageId=100529&orgId=aascp; Alaska
Peace Officers Association (lists among its goals "[t]hrough involvement
with the legislature and the governor, offering suggestions to improve Alaska's
justice system"), accessed Sept. 1, 2010, at http://www.apoaonline.org/about.
htm; Arizona Police Association (listing political endorsements and a
comprehensive legislative agenda, and including extensive reports of
political activity supporting Arizona's immigration law, S.B. 1070, explaining that it uses its big "voice" in the state to, inter alia, "effectively communicate with and lobby the state legislature, our federal representatives, and when
needed, local city and town councils, board of supervisors. . . ."), accessed
Sept. 1, 2010, at http://www.azpolice.org/; California Police Chiefs Association (listing, under "Advocacy," numerous tools for opposition to Proposition 19, 2010 primary election endorsements, and a menu of the organization's positions on legislation), accessed Sept. 1, 2010, at http://www.
californiapolicechiefs.org/nav_files/legislative.html; Colorado Association
of Chiefs of Police (CPCA) (stating, under "CPCA's Values," "We believe
that the Association should take an active, nonpartisan role in developing,
monitoring and supporting quality law enforcement legislation—working
closely with community groups, legislators, the media, private business, and
other law enforcement organizations toward this goal") and also providing
"Legislative Information" for members only, accessed Sept. 1, 2010, at http://
www.colochiefs.org/geninfo.shtml; Connecticut Police Chiefs Association
(written testimony from association for the state legislature's Judiciary
Committee on Feb. 27, 2006, in support of bill expanding police authority
to make arrests for nonfelonies, noting association's history of advocating
"for similar bills in past sessions"), accessed Sept. 1, 2010, at http://www.cga.
ct.gov/2006/JUDdata/Tmy/2006HB-05464-R000227-CPCA%20
-20Chiefs%20Anthony%20Salvatore%20&%20James%20Strillacci-TMY.
PDF; Florida Police Chiefs Association (FPCA) (under "Legislative Issues,"
stating that "[t]he Florida Police Chiefs Association was originally organized in 1952 to promote legislation that would enhance public security by
providing superior police protection for the residents of Florida as well as
our many visitors. For more than fifty years, the Association has maintained
a strong presence in Tallahassee and regularly testifies on legislative issues
of a public safety nature. FPCA members are frequently recognized by the
legislative leaders to provide insight into public safety issues and problems
facing the criminal justice system."), accessed Sept. 1, 2010, at http://www.
fpca.com/fpcalegislation.htm; Georgia Association of Chiefs of Police
(GACP) (listing "legislative activities" on its website, with a link to monthly
"legislative alerts" that contain notations such as those in the April 2010

alert in which a particular pending bill is described as "GACP's Bill and a good one for law enforcement"), accessed Sept. 1, 2010, at http://www. gachiefs.com/News_LegislativeNews.htm and http://www.gachiefs.com/ pdfs/Legislative/LegislativeAlert2010_4.pdf; Idaho Chiefs of Police Association (ICOPA) (web page for "Legislation" gives information on "current legislation initiated by ICOPA" and "current legislation watched by ICOPA"), accessed Sept. 1, 2010, at http://www.icopa.org/leg.htm; Illinois Association of Chiefs of Police (noting in its "mission and values statement that "[w]e make a positive impact on the quality of life in the communities we serve through proactive leadership in . . . [l]egislation"), accessed Sept. 1, 2010, at http://www.humanspan.com/uploads/archives/4341/site/subpage. asp?pagenumber=46353; Indiana Association of Chiefs of Police (providing a "legislative report" with recommended positions on particular bills, and setting out the membership of a "government relations committee" that includes representatives of the firm Short Strategy Group, Inc., a lobbying and public policy firm), accessed Sept. 1, 2010, at http://www.iacop.org/ government_relations.html and http://www.iacop.org/govt_relations_com-mittee.html; Iowa Peace Officers Association (formerly Iowa Association of Chiefs of Police and Peace Officers (web page of legislative priorities for work with state legislature during 2009-2010), accessed Sept. 1, 2010, at http://www.iowachiefs.org/legislative/legislativereport.html; Kansas Association of Chiefs of Police (KACP) (declaring that KACP "works hard to identify and consult with the legislature regarding needed changes in state laws to improve public safety and to help law enforcement better respond to changes and challenges in crime," through its Legislative Committee), accessed Sept. 1, 2010, at http://www.kacp.cc/legisact.php; Kentucky Association of Chiefs of Police (web pages containing "Bills of Interest to Law Enforcement signed by the Governor" and "2010 Bills Filed of Interest to Law Enforcement"), accessed Sept. 1, 2010, at http://www. kypolicechiefs.org/joomla/; Louisiana Association of Chiefs of Police (web page containing "Final Legislative Report for 2009" indicating comprehensive tracking of legislation, testimony, and other efforts in the state legislature by the organization), accessed Sept. 1, 2010, at http://data.member-clicks.com/site/lacp/2009_Final_Legislative_Report.pdf; Massachusetts Chiefs of Police Association (executive director's report featuring comment on many actions by association in the legislative arena, and declaring that executive director reads reports from the legislature every day and is tracking over two hundred bills that could affect association members), accessed Sept. 1, 2010, at http://www.masschiefs.org/page.php?pageid=122; Michigan Association of Chiefs of Police (website offering organization's

"Priorities for the 2009–2010 Legislative Session," as well as legislative reports and bill tracking reports for members), accessed Sept. 1, 2010, at http://www.michiganpolicechiefs.org/page.cfm/10/; Minnesota Chiefs of Police Association (stating that the organization is "the voice of police executives in Minnesota" on legislative issues), accessed Sept. 1, 2010, at http://web.memberclicks.com/mc/page.do?sitePageId=39883&orgId=mcpa; Mississippi Association of Chiefs of Police (website notes that group "strive[s] to endorse legislation which has positive effects on law enforcement's ability to reduce crime and the fear of crime in the State of Mississippi"), accessed Sept. 1, 2010, at http://www.mschiefs.org/legislation.htm; Missouri Police Chiefs Association (MPCA) (explaining "the importance of legislative affairs work to the organization, stating that "Legislative Affairs is one of MPCA's major areas of interest and attention because the laws passed by the General Assembly and the regulations mandated by government agencies affect every law enforcement officer in Missouri" and making available numerous legislative reports and updates on MPCA's activity in the legislature), accessed Sept. 1, 2010, at http://www.mopca.com/mpca/la-updates.html; Montana Association of Chiefs of Police (stating that the group "supports legislation" and showing the name of the group's legislative chairman), accessed Sept. 1, 2001, at http://www.macop.com/Home_Page.html; Police Officers Association of Nebraska (stating that legislative advocacy is part of association's mission, and listing many proposed and enacted statutes with indication of group's support or opposition), accessed Sept. 1, 2010, at http://www.poan.org/about/mission_and_vision.php and http://www.poan.org/newsroom/legislative_bills.php; New Jersey State Association of Chiefs of Police (stating that the organization "takes an active role in legislative affairs by drafting, tracking and lobbying for the needs and interests of the law enforcement profession" and linking to lengthy legislative activity report concerning state legislature), accessed Sept. 1, 2009, at http://www.njsacop.org/content.asp?pl=19&contentid=45; New York State Association of Chiefs of Police (including on legislative affairs web page numerous "legislative memoranda in support/opposition" that group would submit to legislators to detail the group's stances in order to try to shape law and public policy as it emerges), accessed Sept. 1, 2010, at http://www.nychiefs.org/legislative_memoranda.php; Ohio Association of Chiefs of Police (featuring comprehensive "Law & Legislation" page, and numerous summaries of the law written by the organization's "legislative counsel"), accessed Sept. 1, 2010, at http://www.oacp.org/lawleg.html; Oregon Association of Chiefs of Police (noting in its comprehensive annual legislative report for 2009 that the association and its members frequently "engage[ed] with the legislative process" through giving testimony, writing to and calling legislators, and participating in working groups and that this helped defeat legislation that ran counter to law enforcement's interests), accessed Sept. 1, 2010, at http://www.policechief.org/index.php?c=State%20 Legislation_OACP_2009_End_Report.pdf; Pennsylvania Chiefs of Police Association (engaging in legislative advocacy by "promoting legislation which advances the mission of the Association before the United States Congress and the Pennsylvania General Assembly"), accessed Sept. 1, 2010, at http://www.pachiefs.org/MissionStatement.htm; South Carolina Police Chiefs Association (association monitors developments in the state legislature, and advocates for or against legislative proposals by "adopt[ing] resolutions to be forwarded to our state lawmakers"), accessed Sept. 1, 2010, at http://www.scpolicechiefs.org/; Utah Law Enforcement Legislative Committee (ULELC), an organization uniting the Utah Chiefs of Police Association, Utah Sheriffs Association, Utah Peace Officers Association, and a number of other organizations and public officials to influence the legislature on law enforcement issues ("The ULELC is located at the Utah State Capitol during the General Sessions of the Utah State Legislature. . . . The ULELC publishes a weekly position paper on this website, listing all bills in which the ULELC has taken a position by majority vote. The final 2010 ULELC bill list, showing ULELC positions taken and the passage/failure status of the bills, is posted on this site."), accessed Sept. 1, 2010, at http://www.ulelc.org/; Virginia Association of Chiefs of Police (stating that association actively monitors the state General Assembly "to promote and protect the interests of Virginia's police agencies"), accessed Sept. 1, 2010, at http://www.vachiefs.org/about/; West Virginia Chiefs of Police Association (stating that "[t]he West Virginia Chief's Association will actively participate in the legislative process. We have and will continue to meet with elected and other officials from City, County, State and National Government."), accessed Sept. 1, 2010, at http://www.wvcop.com/main/legislative.php; Wisconsin Chiefs of Police Association (group has taken public positions and advocated for and against legislation for at least a decade, according to legislative activity web page), accessed Sept. 1, 2010, at http://www.wichiefs.org/legislation.asp.

106. E.g., California State Sheriffs' Association (full-scale effort in legislature as well as a political action committee that works on issues of candidate endorsements, state referenda, and gubernatorial appointments), accessed Sept. 3, 2010, at http://ct2k2.capitoltrack.com/report.asp?rptid=U33332 and http://www.calsheriffs.org/index.php/legislativepac/political-action-policy; Florida Sheriffs Association (FSA) (offering members a "Legislation" web

page, where for each year members can "[f]ind out all the details on FSA-supported legislation, including the politicians and players"), accessed Sept. 1, 2010, at http://www.flsheriffs.org/index.cfm/referer/content.contentList/ID/319/; Georgia Sheriffs' Association (listing as among its activities and services "advocacy in the Georgia General Assembly" on various crime control and law enforcement issues), accessed Sept. 1, 2010, at http://www.georgiasheriffs.org/Display.asp?Page=AboutUs; Idaho Sheriffs' Association (listing as part of its mission "[t]o study, prepare, and present to the Legislature such changes or additions to the current laws as the experience of the sheriffs would indicate, and would be beneficial in the effective enforcement of the laws, and in the better conduct of the business of the sheriff's officers"), accessed Sept. 1, 2010, at http://www.idahosheriffsassociation.com/ISA%20Mission.html; Indiana Sheriffs' Association (showing membership of large legislative committee and legislative advisory committee), accessed Sept. 1, 2010, at http://www.indianasheriffs.org/ns/legislative.php; Iowa State Sheriffs and Deputies Association (listing a legislative committee that "promotes the legislative goals of the Association in the Iowa Legislature"), accessed Sept. 1, 2010, at http://www.issda.org/LegislativeCommittee.htm; Kansas Sheriff's Association [sic] (listing a legislative committee's membership, and listing among the organization's goals "support[ing] legislation that is beneficial for the community safety and security"), accessed Sept. 1, 2010, at http://www.kansassheriff.org/about.htm and http://www.kansassheriff.org/comitee.htm; Maine Sheriffs' Association (noting that among association activities, "We actively promote and support legislation to provide sheriffs with the authority and responsibility necessary to properly administer their departments and to upgrade conditions of employment to be able to attract and retain the most qualified personnel in order to best serve the citizens of Maine"), accessed Sept. 1, 2010, at http://www.mainesheriffs.org/index.cfm?fuseaction=browse&id=103740&pageid=63; Michigan Sheriffs' Association (declaring that it "[m]aintain[s] a leadership role in support and enactment of appropriate law enforcement legislation" and actively monitors pending legislation), accessed Sept. 1, 2010, at http://www.michigansheriff.com/about/about.htm; Minnesota Sheriffs' Association (organization's mission includes studying, preparing, and presenting proposed legislation to the legislature), accessed Sept. 1, 2010, at http://www.mnchiefs.org/mc/page.do?sitePageId=32472; Montana Sheriffs and Peace Officers Association (claiming that the association "scored many other victories through legislative work" and noting its "persistence in the legislature"), accessed Sept. 1, 2010, at http://www.mspoa.org/history.htm; New York State Sheriffs' Association (noting that the group made it a practice to advise the state legislature and the governor's office "concerning the feasibility and implications of proposed legislation or administrative rules"), accessed Sept. 1, 2010, at http://www.nysheriffs.org/who-we-are; North Carolina Sheriffs' Association (stating that the group advocates for sheriffs by monitoring the General Assembly, and website containing annual and weekly legislative reports that include bill descriptions and information on whether the group supported or opposed the bills), accessed Sept. 1, 2010, at http://www. ncsheriffs.org/Weekly%20Legislative%20Report/2009/NCSA.FLR.2009. pdf; South Dakota Sheriffs' Association (Association states that it "represents law enforcement issues at the legislature in Pierre every year."), accessed Sept. 1, 2010, at http://www.southdakotasheriffs.org/assoc.htm; Tennessee Sheriffs' Association (stating that it provides and funds "a legislative liaison service for improving laws that protect the citizenry"), accessed Sept. 1, 2010, at http://www.tnsheriffs.com/MissionStatement.htm; Sheriffs Association of Texas (organization's legislative committee members "are active participants in the legislative process and insure that all bills introduced which affect the duties, responsibilities, training, court and jail functions of the Sheriffs are given proper consideration"), accessed Sept. 1, 2010, at http://www.txsheriffs. org/; Virginia Sheriffs' Association (claiming to be "in the forefront of the legislative process" and "a driving force" with the state's General Assembly over the course of many years, influencing many criminal justice issues as well as issues of working conditions and salaries), accessed Sept. 1, 2010, at http://vasheriff.org/legislative/; Washington Association of Sheriffs and Police Chiefs (noting organization's taking part in the legislative process, and presenting a detailed legislative agenda for 2010), accessed Sept. 1, 2001, at http://www.waspc.org/index.php?c=Legislation; West Virginia Sheriffs' Association (featuring a legislative update section on organization's web page and "watch list" on bills of special interest to law enforcement), accessed Sept. 1, 2010, at http://www.wvsheriff.org/pdf%20files/2008_Legislative_Final_List.pdf; Wisconsin Sheriff's and Deputy Sheriff's Association [sic] (declaring that the association's Government Relations Office "monitors thousands of legislative proposals . . . and advocates for member interests in the Governors [sic] Office and before the Wisconsin Legislature at the State Capitol in Madison. These efforts greatly benefit Wisconsin's 72 county sheriffs, and thousands of their deputies, jailers, and retirees"), accessed Sept. 1, 2010, at http://www.wsdsa.org/legislative.

107. As enumerated in notes 105 and 106, the fourteen states that have both police officers' associations and sheriffs' associations are California, Florida, Georgia, Idaho, Indiana, Iowa, Kansas, Michigan, Minnesota, Montana, New York, Virginia, West Virginia, and Wisconsin.

108. Telephone interview with Rachel Bloom, Advocacy and Policy Strategist, national ACLU, Sept. 16, 2010 (notes on file with the author).

109. *Id.*

110. *Id.*

111. Email correspondence with ACLU state legislative coordinator who wishes to remain anonymous, Aug. 18, 2010 (copy on file with the author).

112. *Id.*; telephone interview with Rachel Bloom, *supra* note 108.

113. Email communication with Steve Saloom, the Innocence Project, Sept. 10, 2010 (copy on file with the author).

114. S.B. 77, 128th Ohio General Assembly (2010); Jim Siegel, *Ohio's New DNA Law Called Model,* Columbus Dispatch, April 6, 2010, accessed Sept. 15, 2010, at http://www.dispatchpolitics.com/live/content/local_news/stories/2010/04/06/copy/ohiosnewdnalawcalledmodel.html?sid=101.

115. Aaron Marshall, *Ohio House OKs Bill Setting DNA Standards, Lineup Procedures*, Cleveland Plain-Dealer, March 16, 2010, accessed Sept. 15, 2010, at http://www.cleveland.com/open/index.ssf/2010/03/ohio_house_oks_bill_setting_dn.html ("The legislation was sparked by the Innocence Project, a University of Cincinnati Law School project, which has helped eight men get freed primarily because of problems with eyewitness identifications.").

116. Email communication from Mark Godsey, University of Cincinnati College of Law, Sept. 10, 2010 (copy on file with the author).

117. *Id.*

118. *Id.*

119. Email communication with Stephen Saloom, *supra* note 113.

120. Telephone conversation with Angelyn Frazer, state legislative affairs director, National Association of Criminal Defense Lawyers, Sept. 8, 2010 (notes on file with the author).

CHAPTER 6

1. See chapter 2.

2. Gary L. Wells, Mark Small, Steven Penrod, Roy S. Malpass, Solomon M. Fulero, and C. A. E. Brimacombe, "Eyewitness Identification Procedures: Recommendations for Lineups and Photospreads," 22 Law and Human Behavior 1 (1998).

3. *Id.* at 1.

4. Technical Working Group for Eyewitness Evidence, National Institute of Justice, U.S. Department of Justice, *Eyewitness Evidence: A Guide for Law Enforcement* (hereinafter NIJ *Guide*) (NCJ 178240, October 1999).

5. *Id.* at v-vi (listing as members twenty-three persons from law enforcement or prosecutors' offices, seven social scientists, and four criminal defense attorneys.

6. Gary L. Wells, Mark Small, Steven Penrod, Roy S. Malpass, Solomon M. Fulero, and C. A. E. Brimacombe, *supra* note 2, at 21.

7. *Id.* Interestingly, the NIJ *Guide* does not recommend the use of blind administration of lineups, but the reason for this is not that these procedures do not work to prevent bias or inaccuracy, or would not work in the setting of a police lineup. The *Guide* notes that "investigators' unintentional cues [which] may negatively impact the reliability of eyewitness evidence . . . could be avoided if 'blind' identification procedures were employed." But "this may be impractical for some jurisdictions to implement," i.e., blind lineups may present costs or inconveniences that law enforcement agencies would prefer to avoid. Thus the issue is not efficacy, but cost and convenience. This seems unpersuasive, to put it mildly. For all but the smallest departments, finding an officer to conduct a lineup means finding a single person in the entire department not involved in the case. There is no increased cost overall, because if the uninvolved officer did not conduct the lineup, the involved one would; the task is simply shifted from one officer to another. So at worst, the uninvolved officer's work is interrupted. It would have been much better to recommend blind administration, but to add something to the recommendation indicating that very small departments should be exempt if, after attempting to find an uninvolved person (it need not be an officer, after all) to conduct the lineup, they could not find one.

8. Gary L. Wells, Mark Small, Steven Penrod, Roy S. Malpass, Solomon M. Fulero, and C. A. E. Brimacombe, *supra* note 2, at 23 (The administrator of the lineup "should not only be blind as to which person in the lineup is the suspect but should also be *perceived* (by the eyewitness) to be blind ").

9. *Id.* (citation omitted).

10. *Id.*

11. *Id.* at 25.

12. The practice of using showups—essentially, one-person lineups in which police show the suspect to the witness, alone, sometimes at the scene of the apprehension, or perhaps at the police station—would not comply with this recommendation. All showups carry the implicit question, "We (the police) think this is the guy; do you agree?" The suggestiveness of the showup procedure seems too obvious to require further explanation; the U.S. Supreme Court has acknowledged this (but still, unaccountably, allows the use of showups in court, as long as they are still deemed reliable). *Neil v. Biggers.*

But there is no question whatsoever that the science does not support the use of showups because they produce more false identifications than properly constructed lineups of either live suspects or photographs; researchers have found a measurable, statistically significant difference between showups and other methods. Gary L. Wells, Mark Small, Steven Penrod, Roy S. Malpass, Solomon M. Fulero, and C. A. E. Brimacombe, *supra* note 2, at 24. Either kind of lineup (photographs or live persons) presents at least a possibility for the selection of a filler, and with it the disproof of the police hypothesis that the suspect is the actual perpetrator. A showup does not present this choice to the witness, and therefore cannot qualify as a bona fide test of the question of whether the police have focused on the right person. Showups also present the distinct possibility of contaminating the witness's memory for any subsequent, correctly staged eyewitness procedure or an identification in court. The witness who has experienced a showup will have the memory of that person fixed in his or her mind, and is therefore much more likely to pick him or her out later; if the witness selected the suspect at the showup, the witness will almost certainly select the suspect later. Thus police should not use showups at all. Here the NIJ *Guide* differs from *Eyewitness Identification Procedures*: the *Guide* allows the use of showups, saying that "[w]hen circumstances require the prompt display of a single suspect to a witness, the inherent suggestiveness of the encounter can be minimized through the use of safeguards. The investigator shall employ procedures that avoid prejudicing the witness." NIJ *Guide*, *supra* note 4, at 27.

13. Gary L. Wells, Mark Small, Steven Penrod, Roy S. Malpass, Solomon M. Fulero, and C. A. E. Brimacombe, *supra* note 2, at 15.

14. Even the one study cited in the white paper in support of a correlation between witness confidence and accuracy only says that those who express strong confidence are only somewhat more likely to be accurate than those who express little confidence. *Id.* at 17.

15. *Id.* at 27.

16. NIJ *Guide*, *supra* note 4, at 33.

17. Saul M. Kassin, Steven A. Drizin, Thomas Grisso, Gisli H. Gudjonsson, Richard A. Leo, and Allison D. Redlich, *Police-Induced Confessions: Risk Factors and Recommendations*, 34 Law & Human Behavior 3 (2009).

18. *Id.*

19. *Id.*

20. *Id.*

21. Brandon L. Garrett, *The Substance of False Confessions*, 62 Stan. L. Rev. 1051 (2010).

22. *Id.*

23. Saul Kassin, Richard Leo, and other leading researchers on suspect interrogation have put together a white paper that brings together the best recent research. Just as Gary Wells and his colleagues did in the field of eyewitness identification in 1999, Kassin and his colleagues have created a blueprint for the kinds of reforms necessary to bring the practices of suspect interrogation into line with the most recent research. Saul M. Kassin, Steven A. Drizin, Thomas Grisso, Gisli H. Gudjonsson, Richard A. Leo, and Allison D. Redlich, *supra* note 17. They explicitly modeled their effort on the eyewitness identification white paper. *Id.* at 4.

24. See Stephan v. State, 711 P.2d 1156 (Alaska, 1985), and State v. Scales, 518 N.W.2d 587 (Minn., 1994).

25. Those jurisdictions are Illinois, Maine, New Jersey, New Mexico, North Carolina, Washington, DC, and Wisconsin.

26. Commonwealth v. DiGiambattista, 813 N.E.2d 516 (Mass., 2004).

27. Thomas P. Sullivan, POLICE EXPERIENCES WITH RECORDING CUSTODIAL INTERROGATIONS (2004), accessed September 22, 2010, at http://www.jenner.com/files/tbl_s20Publications/RelatedDocumentsPDFs1252/748/CWC_article_with%20Index.final.pdf.

28. Thomas P. Sullivan, Andrew W. Vail, and Howard W. Anderson III, *The Case for Recording Police Interrogations*, 34 Litigation Magazine 3, 4 (Spring 2008) ("We have spoken to officers from more than 600 police and sheriff departments that electronically record—by audio, video, or both—the entirety of most of their stationhouse interviews in serious felony investigations, starting with the *Miranda* warnings.").

29. *Id.* at 6.

30. Saul M. Kassin, Steven A. Drizin, Thomas Grisso, Gisli H. Gudjonsson, Richard A. Leo, and Allison D. Redlich, *supra* note 17 (describing Sullivan's findings).

31. Thomas P. Sullivan, Andrew W. Vail, and Howard W. Anderson III, *supra* note 28, at 4-5.

32. *Id.* at 5.

33. *Id.*

34. *Id.*

35. International Association of Chiefs of Police National Law Enforcement Policy Center, *Model Policy on Electronic Recording of Interrogations and Confessions* (February 2006).

36. International Association of Chiefs of Police National Law Enforcement Policy Center, *Concepts and Issues Paper on Electronic Recording of Interrogations and Confessions* (February 2007).

37. *Id.* at 1.

38. Thomas P. Sullivan, Andrew W. Vail, and Howard W. Anderson III, *supra* note 28, at 6.

39. *Id.*

40. *Id.*

41. *Id.*

42. U.S. Department of Justice, Federal Bureau of Investigation, *Uniform Crime Reporting (UCR) Summary Reporting Frequently Asked Questions,* accessed Sept. 24, 2010, at http://www.fbi.gov/ucr/ucrquest.htm.

43. Saul M. Kassin, Steven A. Drizin, Thomas Grisso, Gisli H. Gudjonsson, Richard A. Leo, and Allison D. Redlich, *supra* note 17.

44. Maryland Criminal Code Ann. § 7-104(g)(1) (person convicted of theft of property or services valued at one thousand dollars or more is guilty of a felony).

45. International Association of Chiefs of Police National Law Enforcement Policy Center, *supra* note 36, at 3.

46. For example, Illinois requires electronic recordings of interrogations in homicide investigations but creates an exception for when recording could not be accomplished: "Nothing in this Section precludes the admission . . . (ii) of a statement made during a custodial interrogation that was not recorded as required by this Section because electronic recording was not feasible." 705 Ill. Comp. Stat. Ann. 405/5-401.5(e) (West 2007). In a recent article, Thomas Sullivan and his coauthor append a revised version of their own model recording requirement statute, and it has an exception section as well: "A statement need not be Electronically Recorded if the court finds: . . . [t]he law enforcement officer in good faith failed to make an electronic recording of the interview because he or she inadvertently failed to operate the recording equipment properly, or without his or her knowledge the recording equipment malfunctioned or stopped operating." Thomas P. Sullivan and Andrew W. Vail, *The Consequences of Law Enforcement Officials' Failure to Record Custodial Interviews As Required by Law,* 99 J. Crim. L. & Criminology 215, 224-25 (2009).

47. This last alternative is the path taken by the Supreme Judicial Court of Massachusetts in Commonwealth v. DiGiambattista, 813 N.E. 2d 516 (Mass., 2004).

48. E.g., David A. Harris, *How Accountability-Based Policing Can Reinforce—or Replace—the Fourth Amendment Exclusionary Rule,* 7 Oh. St. J. Crim. L. 149 (2009).

49. E.g., Shari Seidman Diamond and Neil Vidmar, *Jury Room Ruminations on Forbidden Topics,* 87 Va. L. Rev. 1857 (2001).

50. Dennis Wagner, *FBI's Policy Drawing Fire, Interrogations Not Taped*, Arizona Republic, Dec. 6, 2005, accessed Sept. 24, 2010, at http://www.azcentral.com/arizonarepublic/news/articles/1206fbitaping.html.

51. James Trainum, *I Took a False Confession—So Don't Tell Me It Doesn't Happen!* The California Majority Report, accessed Sept. 24, 2010, at http://www.camajorityreport.com/indexphp?module=articles&func=display&ptid=9&aid=2306.

52. Saul M. Kassin, Steven A. Drizin, Thomas Grisso, Gisli H. Gudjonsson, Richard A. Leo, and Allison D. Redlich, *supra* note 17, at 28.

53. *Id.*

54. *Id.*

55. Fred E. Inbau, John E. Reid, Joseph P. Buckley, and Brian C. Jayne, CRIMINAL INTERROGATIONS AND CONFESSIONS (2001, 4th ed.).

56. *Frazier v. Cupp*, 394 U.S. 731 (1969).

57. *Id.* at 739.

58. Saul M. Kassin, Steven A. Drizin, Thomas Grisso, Gisli H. Gudjonsson, Richard A. Leo, and Allison D. Redlich, *supra* note 17, at 28.

59. *Id.*

60. These facts are described in Saul M. Kassin, Steven A. Drizin, Thomas Grisso, Gisli H. Gudjonsson, Richard A. Leo, and Allison D. Redlich, *supra* note 17, at 15.

61. *Bram v. U.S.*, 168 U.S. 532, 542-43 (1897), citing 3 RUSSELL ON CRIMES 478 (6th ed.).

62. *Miller v. Fenton*, 796 F.2d 598 (3d Cir. 1986).

63. *Id.* at 602.

64. *Id.*

65. *Id.* at 622.

66. *Id.*

67. *Id.* at 610.

68. Saul M. Kassin, Steven A. Drizin, Thomas Grisso, Gisli H. Gudjonsson, Richard A. Leo, and Allison D. Redlich, *supra* note 17, at 29.

69. Paul G. Cassell, *The Guilty and the "Innocent": An Examination of Alleged Cases of Wrongful Conviction from False Confessions*, 22 Harv. J. Law & Public Policy 523, 573-74 (asserting that false confession problem is very small and limited "to certain narrow, mentally limited populations").

70. National Academy of Sciences, STRENGTHENING FORENSIC SCIENCE IN THE UNITED STATES: A PATH FORWARD (2009).

71. *Frye v. U.S.*, 293 F. 1013 (DC Cir., 1923).

72. For example, the *Frye* rule remains the law in Pennsylvania. *Grady v. Frito-Lay*, 839 A.2d 1038 (2003). However, the standard for whether judges should

allow scientific testimony in federal court and in an increasing number of states is set by *Daubert v. Merrell Dow Pharmaceuticals, Inc.*, 509 U.S. 579 (1993). In the *Daubert* case, the Supreme Court gave judges the role of gate-keepers in deciding whether to allow particular scientific testimony to be admitted into evidence, using a set of measures designed to go beyond the *Frye* principle of general acceptability in the scientific field. *Daubert* will be the subject of extensive discussion later in this chapter.

73. National Academy of Sciences, *supra* note 70, at 173, citing J. A. Kieser, *Weighing Bitemark Evidence: A Postmodern Perspective*, 1 Journal of Forensic Science, Medicine, and Pathology 75-80 (2005).

74. National Academy of Sciences, *supra* note 70, at 173.

75. *Id.* at 174.

76. *Id.*

77. *Id.*

78. *Id.* at 176.

79. *Id.*

80. I. A. Pretty and D. Sweet, *The Scientific Basis for Human Bitemark Analysis: A Critical Review*, 41 Science and Justice 85-92 (2001).

81. National Academy of Sciences, *supra* note 70, at 157-59.

82. See M. M. Houck and B. Budowle, *Correlation of Microscopic and Mitochondrial DNA Hair Comparisons*, 47 Journal of Forensic Sciences 964-67 (2002).

83. *Id.*

84. E.g., State v. West, 977 A.2d 787 (Conn., 2005); Bookins v. State, 922 A.2d 389 (Del. Supr., 2007). Other courts have come to the opposite conclusion, regarding hair analysis as highly unreliable. See P. Giannelli and E. West, *Hair Comparison Evidence*, 37 Criminal Law Bulletin 514 (collecting cases).

85. National Academy of Sciences, *supra* note 70, at 147.

86. *Id.*

87. *Id.* at 25.

88. *U.S. v. Llera Plaza*, 179 F. Supp. 2d 492 (E.D. Pa., 2002). Publication of the opinion was withdrawn after the court vacated its opinion.

89. *Id.* at 516-18.

90. *U.S. v. Llera Plaza*, 188 F. Supp. 2d 549 (E.D. Pa., 2002).

91. *Id.* at 555-56.

92. *Id.* at 558.

93. National Academy of Sciences, *supra* note 70, at 21, 141, 148-49, 155, 160-61.

94. *Id.* at 25.

95. *Id.*

96. *Id.* at 26.

97. See, for example, the numerous news stories about Fred Zain, the forensic scientist in West Virginia who falsified results to support police. E.g., *Court Invalidates a Decade of Blood Test Results in Criminal Cases*, N.Y. Times, Nov. 12, 1993, accessed Aug. 15, 2011, at http://www.nytimes.com/1993/11/12/us/court-invalidates-a-decade-of-blood-test-results-in-criminal-cases.html (Independent scientists examined cases in which Zain had produced evidence for the prosecution; "[i]n the 36 cases it investigated, the team [of independent scientists] said, it discovered that Mr. Zain had lied about, made up or manipulated evidence to win convictions in every single case.").

98. Vera Institute of Justice, *Prosecution and Racial Justice Program*, accessed Nov. 19, 2010, at http://www.vera.org/project/prosecution-and-racial-justice.

99. *Id.*

100. Interview with Wayne McKenzie, Nov. 16, 2010 (transcript on file with the author).

101. *Id.*

102. Email communications with Professor Mark Godsey, University of Cincinnati College of Law, January 2011 (copy on file with the author).

103. *Printz v. U.S.*, 521 U.S. 898 (1997). For example, in 1993, Congress enacted the Brady Act, a gun control law that required the heads of local law enforcement agencies to conduct background checks in connection with some gun purchases; the law essentially obligated these officials to participate in a federal regulatory effort. Two sheriffs, one from Arizona and one from Montana, challenged the law, and the U.S. Supreme Court threw it out. The U.S. government, the Court said, had no business dictating to a local law enforcement agency what it must do, absent some specific constitutional power that gave it such authority.

104. Emergency Highway Energy Conservation Act, 23 U.S.C. § 101 (1974).

105. National Minimum Drinking Age Act of 1984, 23 U.S.C. § 158 (1984).

106. Email communication with Amy Schapiro, special assistant to the director, Office of Community Oriented Policing Services, U.S. Department of Justice, Oct. 13, 2010 (copy on file with the author).

107. *Arizona v. Youngblood*, 488 U.S. 51 (1988).

108. *Frye v. U.S.*, 293 F. 1013 (D.C. Cir. 1923).

109. *Id.* at 1014.

110. Federal Rules of Evidence, Pub. L. 93-595 (1975).

111. Fed. R. Evid. 702.

112. *Daubert v. Merrell Dow Pharmaceuticals, Inc.*, 509 U.S. 579 (1993).

113. *Id.* at 589-90.

114. *Khumo Tire Company v. Carmichael*, 526 U.S. 137 (1999).

115. *Id.* at 147-49.

116. *General Electric Company v. Joiner*, 522 U.S. 136 (1997).

117. *Id.* at 141-43.

118. David L. Faigman, David H. Kay, Michael J. Saks, and Joseph Sanders, *Modern Scientific Evidence: The Law and Science of Expert Testimony* § 1:35, Applying *Daubert:* Criminal Cases (2009).

119. *Id.*

120. D. Michael Risinger, *Navigating Expert Reliability: Are Criminal Standards of Certainty Being Left on the Dock?* 64 Albany L. Rev. 99, 106, 108 (2000).

121. *Id.* at 108.

122. David L. Faigman, David H. Kay, Michael J. Saks, and Joseph Sanders, *supra* note 118.

123. Peter J. Neufeld, *The (Near) Irrelevance of Daubert to Criminal Justice and Some Suggestions for Reform*, 95 American Journal of Public Health S107, S109 (2005).

124. *Maryland v. Rose*, Case No. K06-0545, mem. op. at 31 (Balt. Co. Cir. Ct., Oct. 19, 2007).

125. See, e.g., David L. Faigman, David H. Kay, Michael J. Saks, and Joseph Sanders, *supra* note 118, citing U.S. v. Allen, 390 F.3d 944 (7th Cir. 2004), in which the court gave only the most minimal scrutiny to claims about the accuracy of shoe-print identification, and U.S. v. Hicks, 389 F.3d 514 (5th Cir., 2004), *cert. denied,* 546 U.S. 1089 (2006).

126. Peter J. Neufeld, *supra* note 123.

127. *Id.* at S110. The use of reported cases as a sample in any study is incomplete; only a portion of legal cases generate reported opinions. Most do not. But looking at reported opinions gives one a sense of the lay of the land in respect to the gross qualities of the phenomenon under examination, if not the finer points. On that score, Neufeld's use of reported opinions works acceptably to show us the big picture.

128. *Id.*

CHAPTER 7

1. Executive Order as Issued by Former Governor George Ryan Creating the Commission on Capital Punishment, No. 4 (2000), accessed at http://www.idoc.state.il.us/ccp/executive_order.html.

2. Governor's Commission on Capital Punishment, Report of the Governor's Commission on Capital Punishment (2002).

3. 75 Ill. Comp. Stat. 5/103-2.1 (2008).

4. 725 Ill. Comp. Stat. Ann. 5/107A-5(b) (2004).

5. 75 Ill. Comp. Stat. 5/114-13.

6. 75 Ill. Comp. Stat. 5/115-22.

7. Kent Roach, *The Role of Innocence Commissions: Error Discovery, Systemic Reform, or Both*, 85 Chi.-Kent Law Rev. 89, 109-10 (2010).

8. *Id.* at 110.

9. Bob Egelko, *Governor Vetoes Bills Opposed by Law Enforcement*, S.F. Chron., Oct. 16, 2007, accessed Nov. 7, 2010, at http://articles.sfgate.com/2007-10-16/ bay-area/17264954_1_vetoed-interrogations-jailhouse-informant.

10. Innocence Commission for Virginia, *A Vision for Justice: Report and Recommendations Regarding Wrongful Convictions in the Commonwealth of Virginia* (2005), accessed Nov. 7, 2010, at http://www.thejusticeproject.org/ wp-content/uploads/a-vision-for-justice.pdf. See also Jon B. Gould, THE INNOCENCE COMMISSION: PREVENTING WRONGFUL CONVICTIONS AND RESTORING THE CRIMINAL JUSTICE SYSTEM (2008).

11. According to Mark Rabil, codirector of the Innocence and Justice Clinic at Wake Forest University School of Law, there have been seven cases in North Carolina in which wrongly convicted persons were freed on the basis of DNA testing results, and other exonerations as well. Interview with Mark Rabil, Wake Forest University School of Law, Nov. 9, 2010 (transcript on file with the author).

12. Phoebe Zerwick, *Closed Doors: Case Review Finds That a Series of Troubling Decisions Cast a Shadow of Doubt over a Divisive Case*, Winston-Salem Journal, Nov. 23, 2003; see also Jerome M. Maiatico, *All Eyes on Us: A Comparative Critique of the North Carolina Innocence Inquiry Commission*, 56 Duke L.J. 1345, 1348 (2007).

13. *Id.* at 1348.

14. *Id.* at 1348-49.

15. *Id.* at 1349.

16. *Id.*

17. Interview with I. Beverly Lake, retired chief justice of the Supreme Court of North Carolina, Nov. 18, 2010 (transcript on file with the author).

18. *Id.*

19. Interview with Christine Mumma, North Carolina Center on Actual Innocence, Nov. 15, 2010 (transcript on file with the author)

20. *Id.*

21. *Id.*

22. Interview with I. Beverly Lake, *supra* note 17.

23. *Id.*

24. Interview with Christine Mumma, *supra* note 19.

25. Interview with Mark Rabil, Wake Forest University School of Law, Nov. 10, 2010 (transcript on file with the author).

26. *Id.*

27. Jerome M. Maiatico, *supra* note 12, at 1356.

28. Interview with I. Beverly Lake, *supra* note 17.

29. *Id.*

30. *Id.*

31. *Id.*

32. Interview with Christine Mumma, *supra* note 19.

33. North Carolina Actual Innocence Commission, *Recommendations for Eye-witness Identification*, October 2003, accessed Nov, 7, 2010, at http://www.innocenceproject.org/docs/NC_Innocence_Commission_Identification.html.

34. Interview with Christine Mumma, *supra* note 19.

35. Christine Mumma, *The North Carolina Actual Innocence Commission: Uncommon Perspectives Joined by a Common Cause*, 52 Drake L. Rev. 647, 654 (2004).

36. Under Federal Rule of Criminal Procedure 33, a motion for a new trial based on newly discovered evidence must be filed within three years of the original final verdict, and even then will be granted only "if required in the interest of justice."

37. *Herrera v. Collins*, 506 U.S. at 390 (1993).

38. *Id.* at 400.

39. Associated Press, *Innocence Commission Proposes Review Board*, March 9, 2005, accessed Nov. 7, 2010, at http://www.injusticebusters.com/05/North_Carolina.shtml.

40. Christine Mumma, *supra* note 35, at 654.

41. Jerome M. Maiatico, *supra* note 12, at 1357-58.

42. N.C. Gen. Stat. §§ 15A-1460 to 15A-1475 (Supp. 2006).

43. *Id.* at § 15A-1466.

44. *Id.* at 15A-1460 (1).

45. *Id.*

46. *Id.* at § 15A-1467 (b).

47. *Id.* at § 15A-1468 (d).

48. *Id.* at § 15A-1467 (d)-(f).

49. *Id.* at § 15A-1468 (c).

50. *Id.* at § 15A-1469 (a).

51. *Id.* at § 15A-1469 (h).

52. *Id.*

53. The North Carolina Innocence Inquiry Commission, *Case Statistics (May 2010)*, accessed Nov. 7, 2010, at http://www.innocencecommission-nc.gov/statistics.htm.

54. *Id.*
55. *Id.*
56. See Innocence Project, *Exonerations by State*, accessed Nov. 15, 2010, at http://www.innocenceproject.org/news/StateView.php (Texas had forty cases of defendants exonerated.).
57. *Id.* (Texas had forty exonerations, and Illinois and New York had thirty and twenty-seven, respectively); the Innocence Project of Texas, *Texas Exonerations at a Glance*, accessed Nov. 15, 2010, at http://www.innocenceprojec-toftexas.org/index.php?action=at-a-glance (listing forty-two total exonerations, with twenty coming from Dallas County alone).
58. *Dallas, DNA Target Wheels of Bad Justice*, Chicago Tribune (hereinafter *Dallas, DNA Target Wheels*), April 10, 2007, accessed Aug. 1, 2010, at http://articles.chicagotribune.com/2007-04-10/news/0704100153_1_innocence-project-exoneration-dna.
59. Michael Hall, *Craig's List*, Texas Monthly Magazine, Sept. 2007, accessed Nov. 15, 2010, at http://www.texasmonthly.com/preview/2007-12-01/bird.
60. Steve McGonigle, *A Dream Come True: Judge Backs Man's Exoneration in '82 Rape Case*, Dallas Morning News, April 10, 2007.
61. Jennifer Emily, *Watkins Shifting Goal from Winning to Justice*, Dallas Morning News, Dec. 30, 2007.
62. Michael Hall, *supra* note 59.
63. Wade Goodwyn, *Dallas DA to Review Decades of Convictions*, National Public Radio, Feb. 23, 2007, accessed Nov. 16, 2010, at http://www.npr.org/templates/story/story.php?storyId=7565610.
64. Article 64 of the Texas Code states that

    [a] convicted person may submit to the convicting court a motion for forensic DNA testing of evidence containing biological material . . . only of evidence that was secured in relation to the offense that is the basis of the challenged conviction and was in the possession of the state during the trial of the offense, but: (1) was not previously subjected to DNA testing because DNA testing was not available; or available, but not technologically capable of providing probative results; or through no fault of the convicted person, for reasons that are of a nature such that the interests of justice require DNA testing; or although previously subjected to DNA testing, can be subjected to testing with newer testing techniques that provide a reasonable likelihood of results that are more accurate and probative than the results of the previous test.

65. Wade Goodwyn, *supra* note 63; *see also Dallas, DNA Target Wheels*, *supra* note 58.
66. Wade Goodwyn, *supra* note 63.

67. Telephone discussion with Mike Ware, chief, Conviction Integrity Unit, Dallas County District Attorney's Office, Jan. 28, 2011 (notes on file with the author).

68. Email correspondence with Russell Wilson, Conviction Integrity Unit, Aug. 2, 2011 (copy on file with the author). This does not include cases in which testing was done before CIU was formed or where results were inconclusive.

69. *Id.* This does not include cases in which DNA showed the suspect committed separate crimes, or when DNA just identified different assailants.

70. Evan Smith, *A Conversation with Dallas County D.A. Craig Watkins*, Texas Tribune, June 11, 2010, accessed at http://www. texastribune.org/texas-dept-criminal-justice/craig-watkins/ conversation-with-dallas-county-da-Craig-Watkins-/.

71. *Id.*

72. Michael Hall, *supra* note 59, at 2.

73. Kevin Johnson, *DNA Tests Fuel Urgency to Free the Innocent*, USA Today, Feb. 19, 2008, accessed Nov. 17, 2010, at http://www.usatoday.com/news/ nation/2008-02-18-dna_N.htm.

74. The idea of restoring integrity became the centerpiece of Watkins's 2006 campaign for the office and has continued to serve as his core theme ever since, and it came as a very personal slap in the face to these veterans.

75. Jennifer Forsyth and Leslie Eaton, *The Exonerator: The Dallas D.A. Is Reviewing Old Cases, Freeing Prisoners—and Riling His Peers*, Wall Street Journal, Nov. 15, 2008, accessed Nov. 17, 2010, at http://online.wsj.com/ article/SB122669736692929339.html.

76. Interview with Jeff Blackburn, Nov. 18, 2010 (transcript on file with the author).

77. *Id.*

78. Michael Hall, *supra* note 59.

79. Ralph Blumenthal, *For Dallas, New Prosecutor Means an End to the Old Ways*, N.Y. Times, June 3, 2007.

80. *Patricia M. Lykos, Harris County District Attorney*, accessed Nov. 18, 2010, at http://www.patlykos.com/.

81. *Id.*

82. *Id.*

83. *Written Testimony of Patricia R. Lykos before the Senate Committee on the Judiciary*, Nov. 10, 2009, accessed Nov. 19, 2010 at http://judiciary.senate. gov/pdf/09-11-10Lykos'sTestimony.pdf.

84. Emily Freidman, *Texas Inmates Likely to Be Exonerated after Committee Discovers Wrongful Convictions*, ABC News, July 30, 2010,

accessed Nov. 19, 2010, at http://abcnews.go.com/US/texas-inmates-released-wrongful-convictions-discovered-46-years/story?id=11287347.

85. Interview with Sandra Guerra Thompson, University of Houston Law Center, Nov. 22, 2010 (transcript on file with the author).

86. *Id.*

87. Sandra Guerra Thompson, *Brand New Era of Criminal Justice in Harris County?* Houston Chronicle, Aug. 4, 2010, accessed Nov, 30, 2010, at http://www.chron.com/disp/story.mpl/editorial/outlook/7139733.html.

88. *Written Testimony of Patricia R. Lykos, supra* note 83.

89. Peggy O'Hare, *Odds Still against Clearing Convicts,* Houston Chronicle, Aug. 2, 2010, accessed Nov. 19, 2010, at http://www.chron.com/disp/story.mpl/metropolitan/7135030.html.

90. Stephan v. State, 711 P.2d 1156 (Alaska 1985).

91. State v. Scales, 518 N.W.2d 587 (Minn. 1994).

92. 725 Illinois Compiled Statutes Annotated 5/103-2.1.

93. The Innocence Project, *Reevaluating Lineups: Why Witnesses Make Mistakes and How to Reduce the Chance of a Misidentification* 22, accessed Dec. 2, 2010, at http://www.innocenceproject.org/docs/Eyewitness_ID_Report.pdf.

94. Ohio Revised Code § 2933.8 (2010).

95. Ohio Revised Code § 2933.81 (2010).

96. Wisconsin Statutes Annotated 175.50 (2006).

97. Wisconsin Statutes Annotated 972.115 (2005).

98. U.S. Department of Justice, *National Institute of Justice, Eyewitness Evidence: A Guide for Law Enforcement,* NCJ 178240 (Oct. 1999).

99. *Id.* at 12.

100. *Id.* at 2.

101. Interview with John Farmer Jr., Dec. 8, 2010 (transcript file with the author).

102. *Id.*

103. *Id.*

104. Memorandum of John J. Farmer Jr., Office of the Attorney General, to All County Prosecutors, Col. Carson J. Dunbar, Jr., Superintendant, New Jersey State Police, All Police Chiefs, All Law Enforcement Chief Executives, Re: Attorney General Guidelines for Preparing and Conducting Photo and Live Identification Lineups , April 21, 2001 (copy on file with the author).

105. *Id.*

106. *Id.*

107. *Id.*

108. Memorandum of John J. Farmer Jr., *supra* note 104 ("Two procedural recommendations [blind and sequential lineups] contained in these Guidelines

are particularly significant and will represent the primary area of change for most law enforcement agencies.").

109. *Id.*

110. Gina Kolata and Iver Peterson, *New Way to Insure Eyewitnesses Can ID the Right Bad Guy*, N.Y. Times, July 21, 2001.

111. *Id.*

112. Interview with John Farmer Jr., *supra* note 101.

113. *Id.*

114. For a detailed description of these events, see David A. Harris, PROFILES IN INJUSTICE: WHY RACIAL PROFILING CANNOT WORK (2002), chapter 3.

115. New Jersey Attorney General's Office, Interim Report of the State Police Review Team Regarding Allegations of Racial Profiling, April 20, 1999, at 4.

116. Interview of John Farmer Jr., *supra* note 101, at 4.

117. *Id.*

118. Memorandum of John J. Farmer Jr., *supra* note 104.

119. The Innocence Project, *supra* note 93, at 23.

120. *Id.*

121. *N.J. Hearings to Review Police Lineup Procedures*, Associated Press, Sept. 23, 2009, accessed Dec. 3, 2010, at http://www.nj.com/news/index.ssf/2009/09/nj_hearings_to_resume_on_polic.html.

122. *Id.*; The Innocence Project, *New Jersey Judge to Hear Case on Eyewitness Guidelines*, Sept. 23, 2009, accessed Dec. 3, 2010, at http://www.innocenceproject.org/Content/New_Jersey_Judge_to_Hear_Case_on_Eyewitness_Guidelines.php.

123. *Id.*

124. The Innocence Project, *Special Master Appointed by N.J. Supreme Court Calls for Major Overhaul of Legal Standards for Eyewitness Testimony*, June 21, 2010, accessed Dec. 3, 2010, at http://www.innocenceproject.org/Content/Special_Master_Appointed_by_NJ_Supreme_Court_Calls_for_Major_Overhaul_of_Legal_Standards_for_Eyewitness_Testimony.php.

125. Cybergenetics company website, *Principals*, accessed Aug. 1, 2011, at http://www.cybgen.com/company/principals.shtml; interview with Dr. Mark Perlin, Aug. 16, 2011 (copy on file with the author).

126. *Id.*

127. Cybergenetics company website, *History of Cybergenetics,* accessed Aug. 1, 2011, at http://www.cybgen.com/company/history.shtml.

128. Interview with Dr. Mark Perlin, *supra* note 125.

129. *Id.*

130. *DNA Intelligence and Forensic Failure: What You Don't Know Can Kill You,* The DNA Investigator (Cybergenetics newsletter), Winter 2011, at 2-4.

131. Interview with Dr. Mark Perlin, *supra* note 125.

132. Mark W. Perlin, Matthew M. Legler, Cara E. Spencer, Jessica L. Smith, William P. Allan, Jamie L. Belrose, and Berry W. Duceman, *Validating TrueAllele DNA Mixture Interpretation,* Journal of Forensic Sciences 1-18 (2011).

133. David Templeton, *Local Technology Enhances DNA Analysis*, Pittsburgh Post-Gazette, June 26, 2011.

134. Interview with Dr. Mark Perlin, *supra* note 125.

135. *Id.*

136. David Templeton, *supra* note 133.

137. Letter of Dr. Jack Ballantyne, chair, New York State DNA Subcommittee, to Sean Byrne, Acting Commissioner and Chair, Commission on Forensic Science, Division of Criminal Justice Services, May 20, 2011 (copy on file with the author); David Templeton, *supra* note 133.

138. Interview with Dr. Mark Perlin, *supra* note 125.

139. Mary Pat Flaherty, *Virginia Reevalutates DNA Evidence in 375 Cases,* Wash. Post, July 16, 2011.

140. Interview with Dr. Mark Perlin, *supra* note 125.

141. David Templeton, *supra* note 133.

142. Interview with Dr. Mark Perlin, *supra* note 125.

143. David Templeton, *supra* note 133.

ABOUT THE AUTHOR

David A. Harris is Distinguished Faculty Scholar, Professor of Law, and the Associate Dean for Research at the University of Pittsburgh. He teaches Criminal Procedure, Criminal Law, Evidence, Criminal Justice Policy, and courses in homeland security. His research covers police behavior, police accountability, search and seizure, racial profiling, and community policing. He is the author of *Good Cops: The Case for Preventive Policing* (2005) and *Profiles in Injustice: Why Racial Profiling Cannot Work* (2002). He lives in Pittsburgh.